SPEAKING UP, SPEAKING OUT

SPEAKING UP, SPEAKING OUT

Lived Experiences of Non-Tenure-Track Faculty in Writing Studies

EDITED BY
JESSICA EDWARDS,
MEG MCGUIRE,
AND RACHEL SANCHEZ

UTAH STATE UNIVERSITY PRESS
Logan

© 2021 by University Press of Colorado

Published by Utah State University Press
An imprint of University Press of Colorado
245 Century Circle, Suite 202
Louisville, Colorado 80027

All rights reserved

 The University Press of Colorado is a proud member of the Association of University Presses.

The University Press of Colorado is a cooperative publishing enterprise supported, in part, by Adams State University, Colorado State University, Fort Lewis College, Metropolitan State University of Denver, Regis University, University of Colorado, University of Northern Colorado, University of Wyoming, Utah State University, and Western Colorado University.

ISBN: 978-1-64642-074-2 (paperback)
ISBN: 978-1-64642-075-9 (ebook)
https://doi.org/10.7330/9781646420759

Library of Congress Cataloging-in-Publication Data

Names: Edwards, Jessica, 1984– editor. | McGuire, Meg (Professor), editor. | Sanchez, Rachel, editor.
Title: Speaking up, speaking out : lived experiences of non-tenure track faculty in writing studies / edited by Jessica Edwards, Meg McGuire, Rachel Sanchez.
Description: Logan : Utah State University Press, [2021] | Includes bibliographical references and index.
Identifiers: LCCN 2020049979 (print) | LCCN 2020049980 (ebook) | ISBN 9781646420742 (paperback) | ISBN 9781646420759 (ebook)
Subjects: LCSH: College teachers—United States. | Writing centers—United States. | Academic writing—Study and teaching (Higher)—Social aspects—United States. | Universities and colleges—United States—Faculty.
Classification: LCC LB1778.2 .S64 2021 (print) | LCC LB1778.2 (ebook) | DDC 378.1/20973—dc23
LC record available at https://lccn.loc.gov/2020049979
LC ebook record available at https://lccn.loc.gov/2020049980

Cover illustration © Rinat Khairitdinov / Shutterstock

CONTENTS

Acknowledgements   vii

Introduction: Negotiating Non-Tenure-Track Identities
 Jessica Edwards, Meg McGuire, and Rachel Sanchez   3

PART I: DEFINITIONS

1. Practice Doesn't Always Make Permanent: Directing a Writing Center as a Professor of Practice
 Rachel Azima   15

2. How Student Affairs Praxis Can Aid the Nexus of Emotional Labor for NTTF
 Peter Brooks   28

3. Contingent Faculty in the Gig Economy: A Conversation, Comparison, and Call
 Erica M. Stone and Sarah E. Austin   42

4. "What Are You?": Rethinking Frames for Contingent Writing Center Work
 Liliana M. Naydan   59

PART II: CRITICAL PERSPECTIVES

5. Having It All: The Costs and Opportunities of Non-Tenure-Track Faculty's Institutional Progress
 Lacey Wootton   73

6. Ghosts in the Building: Investigating Contingent-faculty Experiences
 Brendan Hawkins and Julie Karaus   90

PART III: LIVED EXPERIENCES

7. An Inconvenient Truth: Labels and Limits in Writing Center Directorship
   Megan Boeshart Burelle and Elizabeth J. Vincelette   107

8. A Tale of Two Pities: An Inside Look at a Dual Non-Tenure-Track Household
   Jessica Cory and John McHone   119

9. The Sound of Silence: Negotiating Non-Tenure-Track Invisibility within the Institution
   Angie McKinnon Carter, Christopher Lee, and Linda Shelton   131

10. Disunity in a Writing Community: A Post-PhD Memoir of Professional Transitions
    Liz Gumm   145

11. Collective Bargaining, Heterogeneity, and Non-Tenure-Track Writing Faculty
    Denise Comer   158

12. Off Track and Sidetracked
    Seth Myers   177

PART IV: NEXT STEPS

13. Collaboration as Antidote to NTTF Pressures
    Nathalie Joseph and Norah Ashe-McNalley   193

14. Collaboration Is Critical, but Further Considerations Are Needed for NTTF
    Heather Jordan   207

15. Faculty Community Building: Portfolio-Assessment Groups as Teaching Circles
    Dauvan Mulally   221

About the Authors   235
Index   237

ACKNOWLEDGMENTS

We are grateful to Dr. Stephanie Kerschbaum and Dr. Victor Villanueva for their thoughtful guidance as we developed this project. We appreciate Rachael Levay and Darrin Pratt for their diligence and speedy responses to our many inquiries. We also give a shout-out to the reviewers of this edited collection who encouraged us and offered useful suggestions.

We acknowledge our non-tenure-track colleagues, particularly those whose voices and stories are not contained within this collection and have yet to be heard. We hope the experiences shared within will inspire and encourage readers to speak up and speak out whenever and wherever necessary.

SPEAKING UP, SPEAKING OUT

INTRODUCTION
Negotiating Non-Tenure-Track Identities

Jessica Edwards, Meg McGuire, and Rachel Sanchez

This collection began with three non-tenure-track faculty members (NTTF) struggling to understand our professional identities in the context of a tenure system. We were faculty without an understanding of our place in that system and without clear connections to the community of NTTF who comprise our cohort, perhaps in part because the language used to identify us is so inconsistent.

Contingent faculty. Adjuncts. Non-tenure-track faculty. Instructors. Lecturers. Clinical professors. Term faculty. Part-time faculty. Our collective professional identities are wrapped up in language that is not only not controlled by us but is also the language of our commerce—how we are packaged as commodities—because not only are the labels inconsistent, but the work we are asked to do under each label is inconsistent, as you will read in this collection. Some of us do administrative work, and some of us do not. Some of us are in a position to be promoted, and some of us are not; some of us are not interested in promotion. Some of us cobble full-time positions out of many part-time positions, and some of us do not. These staggering inconsistencies make it difficult for our tenured or tenure-track (TT) counterparts to understand the work we do, inside or outside the classroom, and the lengths we must often go in order to remain committed to our students and colleagues.

The rhetorical power of these labels is in defining our worth to our peers and administrators, in framing the scholarship we produce in the name of our institutions, and in defining our worth to our institutions themselves. But we know NTTF are consistently defined by what we are not in all the above contexts. Often, such defining is incorporated into our titles, yet there are other ways the institution identifies NTTF by what we are lacking. We do not only lack tenured status, we lack focus. We do not only lack voting rights, we lack institutional memory. We do not only lack stability in our employment contracts, we lack power to communicate our ideas and woes in proper institutional channels.

DOI: 10.7330/9781646420759.c000

For instance, a contingent-faculty member at one college labeled as an instructor might have the same contract as someone who is labeled an assistant professor at another institution.

This slipperiness of language on a national scale presents a lack of consistency that must be made visual, shared, and challenged in order to curtail the histories that have relegated NTTF to the boundaries. While *non-tenure-track faculty* (NTTF) is imperfect in its deficit approach to labeling, we chose this term for the collection because it most closely encompasses all our titles. As we work to speak up and speak out, providing a space to communicate a few of the many stories that exist, sharing details about our professional and personal lives that give fuller insight into the experiences of NTTF, we hope to open a needed dialogue about how to value the very people who take on such physical, rhetorical, and emotional work. In our discipline's critical work of ensuring the future of writing studies, we must understand who teaches so many of these courses.

The linguists and philosophers George Lakoff and Mark Johnson (1980) use much of their text *Metaphors We Live By* to argue the power conceptual metaphor—and rhetoric—has on our basic understanding of the world around us, including the roles we inhabit, the ways we situate our identities within a larger world. Conceptual metaphors, they tell us, play a role in "the construction of social and political reality" (159), and the political reality of NTTF has and will always be tied to the language used to identify and talk about that body of workers. Because we exist in a tenure system, the labels tied to NTTF replicate that system without replicating any of the associated power.

If we believe in Antonio Gramsci's (2005) idea that sedimentations from one "historic bloc" are often found in another, or Michael Omi and Howard Winant's (1994) claim about rearticulation and how systemic structures are often revamped in different historic blocs to feed hegemony, it is easy to understand the rhetorical vibrato of NTTF conversations. Although this landscape is largely focused on quality teaching and access to teaching opportunities and service for NTTF, there are many mountains to climb, as attention to inequality and struggles for legitimacy cannot be ignored. Adjunct professors and non-tenured folk all over the country are faced with challenges, from material conditions to lack of literal time to just get work done. Faculty of color experience problems at the intersections of race, gender, identity, and even income within and outside NTTF positions. These problems cause disenfranchised people to experience life differently from their white counterparts. Although there are very few data about NTTF demographics related to race, Kimberlé Crenshaw's (2016) work "The Urgency of Intersectionality" underscores the importance of understanding how power works and how disenfranchised people are often hit with multiple types of discrimination at once. Crenshaw notes she "began to use the term 'intersectionality' to deal with the fact that many of our social justice problems like racism and sexism are often overlapping, creating multiple levels of social injustice."

We write of our non-tenure-track faculty in this collection, of our adjunct family, of ourselves, yet we cannot write about ourselves in a singular way. We want to write about ourselves, yet we do not control the language that defines ourselves. We want to reject the homogeneity of an NTTF identity and engage with the tools to establish the myriad, complex identities that comprise more than half the teaching force at most institutions in this country. Throughout this introduction, we editors share our own brief stories about being NTTF and, like the authors who follow, we strive to engage the differences in our experiences, personal lives, and outlook on teaching and administration to paint a clearer picture of NTTF life during another sea change for higher education.

JESSICA

The work of developing a professional identity, of discovering exactly what it means to not be on a TT track, was a long road of soul searching for me as I worked to, as Audre Lorde famously said, "define myself for myself." When I teach writing classes, I often use the first two weeks to encourage students to think about their own identity. I am of the mind that much of what we do and what we write is tied to a set of beliefs we hold; I also think if we can understand who we are and what shapes us, we are in a better position to navigate in meaningful ways. My approaches to teaching have certainly helped me better understand my professional identity, as I now think of myself as a pedagogical researcher dedicated to the scholarship of teaching; in my first teaching job, however, I was challenged to consider my professional identity in ways that required me to dig into the rhetorical nature of job labels and how they affect self-awareness. As Denise Comer notes in this collection, "The Conference on College Composition and Communication offers a deliberately expansive definition of NTTF: 'all faculty who are not protected by tenure.' Still, the range of heterogeneity emphasizes the complex and varied systems that impact NTT labor and may even contribute to the inequities themselves" (chapter 11). Because of possibilities of what an NTTF might look like, NTFF may need to discover their own professional identities. Throughout my journey, not only did I have to take time to consider the realities of my position, I had to think through what was possible in the role to help me define myself and my work.

Immediately, I understood that high-impact practices would not be possible for me to sustain. Heather Jordan notes in her chapter "Collaboration Is Critical, but Further Considerations Are Needed for NTTF," NTTF are often expected to engage in "high-impact practices" that "require significant time and energy contributions on the part of the faculty member" (chapter 14). These high-impact practices vary but can combine consistent excellence in research, teaching, service, mentoring, volunteering, personal life, invisible labor, and more. The reality is that consistent excellence and engagement in high-impact practices is not healthy for any faculty member, especially NTTF. So, for me, determining what was most important to me mattered greatly to my ability to develop an identity I would be able to share with folk in any setting so as to not sacrifice my professional integrity, my health, or my personal life. I had to structure time each day to write, to think, which led me to consider more clearly my professional practices. Focusing on the scholarship of teaching helped me align myself as a professional. Seeing myself as a pedagogical researcher, dedicated to the life of the mind, helped me find footing. Understanding my craft as not only an important part of the larger fabric of the institution but also as an extension of me helped me feel more grounded. Having a strong support system of family, friends, and colleagues who continually remind me of the significance of my contributions mattered. Finding avenues to assert my voice proved valuable. I had to, in many ways, create these conditions using what was available to me, and that made all the difference.

* * *

The potential fracture of identity that comes with taking on an NTTF position and the need to put yourself together deserves more attention. Part of the problem is that there are few places to share that not only validate NTTF experiences but also allow for the experiences to serve as tools for thoughtful engagement. We created this space to amplify those stories and identities so more NTTF can be seen, heard, and understood. In so doing, we create another avenue where NTTF identities are embraced and celebrated.

MEG

From the outside, my NTTF position does not appear to be that different from those that are tenure track. I have full voting rights in faculty meetings; I serve on important and worthwhile committees; overall, I am meant to be a valued member of my institutional community. I get the traditional, more seemingly prestigious title of associate professor. There are no *of* qualifiers like *of* practice or *of* teaching in my title. I had the opportunity to be promoted from assistant to associate professor, and I hope to someday be promoted to full. My membership in my institutional community may be viewed and believed by many to be inclusive, but like everyone in this collection, some areas in which the institution strives for inclusiveness actually reinforce my exclusion.

This mixed message of inclusiveness was most apparent in my recent promotion process. The process was exactly the same as if I were applying for tenure. I compiled a full dossier with statements that outlined my teaching and service. My dossier was sent out to external reviewers, selected from some of the most important people in my field. A number of students gave statements on my teaching. The process was challenging, especially in trying to convey how my workload and the work I do as NTTF matters to the university I work for. It is a different argument than one made by TT faculty, yet the dossier looks similar. The only difference is that I do not have a research section. But I had done scholarship as NTTF, and that scholarship was also included, not in a separate scholarship section but as part of my teaching statement. NTTF are not expected to produce articles or books, yet we are encouraged to do so, so the articles and book chapters acted as a testament to the work I put into my teaching and how the work I do gives me room to strive to be better as a teacher by bringing this knowledge into the classroom. But publishing is not, again, on paper, important to our performance review as teachers. And yet, reading between the lines, if NTTF want to be promoted, we are encouraged to produce articles, or books. In fact, in every letter I received in support of my promotion case, my research was discussed as just that. Almost all comments regarding my scholarship made some point about how impressive it was that I had had such a full teaching load and was still producing scholarship. Not one comment was made about how it strengthened my teaching or discussed what kind of scholarship it was.

What I took from this experience is that NTTF, in order to further succeed at the university, especially in terms of a dossier, must look like TT faculty, even if we are not always valued as such. I am fortunate I am able to include my scholarship, unlike NTTF at some universities that advocate for no scholarship at all, as Angie McKinnon Carter, Christopher Lee, and Linda Shelton discuss in their chapter "The Sound of Silence: Negotiating Non-Tenure-Track Invisibility within the

Institution" about their own promotion experiences. But the review process for contingent faculty is designed for tenure-track faculty, assessed by tenure-track faculty, and decided upon by tenure-track faculty. One could argue this process is one way to make NTTF valued and included. NTTF go through a vigorous process that assesses their work and merits achieved in a certain time frame because they are just as important as the work and merits of TT faculty. Many of my colleagues involved in this collection and I argue that this process exists because, as many NTTF faculty working in writing and English departments nationally know, universities don't know how to account for the work NTTF do. They know what they want NTTF to do; they want them to teach classes. Even the MLA, in its Statement on the Use of Part-Time and Full-Time Adjunct Faculty Members, states, "Adjunct faculty members should be hired, reviewed, and given teaching assignments according to processes comparable to those established for the tenured or tenure-track faculty members" (2020). This advocacy, though made in good faith, does little to create equity and inclusion. Adjuncts are supplemental to the perceived permanency of tenure, a truth tied more to language than to practice, as the ranks of NTTF grow to not only equal those of their tenured counterparts but to surpass them significantly. Adjuncts are supplemental to the idea of tenure but are not supplemental to undergraduate education; their labor is where undergraduate education lives.

* * *

Because NTTF labor can be seen as a threat to the traditional tenure system, as evidenced by such texts as the WPA listserv, where frequent arguments are made about the value and impact of NTTF, the sense of isolation and exclusion felt by NTTF grows even as university administrators create programs and paths that seek to aid in NTTF development. Strange that such labor is viewed as a threat at all when its very existence is contingent, is paid a fraction of what TT labor is paid, and has never contained a back-door or secret, easier path to tenure. What is less strange is that educators would take on an NTT appointment at all, given the vulnerabilities related not only to the position but also to the profession. We are professionals who are as committed to our students, scholarship, and institutions as our TT counterparts, but we are also people with responsibilities that demand our attention, demand we take positions steeped in vulnerability in order to survive the economic and personal realities of being postsecondary writing instructors with significant student debt in a world that increasingly devalues liberal arts education.

RACHEL

I was a month into living in a friend's basement when I received my first contract offer. Knowing there weren't jobs in my hometown for recently minted MAs of English literature, I had developed enough fear that, when I received the email from my former department chair asking if I was looking for a teaching job, I didn't hesitate. The job was part time. I couldn't afford moving back to the college town I had only recently vacated, so I had to borrow from a graduate school friend, also a new MA, to cover my moving expenses. The narrative of MA graduates being what it is, and the preparation of graduate students for professions outside academia being what it is, I believed this offer was the best I should expect.

A *bridge appointment*. That's what our profession calls it, yet the trouble with that label is that it supposes the employer is invested in assisting the employee in crossing that bridge from apprentice to expert. Those first couple of years, I worked under a department chair who did not know who I was. I didn't receive annual reviews. I didn't know I could or should be attending department meetings and had even been encouraged not to go. The work was being sold to me, in most respects, as an extension of graduate school without required seminars. My closest ally and the person responsible for mentoring me was another MA graduate with one year of teaching experience beyond my own, another bridge appointee on her way to a PhD program. TT faculty, whom I saw as treasured and critical mentors, asked about upcoming PhD plans, and regardless of intention, this question implied a limitation to the position that had not occurred to me when I accepted it. Looking back, I understand; a bridge appointment is only that if I am walking across the bridge from the place I was—a space untenable, of unreliable contracts and fewer professional benefits—to the promised land: tenure. And if not tenure, then to the space we rarely discuss in graduate school: the real world. This untenable space is difficult to live within, and it can be difficult to know where you are or where you need to go, especially as a new instructor two months outside her MA, only six years outside high school.

But ours is a position of contradictions, and it is also worth noting that during this half-time employment, I was benefit eligible. My life filled with complications, yet I never worried that my job was in danger as a result. Quickly after I took on significant family responsibilities, my contract stretched to full time, thanks in large part to a new department chair. Later, I brought a toddler with me to class, and nobody cared. A canceled class was not strike one in a three-strike system. My department did not close new teaching opportunities to me after a disastrous attempt at teaching my first upper-division class but instead provided me additional opportunities—I taught new upper-division courses, then I taught online, then I taught courses for multilingual students, then I taught courses for basic writers. For NTTF, life exists within the space of these contradictions, as Seth Myers details beautifully in "Off Track and Sidetracked," in this collection, and what we carry with us in that space is our commitment to the work. Our identities as professors are not contingent, a truth that no doubt contributes to our (dys)functional relationship to our positions. We love the work we do, and we are so lucky to be employed by institutions even though they find us too lacking in one way or another to be seen as permanent; we are so lucky to be housed in departments with such significant service-course responsibilities that what we lack is necessarily overlooked.

It's a phrase I've heard repeatedly as NTTF, a refrain in our nonofficial theme song. *We're so lucky; it could be so much worse.* We could have semester or quarter-long contracts. *We're so lucky.* We could make so little we must seek employment from two or more universities. *It could be so much worse.* We could have classes taken away from us a week before starting class. We could be ineligible for benefits. We could have even less than we have now, we're sooooooooo lucky.

* * *

The contradiction of our employment—our existence—is tough to understand outside the vantage point NTTF call home. It is a space of averages, tallying what we have so we might leverage it against what we do not have, what we're told might never be ours. Consequently, this collection challenges the institution and all who participate within it, asking for clear ways contingent faculty fit into the system. It challenges tenure-track counterparts who often want to support NTTF but lack an understanding of how contingent faculty are seen and valued. Finally, this collection challenges the collective identities within the contingent-faculty cohort across the nation. We have all chosen our careers for a variety of reasons and bring with us our own background experiences. So the authors of these fifteen chapters have been brave to share their stories by speaking up and helping define what the nontenure track is and by beginning to offer suggestions for ways we can come together as a community and how we might better fit within our departments and institutions.

REFERENCES

Crenshaw, Kimberlé. 2016. "The Urgency of Intersectionality." TED video, 18:41. https://www.ted.com/talks/kimberle_crenshaw_the_urgency_of_intersectionality?language=en.

Gramsci, Antonio. 2005. *Selections from the Prison Notebooks*, edited by Quintin Hoare and Geoffrey Nowell Smith. New York: International.

Lakoff, George, and Mark Johnson. 1980. *Metaphors We Live By*. Chicago: University of Chicago Press.

Modern Language Association. 2020. "*Statement on the Use of Part-Time and Full-Time Adjunct Faculty Members.*" https://www.mla.org/Resources/Research/Surveys-Reports-and-Other-Documents/Staffing-Salaries-and-Other-Professional-Issues/MLA-Statement-on-the-Use-of-Part-Time-and-Full-Time-Adjunct-Faculty-Members.

Omi, Michael, and Howard Winant. 1994. *Racial Formation in the United States: From the 1960s to the 1990s*. New York: Routledge.

PART I

Definitions

1

PRACTICE DOESN'T ALWAYS MAKE PERMANENT
Directing a Writing Center as a Professor of Practice

Rachel Azima

"People say 'practice makes perfect,' but that isn't really true," my childhood piano teacher would say. "You can practice something over and over and you'll remember it, but if you're practicing it wrong, you'll remember it like that. So it's more like 'practice makes permanent.'" I've taught this saying to my son, too, as we battle our way through preparing for his cello lessons and recitals. My piano teacher didn't have my current state of employment remotely in mind when he was talking to teenage me, but as someone who presently serves as assistant professor of practice on a fixed-term contract, the connection amuses me anyway: practice does not always make permanent—at least in academia.

When I was first on the job market, I did not particularly want the tenure-track R1 job that was supposed to be my goal, with its attendant pressure to generate scholarship on a strict timeline. I ended up in a tenure-track job with a 4/4 teaching load at a small private university in the Midwest. My experience there was . . . not ideal. At one point, a senior colleague tried to start an insurrection against the department chair, attempting (unsuccessfully) to recruit me and my friend—both new assistant professors—for the cause. How could this possibly have been a good idea for us? That senior colleague was also teaching climate-change deniers in his philosophy of science class while I was discussing global warming in my nature-writing course. You may well imagine whose arguments our mutual students found more authoritative.

While these situations made my job unnecessarily difficult, I don't mean to overstate the role of this particular colleague or even interpersonal dynamics more generally. I simply disagreed with the "holding the line against the fall of Western Civilization" philosophy that undergirded our curriculum and pedagogical practices. I was expected to enforce a Banned Error List that involved docking a student half a grade for a lack of subject-verb agreement, another half a grade for one runon sentence, and so forth. Suffice it to say, my friend left after two years to return to the Pacific Northwest without any specific job prospects. I hung in for four years, but truth be told, I was on the job market in one way, shape, or form from the moment I started.

But that moment was also 2008, and (as we know) the recession did not spare the academic job market. At first, I dutifully applied for other assistant professor positions. But classroom teaching had never been my favorite, and I'd been inspired by wonderful administrative role models: my stepdad, Allan Saaf, who ultimately retired as a community college vice president, and Bradley Hughes, the director of the UW–Madison Writing Center, who is legendary in the writing center world for his mentorship. The strategic, visionary work of program building appealed to me, so I had always intended to seek out an administrative role eventually. Seeing what teaching jobs were out there after a year or two—or, more to the point, what weren't there—I began looking to move into administration sooner rather than later, ultimately narrowing my focus to writing center administration. I had found writing center teaching and leadership far more fulfilling than classroom teaching as a graduate student, and here was a line of work for which my unwillingness to specialize would be an asset!

In the third year of my assistant professor gig, I did indeed land an offer for a writing center directorship, but I was pregnant at the time and turned it down. Instead, I parlayed the job offer into a raise and a semester off from teaching.

This move was truly the beginning of the end for me at that university. It crystal clear my chair and dean had not appreciated the way I'd played hardball, and I was increasingly made to feel as if my pregnancy was a liability. "I'm not jealous or anything, even though that's not something I'm going to experience in my own life," my chair told me—which I found a peculiar thing to say, unless the reverse were actually true. She'd been a major cheerleader at first, but it became more and more evident that I wasn't meeting her (murky, to me) expectations. I had a course release for some administrative duties, which I realize now could be considered WPA work: selecting textbooks, hiring and mentoring part-time faculty, and setting the schedule for all English faculty in the department. I literally lost sleep over the scheduling, but this labor wasn't visible enough: I wasn't going to be seen as a team player if I didn't up my participation in recruitment efforts. My chair assigned me to staff an event that kept me mostly on my feet just weeks before I was to give birth. I was made to feel as if I wasn't pulling my ever-increasing weight, and my third-year review indicated as much: I was doing well with teaching and administrative duties, but I wasn't doing enough to promote the English major.

As a new mother and sole breadwinner, I would have done whatever it took to be successful there if it came to it, but I hoped it wouldn't. I took a hiatus from the job market until my son was a few months old, but when a writing center director position opened up a couple of states away, I applied without hesitation. I was offered the job—a staff director position at a large research university with an engineering and agriculture focus—and this time I accepted. "Congratulations!" said my chair. "This is definitely for the best."

The new position could not have been more different. The writing center was housed in Student Affairs—a division I knew nothing about. It was difficult transitioning from a flexible schedule to a twelve-month, at-your-desk-from-eight-to-five mentality. Still, the pay was excellent, the actual writing center work was congenial and well supported, and although I lived in terror that the vice president for Student Affairs would call me sometime at 8 a.m. and catch me being late, I did okay for a while.

But the job itself ended up not being quite what I had been allowed to believe, in ways that were professionally demoralizing. So, when my current position became available—an assistant professor of practice position in an English department at a different large midwestern research university—I applied for the job.

After I agreed to a campus visit, however, I belatedly remembered this was a public university, so I could look up pay rates—and was enraged to discover professors of practice in the department made $15,000 less than their tenure-track colleagues of the same rank. The salary was also considerably lower than what I was currently making. But it was too late to back out, so I went through with the visit.

When I got an initial offer, I let the chair know I was not prepared to take a pay cut and could not accept. It was true I had liked the folks I met in the department, the university was in a pleasant midsized city with far more to offer than where we were living, and I was constantly frustrated in my present job. The offer did include generous start-up funds, which I had never had access to before; the travel budget was much larger than I'd had on the tenure track, and it also exceeded that of one of my recently tenured graduate-school friends. If I took the job, I would also have the same access to faculty development (sabbatical) leaves as tenure-track members of the department. There were a number of temptations, in other words. So when the chair came back with a better offer that included partial summer support, plus the promise of summer teaching—an offer with a total dollar amount just barely to the threshold at which I was willing to consider it—I found myself tempted to accept. "You'd better be sure this time," said my husband, the long-suffering trailing spouse. Problem was, I was anything but sure. I knew being "of practice" would make me a second-class citizen in many ways; the pay gap was evidence of this. I also knew taking a pay cut in general was ill-advised, to put it kindly, and moving for the third time in six years would be unpleasant at best.

But I just couldn't stay with my current job any longer. I felt as though I should but could not bear to wait for other opportunities. I needed to save my mental health, if possible, and I wanted to move before my son started school and was old enough to put down roots. So, with myriad doubts and hesitations, I accepted the offer.

WORKING AS A PROFESSOR OF PRACTICE

I've now been writing center director and assistant professor of practice in English for over five years. It can't be said I didn't have my eyes open when I took on this role. Nevertheless, while some developments haven't surprised me, others have. I initially found it difficult to make inroads into the campus community. When I sent my first batch of emails to department chairs, introducing myself and offering as much or as little collaboration as they would like with the writing center, only one responded—and in only the most basic fashion. When I arrived, I was one of just three professors of practice (PoPs) in a department with approximately forty full-time faculty members. Like most English departments, we also employ a large number of part-time lecturers, quite a few of whom are recent graduates of our program. Our department chair was just beginning his term as I arrived. I was the first PoP in our department who was hired via a national search.

The most painful moment came during my second year, when we were looking to complete a senior hire. My PoP colleagues had previously served on numerous search committees and voted on hiring decisions; during my first year, I myself had attended job talks and voted on a hire, being only too happy to be back in an English department whose dynamics I understood, for better and worse. Since that time, however, our department chair had found language in the bylaws that questioned PoPs' ability to participate in hiring decisions. After a lot of back and forth over email, my PoP colleagues and I attended a meeting where a hiring recommendation was to be made, expecting to vote as usual. To our surprise, the chair began by talking about interpretations of the bylaws versus established department practices of allowing PoPs to vote, effectively inviting our tenure-track colleagues to decide our fates—while we sat right there. A senior colleague—who, incidentally, knew me from my prior life as an ecocritic—kindly spoke up and said, "I think we should go ahead and follow established practice." I appreciated this immensely, but nevertheless I found it profoundly humiliating to be held up for public judgment about whether we could be considered full colleagues.

Furthermore, it turned out our ability to vote that day was a one-off decision. Our department was again trying to hire during the following semester, but when we inquired, our chair said we would not vote on these decisions again until our department handbook was revised and the by-laws clarified. My PoP colleagues and I had been invited to dinners for prospective candidates; once I found out we couldn't participate in any decision-making, I sat out the hiring process entirely. (The chair said he would have done the same thing himself.) The whole business felt absurd: an associate PoP in our department who had recently been hired as an associate dean in our college interviewed these candidates individually in her new administrative capacity, but she was unable to vote on hiring in her home department! We've since resolved this question and now have separate votes for hiring (a simple yea/nay for joining the community) and hiring with tenure, if the latter is necessary, which allows PoPs to participate. I grant this is better than in other departments on campus where PoPs are not accorded this right at all—though arguably, the inconsistency points to the problems inherent in liminal positions, even if some who occupy them have relatively positive experiences.

Regardless, you never fully recover from feeling the rug pulled out from under you—the sting of having no choice but to confront the notion that your ostensible colleagues do not view you as a full member of the community, just as you had feared.

And yet, the reasons I took this job are still here: I have kind, supportive colleagues in our composition and rhetoric faculty group who have welcomed me into the fold, despite the roundabout way I've come into the field (my PhD is in literary studies). And the nature of the PoP position allows me to distribute my workload sensibly: I spend the bulk of my time focused on directing the writing center, which is considered teaching for the purposes of my appointment, with smaller amounts of time allocated to research and service. I appreciate working in an environment that values research and having it included in my apportionment;

I can set the scholarly agenda I prefer and feel encouraged to pursue it, without the "publish or perish" pressure I was never looking for in the first place.

And part of what I enjoy most about working at an R1 institution, albeit as NTTF, is the opportunity to work with graduate students. Had I stayed in my first TT position, I would never have had the opportunity to do so, as our only doctoral students were in fields well outside English. In particular, being able to mentor graduate students who find themselves on the margins has been one of the most fulfilling aspects of my work. As a biracial woman of color, I find value in being completely honest about my experiences in academia, both positive and negative, and helping graduate students (and undergraduates) make more informed choices than I ever did. My marginal identity assuredly compounds the questions of authority I would have to navigate regardless as an NTT writing center director: visitors to the writing center often seem surprised when they find out I am the director, and more than once, when I have met with people from other parts of the university along with the white graduate student assistant director of our writing-fellows program, they have assumed she is the director, not I. What people perceive as my racial identity is never not part of the equation as I move through the world, and I appreciate the chance to talk frankly with graduate students who get similar reminders of their Otherness as they work in classrooms, in the writing center, and in administration while being marked as different.

But even working with graduate students is a double-edged sword. While I can serve on PhD committees, I can't direct dissertations because of my status. So should graduate students come here to write writing center dissertations? They of course could, and I have excellent colleagues who could support this work, but it does not compare to places where the writing center director can oversee dissertations and contribute in that direct, pivotal way to the field's growth. I can still mentor students into the profession and help shape those who feel they have access to and are encouraged to do the work, but one key aspect of their professionalization is off limits. I wonder, sometimes, if my marginal status and that of many directors explains why it never seems to occur to our PhD students to focus on writing centers.

WRITING CENTERS AND NTT WORK

Here, then, is where my own experience exposes trends and problems in the field at large. If writing center studies is an offshoot of writing studies, which is itself marginalized within the larger field of English, then writing centers are doubly marginalized. While writing center scholars such as Jackie Grutsch McKinney (2013) and Lori Salem (2014) have persuasively argued that writing centers are nowhere near as marginal as they might once have been or seemed—Salem's data in particular reveal how ubiquitous writing centers are, at not-for-profit colleges and universities at least—the fact remains that many institutions have been unwilling to recognize the work of directing a writing center as requiring disciplinary expertise and, consequently, a tenure-track director. According to the National Census of Writing, only 31 percent of writing center directors were on the tenure track in 2013–2014; 22 percent were nontenure track but full time (like me), 20 percent were full-time staff, and the remainder held a smorgasbord of mostly part-time positions (Gladstein and Fralix 2015).

These figures evince the wide range of ways institutions conceive of their writing centers: if writing centers are viewed as sites for disciplinary work, they are likely to feature tenure-track or at least faculty directors; if writing centers are viewed as service units, tenure-track directors hardly seem necessary. Given how much administrative labor a writing center director performs, some degree of confusion is understandable. A director's work runs the gamut from mentoring new tutors/consultants and writing up reports to planning ongoing staff education and collaborating with faculty on writing workshops in the disciplines—and on and on. The work does not map easily onto existing structures for evaluation in academic positions, faculty or not. As WPAs of all kinds are only too-well aware, making administrative labor visible and ensuring it is accounted for and acknowledged can be difficult; within a writing center, the wildly ranging workload with its attendant "disciplinary," "emotional," and "everyday" labor vexes the problem even further (Caswell, Grutsch McKinney, and Jackson 2016).

I don't mean to imply here that full-time-staff director positions lack value; I have done such work myself, and being able to focus all my attention on the center, rather than having curricular responsibilities, was often a luxury and benefit. And, as surprising as it may seem to some tenure-track faculty, not everyone wants a faculty life. Alt-ac is often a career goal, not a fallback plan. Still, I am only too aware of the ways perceived status (or lack thereof) has affected my ability to collaborate with faculty across campus, when I have served as staff and NTTF alike. As Dawn Fels has incisively noted, there are "programmatic, professional, and personal risks" to having contingent faculty serving as writing center directors (2017, 121).

But, as always, once you get down to the personal level, matters get complicated. Do I think universities should invest in and demonstrate their commitment to their writing centers by establishing tenure-track lines for their directors? By and large, yes. Would I want this for myself? Not if it meant adhering to the classic model in play at R1 universities, for which I would have to put more effort into research than into building a strong writing center program. Yes, other tenure models operate successfully at other types of institutions, but universities like mine often engage in an unfortunate kind of institutional exceptionalism in which the school's supposed uniqueness or elevated status gets held up as a reason we need not follow others' leads. I am mostly content with my apportionment as is, with its heavy emphasis on teaching (that is, writing center directing-as-teaching), with smaller components for research and service. It is undoubtedly frustrating that no matter how long I'm here, I'll have to continually prove my usefulness: my contract is currently for three years, and it will never be for more than five years—and that is presuming I make it to full professor of practice. And in an ideal world, I'd prefer a slightly larger percentage for research, particularly since I see my scholarship on social justice in the writing center as intertwined with the everyday decisions I make as a director. I can't imagine doing the teaching and administrative work without also engaging actively with scholarly conversations in the field. That said, given the sorts of job situations I have experienced, no one knows better than I do that every situation has drawbacks. So I have been, so far, willing to put up with the downsides.

THE FIELD AT LARGE, AND POSSIBLE SOLUTIONS

Still, my own willingness to tolerate these labor conditions of relative impermanence and lower status is beside the point: Should I even have to make such a choice in order to direct a writing center at a research university—the kind of institution that so often serves as a gateway to the professoriate? My situation, with all its pros and cons, highlights the underlying issue: What do we do about important academic work that does not fit tidily into the usual mold of the tenure-track faculty position at an R1 institution?

The answer to these larger questions, for some, has been to argue for creating a teaching tenure track to complement the typical research-focused track at universities like my own. Important, emphasizing research in tenure decisions is a relatively recent development in the profession: in a statement updated in 2014, the American Association of University Professors (AAUP) documents how prior to the 1970s, most tenure-track appointments were in fact teaching intensive. It is only since then that tenure lines have drifted toward being primarily research intensive, with "teaching-intensive" appointments increasingly converted to "teaching-only" appointments excluded from the tenure track. In response, the AAUP calls for the conversion of contingent-faculty positions focused on teaching to tenure-eligible positions, "with only minor changes in job description." It also argues for the inclusion of a research component if faculty members so desire, though it also cautions that "faculty themselves should not perpetuate the false impression that tenure was invented as a merit badge for research-intensive appointments" (2010). Indeed.

In a similar vein, Michael Bérubé and Jennifer Ruth call for a teaching tenure track in their 2015 text *The Humanities, Higher Education, and Academic Freedom: Three Necessary Arguments*. Bérubé and Ruth focus on contingent faculty who are terminal degree holders; following their proposal, "the tenure process for such faculty would involve rigorous peer review, conducted by their tenured colleagues at the same institution, but would carry no expectations for research or creative activity" (19). They do not entirely preclude the possibility of research expectations, but they make it clear such requirements should not be foisted on anyone. Crucially, they maintain that only faculty on tenure lines (which would include many more people, under their proposal) should participate in shared governance. While their plan as a whole seems sensible, their insistence on this point, in contrast to the AAUP's call for contingent-faculty participation in shared governance, seems to exaggerate both contingent faculty's susceptibility to voting based on self-interest and tenure-line faculty members' ability to rise above said interests. Their argument also elides positions like mine, which involves a fixed-term contract but was filled via a national search and is promotable (they include "professors of the practice" in their overall category of contingent faculty). And it's hard to see where a teaching/administrative position like mine fits in.

As folks in the academic blogosphere have pointed out, most of the published responses to Bérubé and Ruth have been written by individuals occupying positions of academic privilege. In an essay in the *Chronicle of Higher Education* about the possibility of a teaching tenure track, Leonard Cassuto (2017) worries, "And what about the prospect of a caste system? The two tenure tracks could turn into castes (it's not hard to guess which would be the higher), or worse, warring camps." To which I say: the caste system is already in operation; we can do what we can to make the situation more equitable and sustainable, or we can leave it untouched and thus tacitly continue to accept it. And while one's departmental colleagues would inevitably know which track one was on, others need not have ready access to that information. An assistant professor could be an assistant professor, full stop, and so on up the ranks. Moreover, if pay were the same, universities would send the message that both tracks were equally valued, at least on paper—which, in my own case, would be a distinct improvement. In some ways, the question of compensation outweighs gaps in prestige: I have often commented that if my university would like to pay me $120K, as they do my fellow assistant PoPs in finance, they can call me whatever they want!

In all seriousness, pay equity is no laughing matter, nor am I unaware of my considerable privilege. Despite the pay gap between my tenure-track colleagues and me, I am at least paid a livable wage, which can't be said for the ever-growing number of colleagues around the country who disproportionately bear the teaching load in writing courses. As Liliana M. Naydan points out in her chapter in this collection, it is imperative for people like me to ally with those colleagues and avoid complacency. And, to be transparent, I recently managed to partially close the wage gap by (reluctantly) reentering the job-market fray. But the compensation problem can, in fact, be addressed systemically: the University of Delaware, for instance, has a "Continuing Track" for teaching-focused faculty (a deliberate choice of terminology, as it "makes the name an affirmative statement instead of a negative one"), with pay equity between CT and TT faculty (University of Delaware 2016; Dhurjati et al. 2015). While this resolution isn't, perhaps, quite as satisfying as including all these positions on the tenure track, pay equity sends a significant message about the value the institution places on the work of teaching. It seems hardly a coincidence that UD has a collective-bargaining agreement in place. But depending on the climate of one's campus and state, unionizing may be more or less feasible; it is also obviously not a guarantee, or we would see more solutions like Delaware's across the country.

That is not to say other colleges and universities haven't been trying: the AAUP documents a number of attempts to convert contingent-faculty positions to tenure track, including within the Penn State system (where Bérubé has played an active role) and St. John's University—but as the AAUP notes,

> Many of these practices and policies are less than ideal in one respect or another—they may convert the status of one group of faculty members while disregarding another group, or they may convert an existing pool of faculty to the tenure line at once, while putting in place no system for

further regularization of faculty appointments or checks on further hiring of non-tenure-track professors. (2014, Appendix A: Conversion Practices and Proposals, para. 1)

The adjunctification of higher education has been a runaway train, and the bifurcation of teaching- and research-intensive faculty roles at research universities has been so extreme it is unsurprising even schools with good intentions have struggled to reverse this trend.

A teaching track for tenure at research-intensive institutions is far preferable to the situation we have now, but if such lines are adopted wholesale while maintaining large fleets of underpaid, overworked, and undersupported adjunct faculty, we will have done nothing more than put a band-aid on a gaping, festering wound. Truthfully, I have worried about my own complicity: if I, on principle, oppose the idea of important work, especially the teaching of writing, being shouldered by folks off the tenure track, I am still tacitly agreeing to the system by occupying this NTTF job. I have seen and experienced alternatives, and I chose opt out of the tenure track but not leave the faculty life behind altogether. I am lucky to have been able to make such choices, but they are not without consequences, for both myself and others.

Regardless of what position one occupies within this system, for any right-thinking person, the current situation is unacceptable. And given that teaching-intensive tenure-track positions are not presently flourishing at R1 universities, there's something to be said for opting, at minimum, for more positions like my own. I am grateful for the relative autonomy I have as NTTF. I can pursue my research in whatever form I choose; I need not shy away from collaborative work or worry about producing a monograph to get promoted. I appreciate being back on the academic side of the house, in a large enough department to find a support network. I wouldn't say I have achieved work-life balance, but I am able to cook dinner every night for my family (I have to, since we have a number of food restrictions among us). It is a benefit that the work I do to sustain and develop our writing center is accounted for in my apportionment, not seen as a distraction from my scholarship—which would be all but inevitable were my position tenure track at this kind of institution. As Laura Brady and Nathalie Singh-Corcoran (2013) document, it is, in fact, possible to design equitable NTTF administrative positions that are evaluated fairly.

And yet, we can do better. I've made my peace with how, as long as I'm at my current institution, practice is never going to make permanent—but we can and should agitate for more. My NTT status has downsides not only for me personally but also, as a consequence, for the writing center I direct—a unit that deserves more visibility, support, and recognition for the work of our entire staff. To be blunt, I have always had difficulty seeing what I do as any less important or valuable than what my colleagues do—a common phenomenon among NTT/contingent directors, as Fels points out. Many of us in writing centers specifically and writing studies generally are doing essential, exciting work whose importance and impact are sometimes hard to measure period, let alone by a research-centered tenure-track yardstick. For these reasons, I believe a teaching track for tenure is worth pursuing—positions that would offer equity with respect to pay, benefits, and status, as well as equal access to affordances such as sabbatical leaves and course reductions for curricular work and research. I am, however, fully aware that recapturing the earlier "big-tent" definition of tenure would involve a fundamental rethinking of current institutional values at R1s, particularly the value (or lack thereof) placed on teaching. Writing studies shines a particularly hard light on the situation, as instructors who come into contact with so many students in first-year and other writing classes are so often contingent. Our current professional situation is untenable—and it can't be up to those of us with less institutional clout to lead the charge. We need our TT colleagues to be our accomplices and noisy advocates—to listen, to consider the myriad implications of their roles as gatekeepers, and to act, with an understanding that including us and agitating for equitable treatment is truly in the best interests of the profession, our institutions, and the well-being of both teaching-focused professionals and the many students whose lives they touch.

REFERENCES

American Association of University Professors. 2010. "Tenure and Teaching-Intensive Appointments." Last updated 2014. https://www.aaup.org/report/tenure-and-teaching-intensive-appointments.

Bérubé, Michael, and Jennifer Ruth. 2015. *The Humanities, Higher Education, and Academic Freedom: Three Necessary Arguments.* New York: Palgrave MacMillan.

Brady, Laura, and Nathalie Singh-Corcoran. 2013. "Non-Tenure-Track Faculty Members as Administrators: Planning and Evaluation." *ADE Bulletin* 153, *ADFL Bulletin* 42 (3): 71–81.

Cassuto, Leonard. 2017. "A Tenure Track for Teachers?" *Chronicle of Higher Education* 63 (38). https://www.chronicle.com/article/A-Tenure-Track-for-Teachers-/240015.

Caswell, Nicole, Jackie Grutsch McKinney, and Rebecca Jackson. 2016. *The Working Lives of New Writing Center Directors.* Logan: Utah State University Press.

Dhurjati, Prasad, Nicole Donofrio, Jill Flynn, Laura Glass, Thomas Kaminski, Matthew Kinservik, Robert Opila, Thomas Powers, Anuradha Sivaraman, and George Watson. 2015. *Report of the Provost's Commission on Continuing Non-Tenure-Track Faculty.* University of Delaware. http://facsen.udel.edu/Sites/Executive/CNTT-Commission-Report.pdf.

Fels, Dawn. 2017. "The Risks of Contingent Writing Center Directorship." In *Contingency, Exploitation, and Solidarity: Labor and Action in English Composition*, edited by Seth Kahn, William B. Lalicker, and Amy Lynch-Biniek, 119–31. Ft. Collins, CO: WAC Clearinghouse.

Gladstein, Jill, and Brandon Fralix. 2015. "2013 Four Institution Survey." https://writingcensus.swarthmore.edu/survey/4.

Grutsch McKinney, Jackie. 2013. *Peripheral Visions for Writing Centers*. Logan: Utah State University Press.

Salem, Lori. 2014. "Opportunity and Transformation: How Writing Centers Are Positioned in the Political Landscape of Higher Education in the United States." *Writing Center Journal* 3 (1): 15–43.

University of Delaware. 2016. *Collective Bargaining Agreement Between the University of Delaware and the University of Delaware Chapter American Association of University Professors July 1, 2016–June 30, 2021.* https://www.udel.edu/content/dam/udelImages/human-resources/EmployeeRelations/cbas/AAUP.pdf.

2

HOW STUDENT AFFAIRS PRAXIS CAN AID THE NEXUS OF EMOTIONAL LABOR FOR NTTF

Peter Brooks

There is a cost to emotion work: it affects the degree to which we listen to feeling and sometimes our very capacity to feel . . . [it] is an art fundamental to civilized living, and . . . the cost is usually worth the fundamental benefit.

Arlie Hochschild, *The Managed Heart*

Two young boys sit at a cloth-covered table. Plates and glasses hold breakfast foods and drinks: waffles, watermelon, eggs, milk, red punch with miniumbrellas. Both wear caps. The room's aglow with sunbeams, blaring in from big windows, cutting through lush palms. Writing students viewing this photo conclude the boys are in some tropical locale. A Goofy cameo helps. And the boys' wide smiles affirm. What students don't see, hidden behind happy displays, is hurt. Invisible to the eye, both boys have buried being bullied; their caps hide what causes this pain.

I am one of the boys.

On our last class day, I share this photo and other time-frozen moments. Most are candidly positive: pole vaulting in high school with my wild, curly hair; our Arizona State University leadership team clad in school colors; me crying after said team received the Most Spirited Delegation award, a personal goal realized. Coupled with closure activities that attempt to bring students' learning full circle and ease end-of-quarter anxieties, I conclude with stories tied to why I teach. Among the course-long steps I take to bridge my identity as a white, cisgender male professor with the diverse students I serve, this vulnerable moment reinforces our safe community space. Likewise, when I reveal the multiple reasons I got teased—wild hair, big ears, "nerdiness"—I hope fellow bullied students find inspirational options to assuage invisible pain instead

DOI: 10.7330/9781646420759.c002

of hearing *rub some dirt in it*. We can heal without harming others. We can feel whole while reclaiming scars. We can have a voice even if we've been silenced.

I tell students how writing helped. Postbullying, I kept a journal that helped me process through anxieties. I share how writing stories provided a healthy escape and opportunity to reconstruct an identity others had slowly chipped away. And I confess how I wish Rick, my cap-clad friend, had written more with me. My cap hid wild hair, big ears; his hid surgical scars of a young African American boy dying from brain cancer.

Back in school, when Rick wasn't feeling too tired to play tag football, a bully pushed him, shoving a medical tube deeper into his chest. In visible pain, Rick walked away, pulling out the tube while the boy yelled *you fucking pussy, get back here, what's wrong with you?!* I stood sad. Worse, I stood helpless. My fear made it difficult to defend him. My parents transferred me to another school; Rick stayed. Years later, we reconnected. He beat cancer, and I was trying to find an identity. He graciously forgave me after I apologized for not having had the emotional fortitude to support him. Rick's survival spirit is why I teach. And, important, why I choose to carry the emotional labor that complicates my stretched-thin time as a full-time lecturer.

When we non-tenure-track faculty (NTTF) become emotionally empty, we struggle to be present for others. We often hide our own trials when weathering students' emotional storms. Simultaneously, we feel our levees crack due to our precarious teaching positions. Completing our routine labor requirements to stay afloat already creates stress fractures. However, our employment procedures (renewal, promotion, etc.) fail to formally recognize, because of either poor categorization or support, the emotional work we extol. My emotional-labor practice began with Rick and was fostered during my time as a student affairs (SA) professional. Yet, emotional work is highly valorized in SA, validated through training and evaluations. During my first year as a full-time lecturer, I felt a whiplash contrast, which sparked a deeper self-reflection regarding emotional labor's intensifying relationship to being contingent faculty.

I wish to make more visible the invisible work of NTTF's emotional labor, starting with how writing classes are a nexus for students' emotional development and our employment demands. Next, I cover the seldomly discussed emotional-labor scholarship, highlighting Alice Gillam's (2003) concept of the *lean and lien* labor effect—the tension between our natural feelings and institutional requirements. Following that, I introduce the "hairball," a metaphorical representation of administrative systems containing the (in)visible policies, procedures, and personalities that impact instructors. Since professional systems are difficult to change, I discuss how student-development theory, student affairs' scholarly underpinning, can help contingent faculty understand and prepare for the emotional challenges students face. I don't expect faculty to become fully credentialed counselors, yet I think we can manage our emotional weight and dialogues with academic leadership regarding how to recognize this vital work.

THE (UN)EXPECTED NEXUS

Choosing the NTTF[1] lifestyle, I was mostly mentally prepared. I knew we didn't share publishing expectations like our tenure-track colleagues but wasn't fully prepared to spend more time, according to National Survey of Student Engagement data, negotiating service and teaching (2017, 15). The data show disproportionate time is given to service work alone, which surprised me. Sarah Austin and Erica Stone's chapter in this collection wonderfully illustrates the complexities and restraints our positions hold. Moreover, the responsibility to categorize, calculate, and commodify work was unfamiliar to me. In student affairs I never had to justify my existence. In full transparency, I did (and still do) feel support as a first-year composition (FYC) lecturer at my current institution. Yet, in that same year, several moments made me realize how much emotional labor is woven into teaching and service and how it extracts an immeasurable amount of time from our daily work; this "cost," as the Hochschild epigraph indicates, is time multiplied by emotional wear and tear.

Teaching writing specifically carries additional emotional expectations and pressures. Multiple composition pedagogies address student writing anxieties (Clark and Hernandez 2011; Driscoll and Wells 2012). Lecturers care, and we know such anxieties can be assuaged with individual conferences. Beneficial? Yes! Yet, the working week elongates when I meet with forty-eight students for twenty minutes each. FYC instructors carry additional pressures. The article "It Matters a Lot Who Teaches Introductory Courses. Here's Why" synthesizes several studies that corroborate how first-year students need a positive experience with their initial instructors for retention (Supiano 2018). Entering college, students attempt to (re)learn life. *Adulting* as they call it. A Harris Poll confirms this: "[First year] students report feeling more prepared academically than emotionally when they first started college" (2015, slide 22). Top concerns: *How do I afford college? How do I balance school with work, extracurriculars, personal wellness? How do I form meaningful relationships?* (slide 35). The Pew Research Center adds that 70 percent of future students rate anxiety and depression as their highest concerns (Pew Poll 2019). Student anxieties hide within academic work, yearning to be heard.

My own lecturer experience emblemizes the data. During individual writing conferences, a student revealed her high-school trauma and how she created motivational videos to survive. I opened up about my bullying, and we established a supportive rapport. Weeks later, she was sexually assaulted after a party. By listening, validating, and reminding her of how she coped, I hoped to ease her pain. Another student revealed her sexuality. She struggled with her father's unsupportiveness, but she *needed an adult to talk to* because, while she had friends, they didn't have any emotional strategies or guidance. With these moments, I stand with Hochschild: helping these students was worth the cost of my time multiplied by my emotional labor. However, faculty colleagues expressed anxieties about dealing with these common student situations. One asked, *How can you read all those student papers?* and another, in a different setting, *If a student came into my office crying, I wouldn't know what to say.* Neither comment, I feel, was incredulous or insensitive. However, coupled with unforeseen student crises (big or small, yet valid all), these quotes reveal the unpreparedness instructors feel regarding emotional labor and how we all share the cost.

THE LEAN AND LIEN OF EMOTIONAL LABOR

Emotional-labor scholarship is like NTTF labor discussions: present but not yet prominent; felt by contingent faculty, yet mostly unfamiliar to tenure-track faculty. Here, I wish to elucidate emotional-labor research and definitions for all to understand and embrace. Hochschild's *The Managed Heart: Commercialization of Human Feeling* commences with emotional-labor conversations: "What do we do when we manage emotion? What are the costs and benefits of managing emotion, in private life and at work?" (1983, 9–10). To answer, she analyzed college student surveys that had language that signaled emotional management, flight-attendant interviews (a profession tasked with portraying positivity), and bill-collector interviews to see how emotion unravels in unpleasant situations. Her findings:

> To manage the private loves and hates is to participate in an intricate private emotional system. When elements of that system are taken into the [public] marketplace and sold as human labor, they become stretched into

> standardized social forms. In these forms, a person's contribution of feeling is thinner, less freighted with consequence; but at the same time, it is seen as coming less from the self and being less directed to the other. (13)

As instructors, we emotionally support and challenge students, making Hochschild's study relevant to our position. Mary Guy, Meredith Newman, and Sharon Mastracci shift the discussion to public-service professionals, a classification common to most NTTF. Observing and interviewing government leaders, corrections officers, and 911 operators, *Emotional Labor: Putting the Service in Public Service* expands Hochschild's questions: "What are the positive aspects of performing emotional labor? What does burnout look like to those in the human service trenches?" (2014, 28).

Closest to contingent writing faculty contexts is research regarding writing program administration (WPA) and writing centers. Three narratives illuminate emotional labor's complexity in relation to teaching writing. Mara Holt, Leon Anderson, and Albert Rouzie's "Making Emotion Work Visible in Writing Program Administration" and Gillam's (2003) "Collaboration, Ethics, and the Emotional Labor of WPAs" detail the emotional miasma. Gillam writes,

> WPAs show empathy and give encouragement to new writing teachers. WPAs teach this kind of emotion work to new teachers, who engage in it with their first-year students, who need it to gain the courage to write. . . . WPAs must graciously explain to faculty senates why first-year students pass English courses and still don't write to please their engineering professors. (2003, 151)

This mirrors our specific sandwiched situation: we enact empathy and encouragement for students while justifying to tenured faculty why that difficult-to-measure output is relevant to employment expectations. Related, in "Writing Center Administration and/as Emotional Labor," Rebecca Jackson, Jackie Grutsch McKinney, and Nicole Caswell reaffirm how much we as educators are un(der)prepared to navigate emotional hardships: "Our sense at the end of the yearlong study was that it was a shame or problematic, not that the directors have to devote so much time to emotional labor, but rather that they hadn't been prepared to expect and negotiate it" (2016).

Hochschild's term "emotional labor" encompasses all these conflicted narratives because of this public/private system of feelings. "Emotional labor [is] the management of feeling to create a publicly observable facial and bodily display . . . [that] requires one to induce or suppress feeling in order to sustain the outward countenance that produces the proper state of mind I others" (1983, 7). Hochschild's definition reveals the invisible mental work that takes up time during emotional moments at work, and afterward when we're personally decompressing, impeding opportunities to accomplish other employment expectations.

Gillam further illustrates the additional pressure emotional labor places on writing contexts. Through her WPA experience negotiating expectations from academic leadership with student demands and needs, she introduces the homonyms *lean* and *lien* (building from Sandra Bartky), to emphasize this emotional push/pull:[2]

> Bartky uses . . . *lean*, "to bend or slant away from the vertical," "to incline the weight of the body so as to be supported," "to exert pressure." Metaphorically, Bartky suggests that the pressure or weight of supporting another psychically and emotionally bends or hobbles the posture or position of the one serving as the ballast or support. But it seems to me that the term "lien" is an equally suggestive metaphor. A "lien" is, of course, an economic and legal hold on one's proprietary claim on one's material status. (quoted in Gillam 2003, 118)

The occupational gossamer chains we feel strain the labor we must complete and the emotional labor we choose for the betterment of others. Rachel Azima's chapter in this book amplifies these common themes via her own experience. And there is this important, related distinction: emotional-labor researchers are primarily *women*, pioneering this important field. Tragically, as Azima and others point out, women certainly experience more emotional inequity too, typically from disrespectful male students and/or from colleagues/administrators who see emotional labor as women's work (Holt, Anderson, and Rouzie 2003, 150). Emotional labor is ingrained into our daily labor, yet we must fight the systemic procedures that unduly minimize such work.

THE LIEN AS A HAIRBALL

Cat hairballs are unpleasant. These squishy, furry globs are by-products of mostly unseen systems working in concert to achieve one objective: keep the cat clean. The metaphorical hairball-as-lien system emerged from Gordon MacKenzie's (1998) employment within Hallmark's corporate structure. Synthesizing his hairball concept with activity theory (AT)—a methodological lens that unpacks systems' (in)visible structures—we have a framework to better identify invisible ills. Among the various AT iterations, I find Elizabeth Wardle and Doug Downs's (2011) clearest. Within their terminology, all hairballs contain connections between a subject (us) and our job's objectives, tools, rules, and roles and the community who creates/fosters these components. As scholarship shows, complex administrative systems can lead to employee burn out (Guy, Newman, and Mastracci 2014, 105–06), emotional indifference (Gillam 2003, 121), and academic-leadership disappointment if/when we attempt to improve our hairball (Jackson, Grutsch McKinney, and Caswell 2016). All are risks for contingent faculty because, if we have time and energy to fight, we're vulnerable during (in)visible reappointment processes. I'm not suggesting we don't fight the fights that need fighting, yet we should pick our battles.

Knowledge about how/when to change the hairball developed during my less precarious SA years. MacKenzie's hairball provided a language to make visible my employment tendrils that caused anxiety. Two other readings also helped me cope with structural (dys)function as I later matriculated through various writing programs. First, Jerry Harvey's (1988) article "The Abilene Paradox: The Management of Agreement" taught me how to avoid emotionally draining activities. An Abilene Paradox occurs when all participants lose faith in an initiative's function, yet no one is willing to speak up, disband, or leave due to fear. When I worked at Grand Lakes University, writing instructors (full time, part time, and graduate) participated in a pass/fail blind portfolio review for FYC classes. Privately, many instructors expressed dread and drain: there was little curricular freedom, meetings became battlegrounds over microscopic details, and review day was an eight- to ten-hour affair during which we read thirty to forty student portfolios with ten pages of writing each. Students expressed anxiety concerning the high-stakes process, increasing our emotional strain as we attempted to support them. Even decision makers chose to minimize their own misgivings. Yet, no one had the temerity to stop the process. When Abilene Paradoxes exist on a macro level, we can choose to speak up, but we might have to locate the small gaps within the system to find professional solace.

I also introduce this concept to caution us to against creating hairballs of our own. The question *how can you read all those papers?* initially sounded like *reading papers feels torturous.* Anecdotally, I worry this is due to the disconnect between our strong passion for writing and students' writing ambivalence or loathing. As David Bartholomae (1986) reminds us, evaluating papers is complex work and consumes the most labor. So how can we design assignments in which all participants feel positive investment? We want our leaders to abandon unfair/unreasonable expectations; we should do so for students too. Homework is a must. Yet, I'm calling for humble self-reflection when designing assignments to achieve an equitable, challenging, and supportive experience for students.

Related, Daniel Seymour's (1995) *Once Upon a Campus* is another good read that helps us avoid building systems that cause extra emotional labor. His eleventh lesson, "universal solutions to exceptional problems create universal problems" (1995, 121), teaches us to avoid overreacting to rare problems with broad policy shifts. Circling back to Grand Lakes University, decision makers reacted to one administrator's concern that portfolios were not interesting reads. The rubric was changed to require "intriguing" papers. We instructors felt additional stress as we tried to collectively interpret what that meant. To lessen the lien, we must be courageous and avoid participating in or creating problematic structures.

THE LANGUAGE OF STUDENT DEVELOPMENT

I support my colleague who said *If a student came into my office crying, I wouldn't know what to say*. As professors, we're barely trained to counsel/console young adults. When we're leaned on emotionally, we ask ourselves two questions: "'What, in this situation, should I be feeling?' and 'Who am I?'" (Hochschild 1983, 22). The internal labor here is twofold: first, we must consider an appropriate, supportive response; second, we must prepare for the risk that another person's narrative may unearth our own traumas. Both questions require reflective time. Even with an MEd and professional training, I still spend time processing students' woes. The quantity/quality chasm between SA professional training and NTTF training related to emotional labor is gigantic. I know colleagues want to feel more prepared, yet time and training must be provided in ways that don't detract from our routine work schedules.

To further assuage emotional-labor preparedness, we should draw from scholarship that guides SA professionals: student-development (SD) theory. As with the hairball, when language demystifies the invisible, we feel better. When we're ill, knowing why matters. Holt, Anderson, and Rouzie even suggest that "we might explore a vocabulary" (2003, 159) that deconstructs emotional labor. When I was a first-year student, my friend Joanne confided in me the sexual abuse she experienced as a child. Her story, like Rick's, inspired me to learn more. I felt intuitively comfortable to help, but once I came across terminology and language developed by SA scholars, I gained more avenues to support others and myself emotionally.

Student-development theory attempts to make sense of college life's invisible threads. While graduate programs vary by title and curriculum, every SA practitioner comes across Nancy Evans's *Student Development in*

College: Theory, Research, and Practice, which covers the genesis, applications, and challenges of SD theories. Student narratives show how theory works in practice, and the critical analysis of each theory is thorough, credible, and passionate. SD researchers consider these questions:

- What interpersonal and intrapersonal changes occur while the student is in college?
- What factors lead to this development?
- What aspects of the college environment encourage or [restrict] growth?
- What developmental outcomes should we strive to achieve in college? (Evans et al. 2010, 7)

Weave *writing* into these questions, and we start to see how writing pedagogy parallels SD theory. In fact, just as we have key theorists and movements—Peter Elbow/expressivists, Andrea Lunsford/cognitivists, and Patricia Bizzell/social constructionists—so too does SD theory: Chickering's Identity Development, Perry's Intellectual and Ethical Development, and Kolb's Experiential Learning. Moreover, instructors study writing pedagogy for specific learning experiences (ELL, cognitive disabilities, etc.) and rhetorics representing different identities (feminist, cultural, queer, etc.); these areas align closely with SD subdisciplines that also speak to socioeconomic identity, race, religion, gender, and sexuality.

As an example, Nancy Schlossberg's theory of transition unveils the emotional labor within (semi)traumatic events, providing guidance to help students in those moments. When I was bullied, I prayed. Speaking aloud eased the pain. After I transferred schools, things weren't perfect. Similar to praying, I used self-talking reflection to cope. I continue to use self-reflective walks to assuage my anxiety. This discovery process is the basis of Schlossberg's studies. Developed in 1981, Schlossberg's model (Figure 2.1) utilizes language to unpack transitions or "any event, or non-event, that results in changed relationships, routines, assumptions, and roles" (qtd in Evans et al 2010, 218).

You may think *I'm supposed to remember all that?!?* I thought so too, but no. Theory attempts to concretize traumatic ambiguity; learning this language is to become aware of our emotional labor. Additionally, I like this theory's focus on coping. When my former student talked about her second sexual assault, we revisited how she used vlogs to cope, giving her a place to start. SD theory parts are as helpful as the whole.

Another term, the "non-event," characterizes a common occurrence for students and instructors. When overt trauma happens, we all likely have intuitive, empathetic (re)actions. For example, our campus

Figure 2.1. Schlossberg's Theory of Transition (Evans et al. 2010, 218)

A. TRANSITIONS

Events or nonevents resulting in changed relationships, routines, assumptions, and/or roles.

1. Meaning for the Individual Based on:
   Type: anticipated, unanticipated, non-event
   Context: relationship to transition and the setting
   Impact: alterations in daily life
2. The Transition Process
   Reactions over time
   Moving in, moving through, and moving out

B. COPING WITH TRANSITIONS

Influenced by ratio of assets and liabilities in regard to four sets of factors:

1. Situation
   Trigger, timing, control, role change, duration, previous experience, concurrent stress, assessment
2. Self
   Personal and demographic characteristics: socioeconomic status, gender, age, health, ethnicity/culture
   Psychological resources: ego development, outlook, commitment, values, spirituality and resilience
3. Support
   Types: intimate, family, friends, institutional
   Functions: affect, affirmation, aid, honest feedback
   Measurement: stable and changing supports
4. Strategies
   Three categories: modify situation, control meaning, manage stress in aftermath
   Four coping modes: information seeking, direct action, inhibition of action, intrapsychic behavior

---

community came together when someone vandalized a spiritual space, specifically targeting our Muslim students. But sometimes we struggle when things *don't* happen: a student's application for a scholarship/job/academic program is rejected, or a student is "ghosted" (ignored) romantically; an instructor is promised a course release that doesn't materialize. These nonevents slowly chip away at our emotional stability.

A former student, Gina, commutes from her parents' home. Her older sister and husband moved home due to financial issues. Gina was sympathetic, yet became anxious because her sister's schedule made the space inhospitable for studying. Her sister kept promising *It's only temporary, we're looking for a new place to live*; weeks turned into months with no progress. Gina still understood, and tried to adapt; however, her emotional fortification, because she believed everything would resolve, slowly crumbled. Be mindful that when students feel down, the cause may be that something *didn't* happen.

SPREAD HOPE

Emotional labor is a concern. At campus, department, and unit levels, we must "acknowledge the capacity for nurturance, empathy, and care as well as the capacity for anger, fear, sadness and anxiety . . . [and] delete the convention that emotional concerns are not as important as cognitive concerns" (Guy, Newman, and Mastracci 2014, 187–88). Paraphrasing (and adding to) Holt, Anderson, and Rouzie, the following should also be enacted to help instructors:

- Provide emotional-literacy training for administrators, teachers, and students, including counseling.
- Create a collective, holistic understanding of higher education's (in)visible processes through dialogue and transparent practices.
- Recognize, reward, and promote teachers who practice and manage emotional labor well.
- Design role-playing experiences for students and TAs. (2003, 158–59)

Most academic folks (leadership and peers) will likely support the first two suggestions. Partnering our departments with campus resources—especially counseling-center staff who will eagerly support any emotional work involving students—and learning more about our campus's hairballs are both worth the time. I include the fourth suggestion because, as a designer of course-long in-class simulations, I know activities help students navigate emotions and learn in low-risk ways. SA uses simulation all the time. And game-studies scholarship (Juul 2013) reinforces the enjoyment and ethical development inherent in role-playing.

For the third suggestion, a (re)classification of emotional labor is necessary for us as contingent faculty. The language of SD theory can act as an inroad for constructing reappointment/promotion policy that acknowledges emotional work. As a start, walk policymakers through charts like the one in figure 2.1. Even for a brief student encounter, we go through three stages of emotional labor: initially listening, following up/making referrals, and personal processing. I categorize emotional labor as teaching, which is the highest priority for NTTF. Yet, how do we valorize our emotional labor via administrative procedure without then defining student interaction as currency? For *lien* items like merit, renewal, and promotion, I'm comfortable including ongoing mentor-level work and broader required processes (for example, using our mandatory academic-alert system). Yet, I feel less comfortable sharing quantifiable or personal details that reduce my students to statistics.

If our quixotic approaches to changing these policies fall short, smaller strategies can ballast us and our students. First, consider your office space, where students will likely share struggles. Make the space safe and welcoming. In addition to a well-lit room with my window/door shades pulled, I face my desk toward the door and adjust chairs to sit eye level. Personal artifacts and student gifts adorn my shelves more than books and degrees do. Second, I respect instructors' variable (dis)comfort regarding student struggles, yet it is worth the time to establish professional relationships with school counselors. They'll validate your experience and provide advice. Third, learn your departmental policies and dean's expectations about working with students, not just for reappointment/promotion guidelines but also to keep your dean in the loop in case of emergencies. Fourth, it's okay, and helpful, to foster boundaries, including around your time.

Finally, specifically knowing what to say can help. Schlossberg, other theorists, and SA professionals all agree to focus on active listening and validation. Writing scholar Krista Ratcliffe's (2005) rhetorical listening *is* active listening praxis. Make eye contact, nod, and, if you're comfortable, feel free to emote empathetically. Same with validating: *What you've experienced sounds [emotion]; I want you to know I hear you/believe you and I care for your well-being.* Survivors feel at fault. They believe their choices made others harm them. We are not acting as judge when validating; we are, however, publicly acknowledging a survivor's private pain. The best counselors are *not* problem solvers, they're superb listeners and validators.

COMPASSIONATE CODA

I amplify NTTF emotional-labor conversations because emotional labor already amplifies our workload. Our writing classes carry the high potential for students to share personal stories. Our organizations must lessen the lien by supporting emotional labor via preparation and recognition. And for ourselves, we must develop student-support strategies and personal coping mechanisms to minimize the lien that cannot be changed instantly. Determining when to emotionally lean in or away won't be easy. Nor is it easy to (re)create an identity after being bullied. Or to find the strength to fight cancer while feeling socially insecure. Or to muster the courage to share trauma with a teacher. Yet, the minute steps we take are worth the few free minutes we have. We can build a supportive culture. We can let students know we've been bullied. We can inspire others because we've beat cancer. We can stand fearless on a digital stage, visible in front of other women, and share our sexual-assault survival so we may be invisible no more.

NOTES

1. I'll flip between this term and *instructor* throughout.
2. Full disclosure: Alice Gillam, a great mentor to me, was also tenure-track faculty. Thus, imagine being responsible for a writing program's success knowing that success depends on such an obtuse measurement.

REFERENCES

Bartholomae, David. 1986. "Inventing the University." *Journal of Basic Writing* 5 (1): 4–23.
Bartky, Sandra L. 1990. "Feeding Egos and Tending Wounds: Deference and Disaffection in Women's Emotional Labor." *Femininity and Domination: Studies in the Phenomenology of Oppression*, by Sandra L. Bartky, 109–129. New York: Routledge.
Clark, Irene, and Andrea Hernandez. 2011. "Genre Awareness, Academic Argument, and Transferability." *WAC Journal* 22 (1): 65–78.
Driscoll, Dana Lynn, and Jennifer Wells. 2012. "Beyond Knowledge and Skills: Writing Transfer and the Role of Student Dispositions." *Composition Forum* 26 (1): 1–15.
Evans, Nancy J., Deanna S. Forney, Florence M. Guido, Lori D. Patton, and Kristen A. Renn. 2010. *Student Development in College: Theory, Research, and Practice*. San Francisco: Jossey-Bass.
Gillam, Alice. 2003. "Collaboration, Ethics, and the Emotional Labor of WPAs." In *A Way to Move: Rhetorics of Emotion & Composition Studies*, edited by Dale Jacobs and Laura Micciche, 113–123. Portsmouth, NH: Boynton/Cook.
Guy, Mary E., Meredith A. Newman, and Sharon H. Mastracci. 2014. *Emotional Labor: Putting the Service in Public Service*. Taylor and Francis.
Harris Poll. 2015. "The First-Year College Experience: A Look into Students' Challenges and Triumphs During Their First Term at College." October 8. https://www.issuelab.org/resources/23720/23720.pdf.
Harvey, Jerry B. 1988. "The Abilene Paradox: The Management of Agreement." *Organizational Dynamics* 17 (1): 17–43.
Hochschild, Arlie Russell. 1983. *The Managed Heart: Commercialization of Human Feeling*. Berkeley: University of California Press.
Holt, Mara, Leon Anderson, and Albert Rouzie. 2003. "Making Emotion Work Visible in Writing Program Administration" In *A Way to Move: Rhetorics of Emotion & Composi-*

tion Studies, edited by Dale Jacobs and Laura Micciche, 147–160. Portsmouth, NH: Boynton/Cook.

Jackson, Rebecca, Jackie Grutsch McKinney, and Nicole I. Caswell. 2016. "Writing Center Administration and/as Emotional Labor." *Composition Forum* 34. https://files.eric.ed.gov/fulltext/EJ1113425.pdf.

Juul, Jesper. 2013. *The Art of Failure: An Essay on the Pain of Playing Video Games (Playful Thinking)*. Cambridge: MIT Press.

Mackenzie, Gordon. 1998. *Orbiting the Giant Hairball: A Corporate Fool's Guide to Surviving with Grace*. New York: Viking.

National Survey of Student Engagement. 2017. "Engagement Insights: Survey Findings on The Quality of Undergraduate Education—Annual Results 2017." Bloomington: Indiana University Center for Postsecondary Research.

Pew Poll. 2019. "Most U.S. Teens See Anxiety and Depression as a Major Problem Among Their Peers." February 20. http://www.pewsocialtrends.org/2019/02/20/most-u-s-teens-see-anxiety-and-depression-as-a-major-problem-among-their-peers/.

Ratcliffe, Krista. 2005. *Rhetorical Listening: Identification, Gender, Whiteness*. Carbondale: Southern Illinois University Press.

Seymour, Daniel. 1995. "Once upon a Campus: Lessons for Improving Quality and Productivity in Higher Education." *American Council on Education/Oryx Press Series on Higher Education*. Phoenix: Oryx.

Supiano, Beckie. 2018. "It Matters a Lot Who Teaches Introductory Courses. Here's Why." *Chronicle of Higher Education*. April 15. https://www.chronicle.com/article/it-matters-a-lot-who-teaches-introductory-courses-heres-why/.

Wardle, Elizabeth, and Doug Downs. 2011. *Writing about Writing: A College Reader*. Boston: Bedford/St. Martins.

3
CONTINGENT FACULTY IN THE GIG ECONOMY
A Conversation, Comparison, and Call

Erica M. Stone and Sarah E. Austin

Authors' Note: This chapter was written in 2018 when Erica and Sarah were both working in contingent-faculty roles. Since its publication, both authors have moved into tenure-track and administrative positions. While this shift in positionality doesn't undo the confessional nature of this chapter, the authors fully recognize the privilege associated with publishing a piece like this from relatively secure places in the academy.

> *Well, I have just decided that if they're going to treat me like a contractor, then I am going to act like an entrepreneurial contractor!*
> —Anonymous adjunct, overheard at CCCC Regional Conference in April 2018

Quotes like the one above are not uncommon, but they are often hushed by an academic culture that seeks to protect its darkest secret: labor abuse. Historically, the professoriate has been largely seen as privileged white men in suits who get summers off and healthy pensions at fifty. But, as middle-aged women and writing studies faculty, we know this identity couldn't be further from the truth. As of 2018, roughly 75 percent of university faculty were off the tenure track and participating (willingly or not) in the gig economy of higher ed; in 1969, only 21.7 percent of faculty were nontenure (Tolley 2018, viii). Similarly, the shift toward neoliberalism within the US university has caused writing studies coursework to be further viewed as a transaction between teacher and student, mechanizing the learning process and automating the role of faculty (Welch and Scott 2016, 10). As a result, the roles of non-tenure-track faculty (NTTF) in writing studies, largely held by women, have been deprofessionalized and disaggregated so

DOI: 10.7330/9781646420759.c003

their workloads, identities, and impacts have been hidden from view. In response to this shift, grassroot efforts have developed within those casual ranks to address the issue from a labor point of view. Maria Maisto, the president of the New Faculty Majority Foundation, an advocacy organization that focuses exclusively on issues related to NTTF, and her coauthors Joseph McCartin and Jacob Swenson, discuss the ways marginalized faculty members "have coordinated their actions nationally, maximizing their impact," and how they "have developed community support in order to minimize retaliation and build the public awareness needed to sustain their activism" (2014). Our stories and reflections, as follows, are attempts to come to terms with the realities of contingent faculty as we live them. In this chapter, we speak out about the need for continued awareness, organizing, and activism in the face of what looks to be a permanent shift in the composition of higher education faculty. We begin this chapter as both a confession and call. It's a confession of our choices to be members of the contingent-faculty community and our complicity in a system we know exploits the time and labor of those members. Conversely, this chapter traces our own experiences and reflects on the kinds of choices that have led us to our current roles.

Our timeline for this chapter stretches across multiple years. The entire chapter is organized around a synchronous conversation between the authors in October 2018. Table 3.1 compares the overall yearly workload for one calendar year (July 1, 2017–July 1, 2018). Table 3.2 lays bare the differences between our pay and benefits. We chose this method of personal-data collection and direct comparison in order to create a transparent picture of the lived realities of two contingent faculty. We recognize the privilege of our positions that allow us to write this piece at all. The vulnerable nature of this chapter was uncomfortable for us during the composing, revising, and editing processes, and we trust our readers will be gracious in their reading and discussion of our experiences.

A DOCUMENTED CONVERSATION ON CONTINGENT LABOR AND IDENTITY

On October 27, 2018, we met at Common Grounds, a coffee shop in Denver, to record this interview. After struggling to work via long distance and in asynchronous writing sessions, we decided an audio-recorded face-to-face conversation might help us talk openly about our lived labor experiences with a focus on our complicit participation in the contingent-labor cycle. By making the invisible *visible* (Warner

2002) through a documented dialog, we contextualize and call back the constellation (Powell et al. 2014) of hushed conversations about how contingency affects the identities of NTTF. Given's Sarah's experiential and research-based knowledge on the subject of contingency, Erica structured the conversation around a few questions about academic labor practices.

> ERICA: Even though we understand that our institutions would collapse without the labor of NTTF faculty, we continue to remain active in contingent-labor positions. Does that make us complicit in our abuse? Should you and I be held to a different standard because we love our jobs?
>
> SARAH: The oddity of my position is that it's technically a contingent position because it's a three-year renewable contract, but it's called *permanent party*. During the second year of the three-year contract, renewal paperwork is submitted by requirement. As a faculty member, I know for certain in year two whether or not my contract is being renewed for another three years (not including the third year of my existing contract). Unless something egregious occurs, I expect renewal. The choice to return becomes mine. It feels like a misnomer for me to say I'm contingent because I know that the position I have is fantastic as far as academic positions. There are tenure-track positions that aren't anywhere near as good as the job I have: jobs with a 4/4+ teaching load, with less funding for conferences, pay that's worse, and benefits that aren't as comprehensive. I know that I could have this position for the next fifteen years and retire with a pension if I wanted to. That's a privileged position.
>
> I often feel like an imposter: Am I really contingent when I know that the job I have is as secure as any other federally funded job? Yes, I'm subject to furloughs and budget cuts, but when is a federal, military academy going to be disbanded in the United States? Likely never.
>
> ERICA: You have a dual awareness of where you are because you recognize that your position is contingent by definition, and you also spent so much of your time and insight studying contingency and writing your master's thesis on it that you're able to recognize some of the parts of your position that are contingent. For instance, your ability to talk about certain things in class when you're working in a military institution—that's part of an oppression that comes with your position, and you have to do it covertly in some ways.
>
> SARAH: That's true. Although it's nowhere near as restrictive as people assume.
>
> ERICA: That part is worth talking about, and I understand why you might feel complicit. I feel complicit in the same way that you do in terms of, or maybe guilty is the right word instead of complicit, because I could wake up after winter break and say, "I don't want to go back." I could find a job somewhere else or not take another job

at all and just finish my PhD because I have the luxury of being married to someone who carries the benefits. I'm not someone who is teaching nine classes at three institutions as a highway flyer trying to feed a family of three. My participation in the system is voluntary, and that makes me complicit.

I've been thinking a lot about this, especially as we write this chapter. I participate in a system I disagree with more out of obligation for relationships than out of obligation for continuing to keep the system afloat. And those two sets of values are really a conflict for me because I love teaching, and it means a lot to me to make a real difference in the world. Part of remaining in the system is not really in support of it but in support of what I feel like I'm able to give.

SARAH: That need to give, though, expands your job description past what's required in your contract, and it plays into that hideous idea that we can be exploited because we like our jobs. It's not okay to exploit people, to pay them less, merely because they love the job and would do it for free.

ERICA: Right. And some of us, if we won the lottery, would do it for free. I would. But that doesn't equate to wanting to be exploited. How would you say this idea of working as an NTTF member affects the way you design your courses and align them with your current scholarship?

SARAH: I think the biggest frustration I have with where I work is that I am locked into the courses that I teach every year. The core structure doesn't change. I'm always teaching the same four undergraduate classes, and they are always similar in regards to their objectives. For instance, this year I can't decide that I want to add current politics to my argument class. Our course content is already set. It isn't that I can't fold controversial readings or discussions into our curricula ever. Right now, I am teaching about ISIS, which is certainly relevant to my military-bound students, and controversial. It's just that it has to be done more carefully and deliberately where I work. We have a course-director model instead of a consistent WPA model. The course director creates the course, the lesson plans, the assignments, the assessments, the grading rubrics, and the homework activities. We keep course content consistent for a couple of years, then revamp them as our people turn over or the content becomes less exigent. We have a higher turnover for our staff because 50 percent of our department is made up of active-duty military members who leave within two to four years. Often, we get new military members in the department who don't have traditional English/composition teaching backgrounds, which means the course director has to be cognizant of the fact that it's hard for new instructors to teach difficult content. We are more cautious in our course content and in the assignments and assessments. This constraint is a structural, staffing one more than it is a political one. And, in fairness, I did know that when I was hired.

ERICA: One reason that I continue to teach as an adjunct, especially as a PhD student, is that it gives me a variety of teaching experiences that I wouldn't otherwise get in a traditional graduate part-time instructor role at a single institution. Also, because my partner designs software and we move often, adjunct roles have given me the opportunity to teach in all types of classrooms, including developmental English and dual enrollment, community colleges, liberal arts colleges, and research universities.

SARAH: That's an awesome opportunity that I'm jealous of. I don't get that where I work, currently. I'd have to get a job elsewhere (or a second, part-time job) if I wanted to teach something different or if I wanted to teach different types of students. Having that flexibility makes you more marketable if you do decide to change. Right now, I almost always know what my students are going to write about and the arguments they're going to make. They're all seventeen to twenty-two, and there are only so many things they can write about within our curricular umbrella. Every institution has a culture, and that culture dictates the types of topics and arguments that students choose for their papers, often. Sometimes, I'm happily surprised.

ERICA: How has your experience at your current institution or elsewhere contributed to your identity as a teacher and scholar?

SARAH: One of the reasons I took the job that I have right now is because I grew up in a very ethnically, racially, religiously, and socioeconomically diverse area, and that's important to me. Seeing disparities growing up, it is important to me to be an agitator, to upend what I perceive as inequities; I chose to work where I do because the student population I have and the mission of the institution is to diversify the officer corps in the military. That's a really important mission to me because I don't want group think. I want critical thinking, especially in what they call here the *profession of arms*. I want people with diverse experiences and backgrounds making the kinds of huge political decisions our government makes that often end in violence and colonization across the world.

ERICA: I think a lot of people can adjunct temporarily or as an extra job and use it as a bridge. I'm hoping that when I finish my PhD, I'll go on the tenure-track market, but that's a long bridge. When you're in a temporary contingent position for a long period of time, like I have been, teaching at multiple institutions day to day, it's not that sort of experience. It doesn't bother me, but when I start thinking about how I'm going to present myself on the job market and how that is considered versus someone who comes fresh out of a PhD program, I do worry about it. I might be more appealing to a teaching institution because I have ten years of teaching experience with a variety of classes and some admin experience. I'm super marketable in that arena, but I'm not sure how my extensive work experience will be perceived on the academic job market, especially when there is such a stigma around adjunct work.

SARAH: I've taught middle school; I've taught high school; I've done professional development; I've done curricular writing for math, science, history, and English. I've done administration; I've done hiring work. To go back—and it does feel like going backwards to an assistant professor position with a smaller salary and in some ways fewer expectations of what I can do—is painful to think about. I can do more. I have done more and it feels insulting. At the same time, I recognize that I didn't come up the traditional way. The onus of explaining why I'm valuable, why I should be hired if I switch positions, is a tricky one.

ERICA: Exactly. There are few common myths about adjunct work: the fact that NTTF faculty teach only because they love it; teach part time as a side gig; or retired from a tenure-track role and teach part time. How have you seen these myths show up in your lived experience?

SARAH: The myths prevail certainly, but that's not the reality for 75 percent of higher ed faculty. For 75 percent of faculty, being contingent is their livelihood. And even though what we're doing is legitimate, it also reinforces the stereotypes of adjuncts that are hindering the rest of the people who are doing it as their only means.

ERICA: I have a colleague who has no intention of leaving adjunct work. She loves it and, in some ways, I admire her. I wonder if I'm not that way too. There are tons of positives. If you have insurance and benefits through a spouse and aren't living paycheck to paycheck, then adjunct work can be really nice and fun. If you're only teaching one or two classes, you really get to have those relationships with your students, build rapport, and get into your curriculum for that particular course. But those are big ifs, and if we continue to perpetuate the adjunct personas, or myths as you called them, we are complicit in reinforcing those beliefs about adjuncting.

As of 2009, only 33.5 percent of positions at higher education institutions were tenure track (Tolley 2018, viii), and they're disappearing. Even people who are teaching across multiple institutions, teaching more classes than someone who teaches full time, the belief is that adjuncting is always a choice. Adjuncts could do something else. But, the data doesn't support that.

SARAH: Exactly. In fact, the Coalition on the Academic Workforce did a study in 2010 and over 75 percent of the part timers interviewed (over ten thousand people) said that if they were given the opportunity to work at one institution full time, they would take it (2012). It isn't that the majority of part timers want to cobble together a full-time paycheck, it's that they can't get a full-time job. That includes non-tenure-track positions like the one I have. It reminds me of my privilege.

ERICA: I've worked at an institution for five years and can usually get a second class, but I feel guilty about it. It makes me feel guilty because I know that there's someone else who likely really needs that second class for money, and I'm taking it because the department chair says here, take this second class. I think, "Who needs this $2,000 more than I do? Am I taking money away from someone who really needs this money?" But my next thought is always, "If I don't take it, will I have the opportunity to?"

SARAH: I think that's a little bit of a myth, which doesn't detract from your teaching abilities at all. I know your worth as a teacher and scholar, but it's simply that most people who teach for a living are good at what they do. The data bear that out (Green 2007, 33).

ERICA: We started this chapter with a quote from someone that I overheard at a regional conference saying that she talks about adjunct work as entrepreneurial, and she thinks that if she's going to be treated like a gig-economy worker that she might as well treat the job like one. What is your reaction to that perspective?

SARAH: I don't think about it that way at all. When I was working in secondary education, I considered going into administration, had an interview to do an assistant-principal position with my former organization, and decided to take this three-year renewable-contract teaching position instead. After working in professional development for seven years, I realized that I'd get more out of being in the classroom than I do even working with teachers. Arguably, if you coach teachers and run professional development, you will affect more students, numerically speaking. But, having done both, I can say that for me, it's not the same thing. It doesn't feel the same; teaching is more important.

ERICA: When I heard her say that, my first reaction was, "What a smart way to think about it." If they're abusing you then you think about them in the same way. But then that's in direct contradiction to the way that higher education was founded, and it's a disservice to the students. If you only do what you're paid to do and it's not in line with your values system then, why remain a teacher? I was offered two full-time jobs outside of higher education this year. I was interested in seeing what was out there, and I still turned them all down. I still decided to stay in teaching, and I don't stay in teaching because I treat it entrepreneurially. I stay in teaching because it makes a difference in the world, and I need to have a job that makes me want to get out of bed in the morning to make a difference in the world.

Just as Liliana M. Naydan acknowledges in this collection (chapter 4), contingent faculty often feel a connection between "worthy work" and self-worth. Perhaps unsurprisingly, loving your work and feeling like you're "making a difference" can sometimes play a role in NTT faculty's willingness to take on more oppressive, low-paying work. Naydan argues "that caring, but institutionally devalued, contingent work paradoxically satisfies yet oppresses writing center workers," and we echo those sentiments in our experiential reflections and in the comparison of workload, salaries, and benefits in the section below. While the impact of emotional labor is implicit in our discussion of "work love," it's not a measurable factor when comparing the monetary benefits of contingent labor in the academy. According to Peter Brooks's piece in this collection (chapter 2), "How Student-Affairs Praxis Can Aid the Nexus of Emotional Labor for NTTF," "Defining emotional labor is more about putting ourselves within this (in)visible process through awareness, analysis, and action." Inevitably, the places we spend our time shape our identity in much the same way our professional contexts shape our workloads. In the next section, we lay bare and compare our workloads, salaries, and benefits as contingent faculty in very different institutions.

A COMPARISON OF THE WORKLOADS OF FULL-TIME NTTF AND A PART-TIME ADJUNCT FACULTY

The daily workload of contingent faculty varies. While much work has been done to understand the impact of the heavy workloads placed on NTTF, not much research has been published about the differences between the workloads of full-time NTTF and part-time adjunct faculty. We developed two quantitative comparisons of the workloads (classes taught, class size, number of sections), as well as the salary and benefits (annual gross income, net earnings, intrinsic and extrinsic benefits) of a full-time, non-tenure-track composition instructor at a single institution and an adjunct who teaches composition and technical writing across multiple institutions (see Tables 3.1 and 3.2). These tables attempt to expose the otherwise privatized data surrounding the differences in how NTTF faculty are compensated for their work. In the same way Brooks (chapter 2) defines emotional labor as an invisible process he seeks to illuminate, here we are attempting to reveal a more quantitative exposure of NTTF labor exploitation. Following Jacqueline Jones Royster and Gesa Kirsch (2012), we're engaging in a kind of strategic contemplation that taps in and out of our experiential knowledge instead of archival materials. While we began our contemplation in conversation, here we tack into our specific lived experiences as contingent faculty. This side-by-side quantitative comparison offers readers, both contingent and tenure track, a rare opportunity to see how the economic circumstances of two types of NTT faculty compare.

If we take seriously our roles as writing teachers, we have an obligation to our students to provide writing instruction that emphasizes process and risk taking in small classes that allow quick and specific feedback on formative and summative work. Additionally, our scholarship, much like this edited collection, should do more than simply observe injustices; we must take tangible steps towards changing them. Table 3.2 is a vulnerable confession of our economic circumstances. Since this

Table 3.1. Quantitative comparison of workloads

Point of comparison	Full-time non-tenure-track	Adjunct multi-institution
Number of institutions	1	3
Semesters/quarters	9-week quarters, 4/year	School 1: 8-week quarters, 5/year
		School 2: 16-week semesters, 3/year
		School 3: 16-week semesters, 2/year
Courses taught/# of preps	1 course per quarter, 4/year	School 1: 2 courses per quarter, 16/year
		School 2: 1 course per semester, 3/year
		School 3: 1 course per semester, 2/year
Number of sections	2 per quarter, 8/year	School 1: 2 per quarter, 16/year
		School 2: 2 per semester, 6/year
		School 3: 1 per semester, 2/year
Number of students per year *(rounded to the nearest 10)*	140/year (20 students per section maximum, usually fewer)	440/year
		School 1: 320 (20 students per section)
		School 2: 90 (15 students per section)
		School 3: 30 (15 students per section)
Delivery mode/class length	Face to face; 75 minutes, 2 back-to-back courses, every other day	School 1: Online, asynchronous
		School 2: Face to face, 75 minutes, twice per week
		School 3: Face to face, 75 minutes, twice per week

edited collection is focused on speaking up and speaking out about the lived experiences of contingent faculty in writing studies, we trust that our readers will review this data with compassion. From a corporate perspective, the data could lead a reader to say, "Sarah's position is overpaid." Yet her circumstances align with the CCCC's highest recommendations for class size, time for course preparation, assessment and grading work, and earning a living wage (Horning 2007). An academic reader might review the data and conclude, "Erica is unethical for teaching so many courses at School 1." But, in reality, hers is the circumstance of many contingent faculty in the current higher education landscape. We resume our conversation here.

Table 3.2. Quantitative comparison of salary and benefits

Annual gross earnings (July 1, 2017–July 1, 2018)	$64,858.20	$63,424.96
Annual net earnings (July 1, 2017–July 1, 2018)	$47,892.88	$51,987.68
Health insurance	Available: medical, vision, dental	Available during semesters in which an overload of 4 classes is taught at one institution
Life insurance	Available and required at basic level	None available
Vacation days	30 days/year plus federal holidays and air-force-wide family days	None available
Sick days	15 days/year; cumulative and rolling (separate from vacation days); accrue at the rate of 4 hours/pay period.	None available; subs can be requested with reasonable notice, but sub pay is deducted from adjunct pay at School 3; classes can be cancelled with some consequences from department leadership
Parental leave	Accrued sick days used for paternity/maternity leave; up to 12 weeks unpaid but with benefits maintained	None available
State and federal pensions	After 5 years—vested; 1% of top 3 highest earned-salary average for each year of service; 1.1% if 20+ years of service; Social Security	No state pensions available; Social Security
Additional retirement	Thrift Savings Plan (matching up to 3%, tax deferred)	None available from institutions; 401k opened individually
Miscellaneous perks	3 hours/week gym time allowed, built into contract with free access to base community center facilities including free exercise classes Flexible hours on nonteaching days Liberal leave days TBD by commander, for which no leave is required 100% paid conference participation Professional development available in-house, including on-campus conferences, reading groups (for which the books are supplied), and scholarship of teaching and learning support	Flexible time for contract work for professional writing and community organizations

continued on next page

Table 3.2—*continued*

Miscellaneous perks (cont.)	Single-occupancy office with a door and window Time-off and pay awards (performance/ratings based) Yearly step increases Locality pay as part of salary, adjusted for cost of living in city of residence Standing desk and double monitor in office Access to a department-specific conference room, microwave, and refrigerator Open access to printers, copiers, and all required office supplies Classrooms with whiteboards, LCD projectors, document cameras, clickers, and speakers Hard and wireless internet Free flu shots, yearly International trip-chaperone opportunities Tutoring opportunities for student-athletes, including traveling with the team when required (not mandatory) Hiking opportunities available Club or Olympic sport-advising opportunities	
Other duties, as assigned	Duty Officer shifts 4–5 times/year (as of AY 2019, no longer required of civilian faculty) In-processing day duties in July Poetry slam for English Dept. Attendance at 4 yearly all-staff review meetings to discuss students' progress Course directing (for advanced faculty)—course design and implementation, class observations, meeting facilitation Grade norming meetings twice a quarter	Faculty meetings at the beginning and end of each semester Occasional committee work and required grade-norming sessions

* * *

ERICA: How have you reconciled your expectations with the workload that you're carrying, and how does your contingency affect your self-worth?

SARAH: Technically, everyone where I work is contingent, and that affects self-worth in a variety of ways, depending on whether or not you're active duty. The people who are military members are in two- to four-year contracted jobs just like the civilians are. Most military members don't stay in a position more than four years, so in that way they also hold contingent positions similar to the civilian three-year contracts. Some of the contingent civilian positions on campus are only one-year contracts due to funding, but for the most part we have three-year renewable contracts for all positions regardless of level: if you're working in the front office or you're an instructor or you're the dean of faculty, you're on a contract. Our job descriptions determine our workload and the position requirements. It doesn't really change for us, though military members make more than their civilian counterparts doing the same job, sometimes by thousands of dollars a year. But, they are active duty. It's a weird reality. If you look at the CAW data, the way that it categorizes our institution, it's 100 percent contingent. Yet, I've been renewed through 2023 and theoretically could continue renewing my position for decades. Certainly, that's the precedent.

ERICA: For me, there is a distinct link between my contingency, how I define my identity and self-worth, which often affects the workload that I am willing to carry. Sure, the job market for tenure-track jobs is bleak (Leverenz 2018), but I continue to subject myself to unreasonable workloads in the hopes that a tenure-track position will open at one of the institutions where I teach as an adjunct instructor. I often wonder if this work is in vain, or if my current institutions would even consider hiring an "inside candidate."

SARAH: I am interviewing as an "inside candidate" for an administrative position. It's still nontenure track, and sometimes I wonder if I should go out on the job market and do the tenure-track search, but I also compare those workloads and salaries to my current one and then I remember that I have it pretty great where I am.

ERICA: Given the precarity of labor and decrease in tenure-track positions, do you think there's a chance tenure will change or be phased out?

SARAH: The traditional reason for tenure was to protect the ability of faculty if they embark on risky research, or have radical views, and to create opportunities for them to ask difficult questions. Higher ed has already begun to undergo a makeover. A lot of institutions now have a teaching track that is separate from a tenure track. They call them *teaching track* or *professors of practice*, among other titles. For instance, the University of Denver has such a track; an initial one-year probationary period is required, and then after that you can earn a three-year contract. If approved, you can earn a five-year, and then a seven-year contract.

ERICA: Yes, the University of Washington has a similar model in their award-winning expository and interdisciplinary writing programs. That kind of model is better than the adjunct alternative, I think. You have job security; you're not working on a six-month contract or a five-month contract where classes are assigned to you at the last minute. But we're also not promising you a job for the rest of your life, or even after your contract ends.

SARAH: It's a similar model to corporate jobs—they don't promise you a job forever. Currently, adjuncts and contingent positions are defined by the fact that they are not tenure track. If tenure goes away, then you have to redefine what it means to be contingent, if contingency is even a thing anymore. It might morph into something else and highlight differences more clearly; without tenure, perhaps we'd look at pay rates between men and women, or white people and people of color, ensuring that the contracts are similar for similar workloads and levels of expertise. Maybe dissolving tenure refocuses us, or maybe it just exacerbates the gaps that are already in place.

Already many institutions are starting to do collective bargaining, which will lead (has led) to the one-, three-, five-, and seven-year contract scale. Or they'll stay, like my institution, at three years so that if something happens and somebody goes off the rails for some reason or they have a major life change, the institution has leeway. Whereas tenure does not allow as much flexibility. And I should say here that my institution, being a federal position, is much more secure and stable than typical contingent positions that offer multiyear contracts even if I have to occasionally contend with furloughs. It isn't as stable as tenure, but it's less likely that low performance or a life change is going to lead to losing that contract unless it becomes egregious and repeatedly an issue. My perspective though is always skewed because I'm white, able-bodied, cisgender, middle class, and in a relatively safe workspace. Would my workspace be as safe, given its military focus, if I wasn't all of these privileged things? Probably not. But I do think it's still better than many contingent, full-time positions.

There've been many publications in the last twenty years that have talked about the state of adjuncts and contingency in higher education. Not enough, in my opinion, regarding people of color in these positions, but that work is coming in a forthcoming special issue of *Academic Labor: Research and Artistry* edited by Rickie-Ann Legleitner and Genesea Carter (2021). And from a corporate standpoint, which is where we're moving in higher education, the lack of tenure, of a guaranteed career/position, is viewed as normal. In the corporate world nobody's promised anything. Certainly not for your entire career. From that perspective, higher education has always looked kind of cushy and ridiculous because outsiders are like, well, nobody gets something forever.

On the other hand, if I spend seven years of my life getting an advanced (and expensive) degree, I want to be appropriately compensated and get a job in-field. Some of this is an issue of supply and demand from an economic point of view. Recent numbers from the National Science Foundation indicate that in English there were 364 tenure-track (assistant professor) positions (in four subfields) available in 2016–2017. Yet, there were 968 newly minted PhDs that same year (Leverenz 2018). We are doing ourselves and our students a disservice by putting out two-thirds more PhDs than there are jobs available, and the number of PhDs earned doesn't include the technical and professional writing PhDs earned or the number of PhDs looking for jobs from the previous year.

I recognize that some individuals who earn PhDs already have full-time jobs like I do, or could get non-tenure-track positions, and some will go for industry positions, but that still leaves hundreds of newly minted PhDs who want tenure-track jobs without potential tenure-track positions. From that point of view, my position at my current institution feels less complicit because I'm not contributing to an unsustainable system.

Higher ed has been reconfigured as corporate—not just four-year universities but higher education writ large. The tenure model is not sustainable financially. I think that's part of the point of this piece too, is that even though the position I have is technically contingent, if everybody had the type of position that I have, higher education would be a wonderful place to work across the board, and it would be more sustainable. A lot more people would be happy. They would be stable, they'd be financially viable, and the students would get what they need. The institution would have flexibility with hiring and personnel that if there was someone who really wasn't doing her job effectively, they would have recourse within a time frame that was legitimate. Of course (and this is a huge caveat, I recognize), the positions and their parameters and expectations would have to be clearly defined. I think that's part of our implicit argument here: though tenure is preferable, it's likely not feasible; and further, contingency can—must—be done well.

Our conversation ends here, not because we didn't have more to say but because this is our call: NTTF members should be included in the conversations that shape their realities.

* * *

Arguments and conversations like the ones above are common in postsecondary education realms and are likely to be familiar to various higher education audiences. However, if we take this conversation outside higher education, as we argue academics should, and into the world of blue-collar workers, or corporate employees, the argument, perhaps even the conversation, doesn't hold up. People who are used to working paycheck to paycheck or who are let go due to consolidation don't want to hear about higher education's issues with renewable contracts, or precarity surrounding how to find a new job when a person is let go. It begs the question, How much of what's important to those of us in higher ed matters to individuals who do not depend on it for daily livelihood? College has become a place where individuals who can afford it go temporarily to purchase a piece of paper that will allow them to get a job. Learning experiences aren't the focus anymore for a large number of students; they're interested in getting the best education they can for the cheapest cost. That the instructor teaching the course gets paid $2,700/course or $75,000 a year isn't important to the "client," especially if the product looks similar to other courses taught by tenure-track and tenured faculty making twice that amount. Thus, our title isn't as surprising or appalling as it might seem. Adjuncts are entrepreneurs in this new neoliberal, corporate university system, and to survive in this gig economy, we're going to have to adapt: organize, unionize, persuade, or leave academe altogether. Labors of love are no longer viable for a majority of postsecondary workers, and though quaint, nostalgia doesn't pay the bills. We deserve more, and we expect it.

A CALL FOR NTT REGIONAL FACULTY UNIONIZATION AND PUBLIC-FACING TEACHER-SCHOLAR ACTIVISM

Contingent-Faculty Unionization

One way to include NTTF in this conversation is through deliberate unionization. Though the current political climate has defanged the National Labor Relations Board—and there are myriad state and national regulations to contend with regarding unionization and local organizing efforts, especially for public institutions (Saltzman 2018)— it has also incited strikes, bargaining discussions, and activism amongst non-tenure-track faculty across the nation. Recently, several institutions successfully engaged in strikes and collective bargaining in order to secure better wages and more rights for NTTF. For example, in December of 2018, Brooklyn College CUNY adjuncts silently protested via a grade-in for $7,000 per course, which is still 60 percent less per class than the full-time faculty there are paid per course (AdjunctNation 2015). Likewise, Barnard's Contingent Faculty Union-UAW Local 2110, formed in 2015, increased the adjunct faculty members' pay by 50 percent in twenty-four months' time, something the AFT, NEA, and AAUP unions haven't done in the past thirty years (Lesko 2017). These examples support our calls for contingent faculty to act and for unionization to be a valid means of making tangible change. Additionally, these examples seem to indicate that the efforts of smaller, local unions are currently more effective than the larger, national efforts. As Adrianna Kezar and Tom DePaola note in "Understanding the Need for Unions" (2018), "Unions . . . like SEIU's Faculty Forward . . . offer [contingent faculty] a viable mechanism to do something" (42). The time to improve NTTF working conditions, campus cultures, and student learning environments is now, and local and regional unions are the spaces where the revolution must begin.

Public-Facing Teacher-Scholar Activism

As teacher-scholar-activists, it is also our responsibility to do public-facing scholarship that communicates outside the echo chambers of academe. "Many of us . . . who identify as adjunct-equity activists are quick to say our work is obviously about social/labor justice, and that we can't imagine not being committed to it.... Labor justice ... *requires active response.* Mea culpas aren't wrong, but they don't fix anything" (Kahn 2017, 265; emphasis in original). In addition to unionizing, which enables contingent faculty to speak out about their own current working conditions, labor practices, and hiring decisions, we advocate for more defined ways for their voices to be included in institutional policies and procedures and in public-facing media.

We recognize contingent-labor research can only function as activism when you put it in front of audiences outside higher ed. We should ask ourselves, "Who is our scholarship for? To whom is it accountable?" (McGregor 2017). What would happen if the parents of first-year college students understood the impact of contingent labor on their kids' education? How would labor unions react if there was a sudden influx of blogs and podcasts about the research-backed effects of adjunct labor? How do we begin to put our research in front of the audiences it impacts, namely students? Just as Christian Weisser identifies public writing "as an extension of radical composition" that both "enables and inhibits participants in their struggles for public democracy and social justice" (quoted in Ervin 2007, 37), contingent-labor research has the power to liberate higher education from the gig-economy mindset by creating an open, transparent dialogue about higher education labor practices with public audiences in the hopes of breaking the shackles of the for-profit publication process. "Scholarship that is both open and public gives us an opportunity not to throw out these institutionalized norms but to fundamentally reconsider the work that we're doing" (McGregor 2017). These moves toward publicly available and relevant scholarship, towards organizing and unionizing, toward deliberate activism, are the only things that will move our profession to a lived reality that is sustainable.

REFERENCES

AdjunctNation. 2015. "CUNY Adjuncts Asking for $7K Per Class. That's Still 60 Percent Less Per Class Than FT Faculty Are Paid." Twitter, December 15. https://twitter.com/AdjunctNation/status/1073949648652550144.

Coalition on the Academic Workforce. 2012. *A Portrait of Part-Time Faculty Members: A Summary of Findings on Part-Time Faculty Respondents to the Coalition on the Academic Workforce Survey of Contingent Faculty Members and Instructors.* June. http://www.academicworkforce.org/CAW_portrait_2012.pdf.

Ervin, Elizabeth. 2007. "Composition and the Gentrification of 'Public Literacy.'" *The Locations of Composition,* edited by Christopher J. Keller and Christian R. Weisser, 37–54. Albany: State University of New York Press.

Green, Donald W. 2007. "Adjunct Faculty and the Continuing Quest for Quality." *New Directions for Community Colleges* 2007 (140): 29–39.

Horning, Alice. 2007. "The Definitive Article on Class Size." *WPA: Writing Program Administration* 31 (1–2): 11–34.

Kahn, Seth. 2017. "The Problem of Speaking for Adjuncts." In *Contingency, Exploitation, and Solidarity: Labor and Action in English Composition*, edited by Seth Kahn, William B. Lalicker, and Amy Lynch-Biniek, 259–70. Fort Collins, CO: WAC Clearinghouse.

Kezar, Adrianna, and Tom DePaola. 2018. "Understanding the Need for Unions." In *Professors in the Gig Economy: Unionizing Adjunct Faculty in America*, 27–45. Baltimore: Johns Hopkins University Press.

Legleitner, Rickie-Ann, and Genesea Carter. 2021. "Intersectional Labor: Sustainability and Solutions in Social Justice." [Special issue]. *Academic Labor: Research and Artistry* 5 (1).

Lesko, Patricia. 2017. "Barnard Adjunct Profs Just Showed Us All Why It's Time for the 25K Maifesto." *Huffpost*. Last modified February, 28, 2017. https://www.huffpost.com/entry/barnard-adjunct-profs-just-showed-us-all-why-its-time_b_58b5f590e4b0e5fdf61977f2.

Leverenz, Carrie. 2018. "Annual Bad News on the Job Market." WPA-L Archives, December 11. https://lists.asu.edu/cgi-bin/wa?A2=WPA-L;42f11a9b.1812&S=.

Maisto, Maria, Joseph A. McCartin, and Jacob Swenson. 2014. "Unethical Academia: The Next Front for Low-Wage Worker Uprising?" *The Blog, Huffpost*. Last modified January 23, 2014. https://www.huffingtonpost.com/maria-maisto/unethical-academia-the-ne_b_4116373.html.

McGregor, Hannah. 2017. "Bonus Episode: Podcasting, Public Scholarship, and Accountability." *Secret Feminist Agenda (podcast)*, November 23. https://secretfeministagenda.com/2017/11/23/bonus-episode-podcasting-public-scholarship-and-accountability/.

National Science Foundation. "2016 Doctorate Recipients from U.S. Universities." March 2018. p. 9. Figure B. https://www.nsf.gov/statistics/2018/nsf18304/static/report/nsf18304-report.pdf.

Powell, Malea, Daisy Levy, Andrea Riley-Mukavetz, Marilee Brooks-Gillies, Maria Novotny, Jennifer Fisch-Ferguson, et al. 2014. "Our Story Begins Here: Constellating 'Cultural Rhetorics.'" *Enculturation*. http://enculturation.net/our-story-begins-here.

Royster, Jacqueline Jones, and Gesa Kirsch. 2012. *Feminist Rhetorical Practices: New Horizons for Rhetoric, Composition, and Literacy Studies*. Carbondale: Southern Illinois University Press.

Tolley, Kim. 2018. "Preface." In *Professors in the Gig Economy: Unionizing Adjunct Faculty in America*, edited by Kim Tolley, vii–xv. Baltimore: Johns Hopkins University Press.

Warner, Michael. 2002. *Public and Counterpublics*. Brooklyn: Zone Books.

Welch, Nancy, and Scott, Tony. 2016. *Composition in the Age of Austerity*. Logan: Utah State University Press.

4
"WHAT ARE YOU?"
Rethinking Frames for Contingent Writing Center Work

Liliana M. Naydan

Most contingent workers in writing programs see contingency as hard because it perhaps involves traveling among institutions, meeting different programmatic expectations, or cobbling together what may never amount to a living wage. Even full-time contingent work may involve feeling as if you're at the periphery of an increasingly corporate institution of the kind Marc Bousquet (2008) describes in *How the University Works*. However, contingent workers who work in writing centers as opposed to writing programs complicate commonly understood notions of what it means to work off the tenure track. As my colleagues and I intimate in "Toward An Investigation into the Working Conditions of Non-Tenure Line, Contingent Writing Center Workers," the extensive one-to-one mentoring full- or part-time faculty or staff contingent writing center workers do is still relatively invisible in conversations about contingency among academic activists (Fels et al. 2016). And, as Emily Isaacs and Melinda Knight explain in "A Bird's Eye View of Writing Centers," because 73 percent of writing center administrators are women, positioning writing centers as "a province of women" in colleges and universities, the hard one-to-one work of mentoring writers emerges as de facto women's work (2014, 49). It emerges as a sort of housework of the twenty-first-century academy—a burdensome and largely invisible kind of work many women in the academy shoulder.

This chapter puts personal narrative into conversation with social-movement theory to expose the invisible labor of predominantly women contingent-faculty workers in writing centers, to explore the nature of writing center faculty work, and to suggest workers in writing centers must rethink frames for the academic labor movement. I begin by telling a personal narrative that underscores differences among perceptions of writing center labor and helps expose writing center work as gendered work of the kind Irene Padavic and Barbara Reskin (2002)

DOI: 10.7330/9781646420759.c004

describe in *Women and Men at Work*. I argue that caring contingent work paradoxically satisfies yet oppresses writing center workers because institutions don't value it. In turn, I suggest that the enticing yet problematic nature of this caring work perpetuates contingency as long as activists in academia resist rhetorically framing or reframing the problem in accord with what David A. Snow and Robert D. Benford (1988) theorize as social-movement framing in "Ideology, Frame Resonance, and Participant Mobilization." Ultimately, I posit that writing center workers might benefit from rethinking their localized frame for contingency as a problem that not only involves a master Marxist frame but also a feminist frame that centers on the issue of gender. Ultimately, doing so will expose tacit acts of institutional sexism colleges and universities engage in. It will also help writing center workers find tenure-line and student allies who might help them make arguments to administrators and more effectively organize for and perhaps realize some semblance of labor justice for themselves and their contingent colleagues.

INVISIBLE WRITING CENTER-WORKER STATUS AND CHALLENGES TO ACADEMIC LABOR LITERACY

"What are you?" asked a student writer with whom I had just had a successful first writing center consultation. It was the middle of my memorably hectic first year as a full-time contingent-faculty member in a writing center staffed exclusively by contingent faculty, mostly women. I laughed at his question, and I remember feeling as if I didn't quite know how to answer him. In a way, he was asking me what kind of a person has time to sit face to face with a student writer for thirty minutes to provide meaningful one-to-one help students don't often feel they can get elsewhere. And I realized I laughed because the answer to his question is a complicated one. I kept my response simple by merely stating my official status at this particular state university. "I'm a lecturer," I declared.

"What's a lecturer?" the student asked. I explained as best I could, saying lecturers are full-time non-tenure-track teachers at our institution. My mention of tenure drew a blank stare, so I didn't say more. But I thought about saying we had union-negotiated, short-term contracts. I thought about saying all contingent faculty working in our esteemed center split their time between teaching writing courses and tutoring students. And I thought about saying I directed a peer writing center staffed by dozens of peer tutors with just a one-course-per-year release. But instead, I said nothing terribly controversial or illuminating. I said nothing about the grueling work of tutoring ten hours per week on top of teaching. I said nothing about the way contingency as a job status affects my identity, a subject Sarah Austin and Erica Stone explore in the conversations and contemplations that they include in this book. I said nothing about feeling like a factory worker because the consultations were so rushed and so filled with emotional labor akin to that Peter Brooks describes in another essay in this collection. And so this student said what made sense to him within the inherently limited frame of his understanding. "So you're a professor," he said. And he thanked me and went on his way as I sat there wondering about how to tell him I wasn't one—even though I certainly wanted to be.

Several years have passed since this exchange. I now have tenure at a different institution, but the exchange stays with me because it illustrates two important points about writing center work—work largely performed by contingent women workers. First, it illustrates that contingent writing center workers have the capacity to make and often do make a remarkable difference in the lives of student writers. They perform markedly caring work in harsh working conditions. Hence they create meaningful learning experiences for students that complement the meaningful writing projects Michele Eodice, Anne Ellen Geller, and Neal Lerner (2016) describe. In the process, they, too, develop as people and professionals, as evidenced by Bradley Hughes, Paula Gillespie, and Harvey Kail's claim that by way of writing center mentoring, "peer tutors are creating one of the most important experiences in their undergraduate careers, a complex, multifaceted experience whose influence persists not just years but decades after graduation" (2010, 13).

Second, however, the exchange illustrates that contingent writing center workers are often invisible within the framework of institutions. Geller and Harry Denny spotlight the invisibility of writing center professionals (or faculty and staff administrators of writing centers), observing that a "professional identity in writing centers is still not understood as a professional identity in English or composition studies" (2013, 123). Yet the invisibility of writing center professionals Geller and Denny write about may well apply to workers of all kinds in writing centers, be they administrators or peer or professional tutors. Unless they happen to have a friend who works in the center, students may not understand the professional qualifications, job status, or working conditions of consultants, especially if they lack a literacy of how the university works, to reference the title of Bousquet's seminal book. They may lack a literacy of the fact that, to quote Bousquet, not too long ago, "75 percent of all college teachers were tenurable; only a quarter worked on an adjunct, part-time, or non-tenurable basis" (2008, 2). But today, "those proportions are reversed" (2). Students lack a literacy of the difference between tenure-line employees and contingent faculty, and they may have yet to attain an understanding of the paradoxical centrality contingency has taken on.

As evidenced by my own reductive rhetoric in the exchange I describe, I see myself and perhaps all contingent faculty as perhaps being in part responsible for an enduring illiteracy involving the difference between contingent and tenure-line workers, their work, and their working conditions, especially when contingent workers fail to frame their situations in full or meaningful ways. As Snow and Benford explain, to frame in terms of social movements such as the labor movement is to "assign meaning to and interpret . . . relevant events and conditions in ways that are intended to mobilize potential adherents and constituents, to garner bystander support, and to demobilize antagonists" (1988, 198). And the master Marxist frame for academic labor suggests that contingent workers exist as exploited low-wage workers in an inherently exploitative system of higher education that has adopted corporate interests and rhetoric. At best, the absence of framing in conversations such as the one I describe exists because there is no ideal moment at which to rupture the rhythm of the exchange. There is no ideal moment to outline the differences or purported differences between contingent and tenure-line faculty. And in part this lack of an ideal moment exists because there is no way to explain the difference—to whatever degree there is one—quickly and clearly. There perhaps also exists a risk that a brief explanation will somehow suggest contingent faculty aren't as qualified to teach or tutor college students as their tenure-line counterparts are, which of course isn't the case. As E. Ian Robinson explains in "Teaching Equality: What the Principle of Equal Pay for Equal Work Means for Lecturer Pay at the University of Michigan," research that tenure-line faculty tend to be required to conduct may help them teach better, but numerous factors beyond research enrich pedagogy. And "on average, Lecturers are somewhat more likely than TT faculty to be seen as excellent teachers" (2012, 34).

Alternately, however, the absence of communication and framing through communication exists because academic workers feel uncomfortable with the dominant frame for the academic labor movement—a frame to which I acclimated through a particularly exploitative act by administration when I was a graduate student but a frame with which not all academics identify or want to identify. To appropriate Snow and Benford's argument, a movement that emerges "later in the cycle" of protest such as the academic labor movement finds its "framing efforts constrained by the previously elaborated master frame"—one that suggests a connection exists between low-wage work and industrial work and one that creates only a tenuous sort of space for academics who may believe themselves to have a certain cultural capital that distinguishes them from low-wage workers (1988, 212). In part, this master frame manifested at rallies I attended or even helped organize as a graduate student and contingent-faculty member. We spoke to it by calling attention to our relatively low salaries and the value of our work. We chatted about getting respect for our teaching and higher pay. And we chastised upper-level administrators for their bloated salaries, one time with a blow-up pig in a pinstripe suit. We involved workers in other unions, including communication and sanitation workers. And hence those among us who identified as workers in accord with labor-movement rhetoric felt a sense of solidarity in our opposition of the values and actions of management, a potentially problematic term in academic contexts that Donna Strickland explores in *The Managerial Unconscious*. As Strickland argues, there exists a "managerial unconscious" in "the field of composition studies" that makes compositionists who prefer to identify as "administration" uncomfortable (2011, 3, 10). And, building on Strickland's argument, I suggest that discomfort with the idea of management transcends the limits of composition or self-identification. Indeed, compositionists and other kinds of academic workers may feel unsettled by the idea of management existing in academia at all. They may, as Christopher Carter puts it, "refuse to view themselves as workers" (2008, 17). Despite growing willingness to strike in recent years, they may reject the master frame upon which the labor movement relies.

In rejecting this master frame that might provide some semblance of community among workers of different ranks in academic contexts, contingent workers arguably open themselves to feeling some semblance of shame about their rank and their labor, especially because many academics tend to measure the quality of an academic job in large part based on whether the job is tenure line. As one particularly offensive administrator candidly mentioned to me in an unsettlingly nonchalant way when I was a contingent graduate student worker, "Academia is about snobbery." And in the face of that sort of perspective—in whatever ways contingent workers have heard it or experienced or lived in the shadow of it—there may be shame, for instance, in not having acquired a terminal degree. There may be shame in not having gotten a tenure-line job in a job market with a high demand for jobs but a low supply of them, or simply in enjoying the work of teaching and not wanting to publish. In turn, there may exist the impulse for contingent workers to attempt to cover their contingent identities just as LGBTQ people, people of color, and women cover their identities, according to Kenji Yoshino's *Covering* (2007), a work that shapes much of Denny's *Facing the Center* (2010). Contingent faculty may opt to conceal that there's a difference not so much between what they and their tenure-line counterparts do (especially since many contingent faculty continue to do research and publish even if it's not required of them) but between their working conditions and the working conditions of tenure-line faculty. They may feel that difference points to some sort of intrinsic personal deficiency as opposed to a problematic corporate mindset that now shapes higher education.

NEW FRAMES FOR CONTINGENCY IN WRITING CENTER WORK

This enduring contingency illiteracy perpetuates problems contingency creates for all inhabitants of colleges and universities because, as the old adage goes, instructors' working conditions are students' learning conditions. And developing new frames for the problem of contingent labor can help create circumstances for contingent academic workers to communicate about their work situations in compelling ways at opportune moments. As Snow and Benford explain, the success of a social movement such as the labor movement in general or the academic labor movement in particular depends on the success of the movement's "framing efforts," or its "frame resonance," because frames function to mobilize—or not mobilize—any given movement's participants (1988, 199). Hence the success of the academic labor movement depends on the success of the Marxist frame on which it relies—a frame that certainly speaks to the "life world of the participants" with the lowest wages, to appropriate Snow and Benford's discussion of phenomenological constraints, but a frame that also has potential to "reduce potential participants to spectators and so make the issue non-participatory" (198, 204). In other words, although the Marxist frame may appeal to activist adjuncts such as those who voice their stories in *Professors in Poverty* (2015), a Brave New Films video campaign, or to the late Margaret Mary Vojtko, the impoverished Duquesne University adjunct whose death received extensive media coverage, it may not appeal to more privileged contingent workers (Kovalik 2013). It may not resonate with the "active, enfranchised" directors Neal Lerner describes in "Time Warp: Historical Representations of Writing Center Directors" (2006, 10). In other words, it may not resonate with contingent writing center directors or other contingent writing center workers who make living wages but still experience injustice at the hands of the corporate university—even if they opt against fully recognizing it.

In lieu of attempting to unearth a new and complementary frame that effectively resonates with contingent workers of different kinds across institutions, labor-movement activists might explore the potential of frames that speak to specific populations of academic workers—frames that intersect with the Marxist master frame that has shaped the labor movement much like social-identity categories intersect with one another. In the case of contingent writing center workers as a small yet cohesive subcategory of academic labor, feminism—meaning the process of advocating for women's rights with the goal of social equality—may provide an organic and compelling frame for everyday writing center work, which, to appropriate Padavic and Reskin's words, US academics seem to consciously or unconsciously "view as 'naturally' female" (2002, 7). As a frame, feminism can help reveal some semblance of complexity in the answer to the question "What are you?" It can underscore the fact that writing center workers are mostly women and that writing centers exist as gendered spaces—homes women often run and inhabit and homes of a notably uncozy sort, to reference Jackie Grutsch McKinney's (2013) dismantling of the master narrative of writing centers as cozy homes in *Peripheral Visions for Writing Centers*. Moreover, it can show that institutions of higher education have designated the caring work that happens within them as women's work akin to housework women have performed without official compensation for centuries—work that may help tidy messy writing by students who, according to the institution as Carter imagines it, are in need of "remediation" institutions aren't willing to "pay much" for (2008, 11). Hence it can show institutions of higher education are participating in a long history of exploitation of women workers—exploitation of the sort Silvia Federici and Arlen Austin portray in *Wages for Housework* (2017), a history of the New York Committee's work as part of the international Wages for Housework movement that developed in the 1970s to draw attention to the invisible work of keeping a home and bearing, delivering, and caring for children.

Feminism as a frame that intersects with Marxism can help counter "sex inequality" of the kind Padavic and Reskin describe (2002, 37). To appropriate Padavic and Reskin's words, it can draw attention to problems with existing and "deeply embedded" cultural perspectives on the teaching of writing and, more specifically, on the work of providing one-to-one mentoring to writers (10). Like the wages-for-housework movement, which, according to Federici's preface in Federici and Austin's book, "contributed to raise consciousness about the importance of housework in capitalist society" (2017, 11), a feminist frame for writing center work can confront patriarchal conceptions of classroom teaching as central and raise awareness about the value of one-to-one mentoring. It can invite audiences within and beyond the writing center to read writing centers in new ways, much like the wages-for-housework movement influenced men and women to read women's labor in new ways, as evidenced by strategic media coverage the movement's members organized by building relationships with predominantly women journalists who had interest in the movement. It can continue to add complexity to the writing-centered theoretical work Grutsch McKinney engages in when she writes that "clinging to the identity of a writing center as cozy home may be problematic in terms of gender" because "female directors who insist on cozy, inviting spaces may be unwittingly narrating their work as non-intellectual in the eyes of some" (2013, 26).

Furthermore, developing new frames for academic-labor activism can help writing center workers find allies, especially tenure-line ones who avoid engaging in what Bousquet calls "an oppositional culture" (2008, 13). And frames such as a feminist frame that intersect with a Marxist one and speak to both contingent and tenure-line-faculty concerns about equality can motivate tenure-line faculty, especially if these faculty see that larger full-time, tenure-track workforces have potential to result in less labor for them—labor that may take the shape of increasing service responsibilities, which tenure-line faculty shoulder. By diversifying and pluralizing the range of frames the academic-labor movement utilizes, contingent faculty activists may be able to help shape tenure-line faculty into the kinds of rhetorical listeners Seth Kahn argues they should become in "The Problem of Speaking for Adjuncts." In Kahn's words, "Too often, tenured faculty—even those of us motivated to work for labor justice—seem to think we understand 'the adjunct problem' without really hearing what adjunct faculty are telling us" (2017, 267). And according to Kahn, tenure-line faculty fail to see that "almost anything we say is likely an overgeneralization, or a misrepresentation of at least some of the contingent faculty population" because "there's nothing approaching a consensus, even a plurality, in survey after survey" among adjuncts on issues such as their "reasons for taking and keeping contingent positions, their goals for workplace reform, their personal priorities" (267).

Ultimately, then, I posit that the answer to the question "What are you?" must be a multifaceted one for writing center workers—one that involves the labor movement's dominant Marxist frame, a wholly relevant feminist frame, and frames beyond and between that speak to the nuances of contingency. And it must be one writing center workers articulate in diverse ways—perhaps not as consultations are coming to a quick close but in thorny moments of everyday conversations that happen in writing centers. To take advantage of or reframe kairotic moments in consultations, contingent workers must listen rhetorically for ways public controversies and conversations about work, contingency, or women in the workplace bleed into everyday writing-centered dialogues they have, to reference the argument my coeditors and I make in *Out in the Center* (Denny et al. 2018). They must listen for moments in which writers reference issues associated with labor, social justice, or women in the workplace. And then they must speak about their complex feelings in those moments with persuasive personal narratives that can uncover their complex personal and professional identities: their identities as contingent workers who are inevitably exploited but who find ways, as Geller and Denny explain, to "make the best of the conditions" they "inherit" and find happiness in the work (2013, 124). In the process, these personal narratives can also uncover the broader body of contingent workers upper-level administrators work tirelessly to conceal for the purpose of saving money.

Moreover, contingent faculty might find ways of speaking about the nuances of the answer to the question "What are you" by unearthing kairotic moments through creative approaches akin to the ones Jonathan S. Coley describes in "Narrative and Frame Alignment in Social Movements: Labor Problem Novels and the 1929 Gastonia Strike," an article that problematizes a precarious void involving form and genre in "social movement literature on framing" and attempts to fill that void by addressing "the forms in which frames are embedded" (2015, 59). As Coley explains, novels about the 1929 Gastonia Strike "provided a particularly useful way for activists to engage in 'frame alignment,'" which he defines as "the task of aligning a movement's understandings about the world with those of individuals" (59). And multimodal works might do the same for contingent writing center workers in the digital age. Social media posts and memes might function to prompt dialogue. And opportunities for dialogue they create are opportunities to reframe students' thinking and thereby galvanize change beyond the confines of the digital world, as evidenced by the success of campaigns such as #blacklivesmatter and #MeToo.

Through one-to-one conversations that exist as the fundamental building block of all writing center mentoring and social-movement organizing, contingent writing center workers might reframe students as allies to complement prospective tenure-line allies they may acquire.

They might build connections with one another to interrogate the current metaphorical frame for disciplinary identity and the limits and possibilities of that frame. And they might push the International Writing Centers Association to develop a statement of its own akin to the CCCC Statement on Working Conditions for Non-Tenure-Track Writing Faculty (2016)—one that transcends the conversation about directors' concerns Jeanne H. Simpson begins in "What Lies Ahead for Writing Centers: Position Statement on Professional Concerns" (1985) and one that considers contingency in forms beyond directorships within our centers. Moreover, they might create opportunities for upper-level administrators to have conversations with constituents who might prompt them to engage in rhetorical listening of their own. If these opportunities for listening manifest, they might help educate administrators about what contingent workers in and beyond writing centers can be. They might complement more conventional and always wholly necessary acts of activism with subtle but steady pressure on administrators to frame contingent workers as respected. Although these workers may not acquire tenure lines as a result of tacit and overt activist acts, they may attain more job security, higher pay, and benefits all workers deserve.

REFERENCES

Bousquet, Marc. 2008. *How the University Works: Higher Education and the Low-Wage Nation*. New York: New York University Press.

Carter, Christopher. 2008. *Rhetoric and Resistance in the Corporate Academy*. Cresskill, NJ: Hampton.

Coley, Jonathan. 2015. "Narrative and Frame Alignment in Social Movements: Labor Problem Novels and the 1929 Gastonia Strike." *Social Movement Studies* 14 (1): 58–74.

Conference on College Composition and Communication. 2016. "CCCC Statement on Working Conditions for Non-Tenure-Track Writing Faculty." https://cccc.ncte.org/cccc/resources/positions/working-conditions-ntt.

Denny, Harry C. 2010. *Facing the Center: Toward an Identity Politics of One-To-One Mentoring*. Logan: Utah State University Press.

Denny, Harry, Robert Mundy, Liliana M. Naydan, Richard Sévère, and Anna Sicari, eds. 2018. *Out in the Center: Public Controversies and Private Struggles*. Logan: Utah State University Press.

Eodice, Michele, Anne Ellen Geller, and Neal Lerner. 2016. *The Meaningful Writing Project: Learning, Teaching, and Writing in Higher Education*. Logan: Utah State University Press.

Federici, Silvia, and Arlen Austin, ed. 2017. *Wages for Housework: The New York Committee 1972–1977: History, Theory, Documents*. Brooklyn, NY: Autonomedia.

Fels, Dawn, Clint Gardner, Maggie M. Herb, and Liliana M. Naydan. 2016. "Toward an Investigation into the Working Conditions of Non-Tenure Line, Contingent Writing Center Workers." *Forum: Issues about Part-Time and Contingent Faculty* 20 (1): A10–A16.

Geller, Anne Ellen, and Harry Denny. 2013. "Of Ladybugs, Low Status, and Loving the Job: Writing Center Professionals Navigating Their Careers." *Writing Center Journal* 3 (1): 96–129.

Grutsch McKinney, Jackie. 2013. *Peripheral Visions for Writing Centers*. Logan: Utah State University Press.

Hughes, Bradley, Paula Gillespie, and Harvey Kail. 2010. "What They Take with Them: Findings from the Peer Writing Tutor Alumni Research Project." *Writing Center Journal* 30 (2): 12–46.

Isaacs, Emily, and Melinda Knight. 2014. "A Bird's Eye View of Writing Centers: Institutional Infrastructure, Scope and Programmatic Issues, Reported Practices." *WPA: Writing Program Administration* 37 (2): 36–67.

Kahn, Seth. 2017. "The Problem of Speaking for Adjuncts." In *Contingency, Exploitation, and Solidarity: Labor and Action in English Composition*, edited by Seth Kahn, William B. Lalicker, and Amy Lynch-Biniek, 259–70. Fort Collins: WAC Clearinghouse.

Kovalik, Daniel. 2013. "Death of an Adjunct." *Pittsburgh Post-Gazette*. Accessed August 16, 2018.

Lerner, Neal. 2006. "Time Warp: Historical Representations of Writing Center Directors." In *The Writing Center Director's Resource Book*, edited by Christina Murphy and Byron L. Stay, 3–11. Mahwah, NJ: Lawrence Erlbaum.

Padavic, Irene, and Barbara Reskin. 2002. *Women and Men at Work*. Thousand Oaks, CA: Pine Forge.

Professors in Poverty. 2015. Brave New Films. https://www.bravenewfilms.org/professorsinpoverty.

Robinson, E. Ian. 2012. "Teaching Equality: What the Principle of Equal Pay for Equal Work Means for Lecturer Pay at the University of Michigan." Lecturers' Employee Organization. Accessed 2012 (no longer available).

Simpson, Jeanne H. 1985. "What Lies Ahead for Writing Centers: Position Statement on Professional Concerns." *Writing Center Journal* 5/6 (2/1): 35–39.

Snow, David A., and Robert D. Benford. 1988. "Ideology, Frame Resonance, and Participant Mobilization." *International Social Movement Research* 1 (1): 197–217.

Strickland, Donna. 2011. *The Managerial Unconscious in the History of Composition Studies*. Carbondale: Southern Illinois University Press.

Yoshino, Kenji. 2007. *Covering: The Hidden Assault on Our Civil Rights*. New York: Random House.

PART II

Critical Perspectives

5
HAVING IT ALL
The Costs and Opportunities of Non-Tenure-Track Faculty's Institutional Progress

Lacey Wootton

Recently, I received a university award for term-faculty service. It's an important award at my institution, given at a faculty-awards dinner that also recognizes tenure-line and adjunct (part-time) faculty. The award even came with money. I was honored to be recognized, and I felt I deserved the award, too. But as meaningful as the recognition was, it couldn't fully capture the years of advocacy work and hours of service that earned it. The award and the citation our provost read brought some of that labor to the surface. But the ability to access the service work that earned me the award—the opportunity to "serve"—resulted from years of incremental progress and activism. Those hard-won gains created new avenues for participation in the university for me and for my term-faculty colleagues, but they also led to new pressures and obligations. Having it all often means being expected to do it all—on a contingent contract, at lower pay, with teaching still considered one's primary obligation.

I explore some of the tensions involved in expanded institutional opportunities for non-tenure-track faculty (NTTF) by considering the nature of that expansion at my university, American University, where the labor conditions for term faculty (full-time NTTF) have changed drastically over the past ten years. While our opportunities might be greater than those at many other universities, they're not unique. For example, a recent *Chronicle* article describes changes at the University of Mississippi to bring NTTF onto the faculty senate and noted similar moves at other universities; notably, the changes at Ole Miss were spearheaded by female writing faculty (Field 2018). (Although I'm focusing on writing faculty here, the expanded opportunities and risks I describe can pertain to all NTTF facing these changes.) I'll contextualize these new opportunities in descriptions of the work

DOI: 10.7330/9781646420759.c005

of NTT writing faculty as gendered labor, focusing on the gendered metaphors that capture not only the conditions but also the perceptions of that labor. Those metaphors—such as the mother or the maid—aren't obsolete, but as NTTF take on new service duties, they are increasingly insufficient. I'll offer a new gendered metaphor to describe the expanded labor opportunities and obligations for NTTF: the second-wave-feminist idea of having it all, with its initial optimism and later criticism. In doing so, I want to examine not only the complexities of expanded roles for NTTF but also the power of metaphor to explain them. The metaphor of having it all can help us understand those complexities—the opportunities and pressures of NTTF participation in faculty labor besides teaching.

This understanding grows increasingly important as higher education expands its reliance on NTTF labor; the already-wavering line between opportunity and exploitation will only become more tenuous. Tenure-line colleagues and administrators should try to understand the complexities of NTTF labor in all its dimensions and avoid complacent back-patting for "allowing" NTTF to participate fully in the university. Their empathetic understanding can help them protect NTTF and attend to their compensation. NTTF should also understand the complexities of their labor so they can move beyond emotional response—that is, "I find this work rewarding, yet I fear I'm being taken advantage of." All these groups can join in this project of understanding to resist the neoliberal tendencies that lead higher education to extract the most work for the least pay under the guise of personal choice and opportunity.

INSTITUTIONAL CONTEXT

When I first started teaching writing at American University (AU) in 1999, my title was writing instructor, and term faculty were commonly referred to as *temps*. There was no possibility of promotion, and we were expected to do little besides teach our classes and get high student evaluations so we could be reappointed by the Department of Literature's rank and tenure committee.

Over the next ten years, full-time writing faculty, and other term faculty, would grow in numbers (AU has retained stable faculty proportions for some time, with about one-third each of tenure-line faculty, term faculty, and adjunct/part-time faculty; all writing faculty are either term or adjunct faculty). Term writing faculty participated in the work of the Department of Literature and began to develop relationships, through faculty development, with faculty in other departments. We were able to capitalize on those relationships when the university revised its faculty manual, arguing for and creating new policies, protections, titles, and promotion opportunities; we were also central to the implementation of those changes. We gained a seat on the faculty senate dedicated to term-faculty representation; I won that first seat and later was elected as senate chair, the first term-faculty member to do so—but not the last. Other writing faculty were later elected to the faculty senate and its committees, led successful advocacy efforts for increased term-faculty salaries, and helped create a term-faculty task force for the College of Arts and Sciences.

Writing faculty, and other term faculty, continue to fill prominent positions at the university. The chair of the general education committee is a member of the writing faculty; she led a radical transformation of that program into a new AU core, which involved extensive negotiation with and faculty development for faculty and administrators. One component of the core is the first-year Complex Problems course; that program is cochaired by two writing faculty. Another writing program faculty member oversees academic integrity for the college; she also works at an institution-wide level, revising the Academic Integrity Code and helping her counterparts across the university deal with academic integrity more effectively. The associate chair of the Department of Literature is term faculty in the writing program. The university's dean of undergraduate studies is a term-faculty member; as past chair of the senate, I chaired her hiring committee. And the dean of our school of extended education is term faculty. All these positions are highly visible, and they all have profound effects on the institution. (And most of these faculty are women.)

This exciting and important work has led to greater respect for term faculty; we are better integrated into the faculty than we were ten years ago, and in fact, our status as term faculty is less visible now. Because of our contributions, we are able to argue for reductions in teaching loads and stipends as compensation for demanding service, and we implicitly argue for more stable employment by demonstrating that we are essential to the university's functioning. In contrast to the "ghostly" feeling of displacement described by Brendan Hawkins and Julia Kaurus in this collection (chapter 6), we have a visible presence in the university.

The benefits, however, are not universally experienced. In some schools and departments, term faculty still cannot vote on curriculum and other local matters. Too many others remain on one-year contracts after years of employment. Insidious signs of tenure-line snobbery still appear occasionally, including that much-hated word, *temps*. And for many term faculty, pay lags well behind that of even junior tenure-line faculty.

And on an individual level, the increased opportunities can verge on overwhelming obligation. I'm no longer on the faculty senate, but I'm now in my third year as the writing program administrator. I chaired the AU core subcommittee developing writing-intensive courses in the disciplines, and I'm on the steering committee for the university's new strategic plan. I'm also a PhD student. I've said no to a variety of requests for participation in work I believe is important for the university and for term faculty, and each time I've felt anxious and guilty out of a sense that with these opportunities come responsibilities—to represent, to advocate, and always to do more. When I reflect on these responses, I find a few causes: my perfectionism and need to be essential; a fear that the opportunities themselves are contingent and might disappear if my colleagues and I don't take advantage of them; and a gendered desire to be of help, to assist the institution.

SAD WOMEN AND SCHOOL MARMS: TRADITIONAL GENDERED METAPHORS

What I don't feel like, however, is the "sad woman in the basement" (Miller 1991b, 121) or the mother or maid, or any of the other gendered metaphors that have long been employed to describe the work of composition faculty. These metaphors linger, however, and writing faculty still bear their weight, as well as many of the conditions, including contingency, that gave rise to them. But just as the limited roles for women laid the foundation for the idea of "having it all," and just as "all" includes motherhood and housework, so too do these metaphors matter in a discussion of writing faculty having it all.

The gendered divisions of labor in academia and the feminization of composition are well documented and theorized, and they serve as the basis for the dominant labor metaphors. Sue Ellen Holbrook explored these gender differences both materially/demographically and metaphorically/symbolically. She established the predominance of actual women in the field of composition and traced their role historically. But she also provided a useful definition of feminization: to "become associated with feminine attributes and populated by the female gender" (1991, 201). Feminization is not just a matter of literal numbers—of demographics; it's also a matter of perception and association. The labor becomes feminized, whether actual women are doing that labor or not. According to Holbrook, feminine labor is associated with domesticity—"servile, family-oriented, and self-effacing, centering their identity on relationships and entering the labor force in order to serve the needs of others"—whereas masculine labor is "competitive, self-concerned, aggressive, and rational" (202). One can see the associations that underlie gendered metaphors for writing-faculty labor.

These long-standing metaphors are primarily domestic—serving the needs of others, occupied by material concerns—but they vary in their emphases and nature. Donna Strickland posits one metaphor: the school marm with the red pen, ever attentive to student error. This domestic labor is hygienic (2011, 44), Strickland claims, cleaning up student prose so those students can work effectively in the world of abstractions. Strickland locates the division of labor in early twentieth-century scientific-management theories. In the corporate world, it was more efficient for the (male) executive to dictate his thoughts and have the (lower-paid, less skilled, female) secretary type them. As universities grew, with more diverse student populations, as writing become more important, the corporate efficiencies were replicated in academia: the conceptual labor belonged to male professors in the disciplines, and the mechanical labor was the purview of contingent faculty and graduate students, many of whom were female. In the popular (and often academic) imagination, this woman is a crabby stickler, toiling away at her basement desk, taking grim pleasure in the dismal papers stacked up before her.

The other traditional domestic metaphor within composition is Eileen Schell's (1998) "mother-teacher." The domestic labor in this case is more caring and nurturing. Schell traces the feminization of composition to teaching as acceptable feminine work. Women's work in composition is often literally linked to motherhood: Schell explains that women take contingent work because they might need to interrupt a career for motherhood, but those interruptions also lead to their work being devalued. Further, this feminized, caring mother-teacher can't escape domestic drudgery; she has hygiene duties in common with Strickland's school marm: "Moreover, teaching composition is still regarded in many circles as a sort of English department 'housework' in which women 'tidy up' student essays with painstaking, careful commentary and hours devoted to students in one-on-one conferencing" (Schell 1992, 58).

The mother and the school marm are implicitly brought together in Susan Miller's analyses of feminized composition labor. Miller (1991b) describes a Freudian mother/maid figure, who embodies a dynamic of desire, shame, and fear, associated with the composition teacher.

Describing composition's relationship to literary study, Miller emphasizes the labor binary: "Composition remains largely the distaff partner in a socially important 'masculine' enterprise" (1991a, 40). "Distaff" connotes literal domesticity, the small world of the home in contrast with the broad, social, masculine enterprise. But while "enterprise" connotes the business world, it is also a world of "play," according to Miller: "relaxed mental contemplation, reflection" (42). The Freudian mother figure is all work and no (intellectual) play. Miller argues that the mother figure carries a heavy burden, too, with multiple layerings of symbolism put upon her—mother, authority, disciplinarian, nurse, religious initiator (47). All this, for low pay, low status, a heavy teaching load, and a marginalized position in the academy: no wonder the composition teacher is, in Miller's words, "the sad woman in the basement" (1991b, 121).

Lest one think these metaphors and their implications have disappeared, Schell's recent foreword to a collection on academic labor should make clear they haven't: "It is also still the case that women are thought to be particularly good at delivering the kind of care work associated with teaching writing or providing language instruction" (2017, xv).

And one should also not assume male composition faculty are exempt from these metaphors; again, even if the labor might have started out originally as literally women's work, the feminized perceptions of the labor, and their accompanying metaphors, have been established and naturalized, whether actual women are doing the work or not, as Holbrook (1991) notes. Miller also locates these gendered labor metaphors, and the identities they construct, within a larger hegemonic system, noting their importance in maintaining the system: "We tacitly accept these identities to maintain the superstructure that we live in, in a process of hegemonic consensus" (1991a, 39). The identities, then, supersede actual individuals. Perceived, accepted identities play a substantive role in the workings and maintenance of the system—perhaps a larger role than the material, physically located individuals do.

As all these writers make clear, the metaphors have meaning and consequences. They reveal conditions of labor but also shape and limit its possibilities. They overburden writing faculty, in Miller's terms, with "symbolic as well as actual functions" (1991a, 47). If work is perceived as hygienic or care work, and if the system relies on that labor for its functioning—as universities rely on first-year writing "cleaning up" students before they proceed to meaningful academic endeavors—then the metaphors take on a force that can create realities. Just as women for centuries were bound not just by laws and policies but by constructions of domesticity, so too are writing faculty bound by metaphoric perceptions that relegate them to marginalized roles in the work of the university.

BEYOND DOMESTICITY: HAVING IT ALL

It seems, then, that more choice and more opportunity would revolutionize the metaphors and the realities of NTTF writing-faculty labor. We would be less bound by domestic perceptions of our labor and move into the intellectual life of the university. But the second-wave feminist idea of "having it all" can offer instructive lessons in the risks of increased choice and opportunity.

In her history of twentieth-century feminism, Gail Collins describes the ways "having it all" infiltrated 1980s popular consciousness and culture. Through pop-culture artifacts and interviews with women, Collins explored the promise and realities of having it all: "It was a new vision of the good life for middle-class young women. Nothing their mothers had wanted had been subtracted. There was just more. Much, much more" (2009, 301). That "more" included increased freedom and opportunity in the workplace but also the continued expectations that they would succeed as wives and mothers—while maintaining an aerobic-exercise-toned body. Moreover, despite encountering heightened expectations and continued prejudices, they were expected to make it look easy. Some women, of course, did successfully have it all and lead happy lives, but many young women were disappointed in the results of their new freedoms—not because they didn't want to work outside the home and have families but because they "had not considered that society might remain pretty much the same as always, and simply open the door for women to join the race for success while taking care of their private lives as best they could" (304). The systems that had supported their oppressions hadn't radically changed; women had to fit themselves into systems designed to foster male success—men who were single or had a woman to manage their domestic lives.

The tensions, pressures, and opportunities of having it all weren't confined to the 1980s, of course, and the myth of having it all became as persistent an idea as having it all. A 1980s self-help book, *Where's My Happy Ending?: Women and the Myth of Having It All* (Morical 1984), was followed twenty years later by *Women Confidential: Midlife Women Explode the Myths of Having It All* (Moses 2006). Both books looked at the experiences of women who thought they could have it all but were overwhelmed and exhausted; both urged women to try find themselves within the competing pressures and demands. These discussions, though, turned the responsibility for happiness back on the individual; life satisfaction became a matter of personal choice and initiative, with the system rendered less responsible for creating conditions that support satisfaction.

Moreover, the "all" women can have is often reduced to two main areas: workplace and home. Women's expanded opportunities comprised job opportunities, retaining the domestic obligations; they did not usually include opportunities to explore leisure activities, be satisfied with a variety of body types, or have free expressions of sexuality. In the discourse of having it all, their "callings," as Julia Wilson labels them, are limited to two: "professional and mother" (2009, 182). Even with such limitations to their expanded choice, women still, as Wilson notes, find little systemic or institutional support for managing these two callings.

Similarly, in her well-known article "Why Women Still Can't Have It All," Anne-Marie Slaughter (2012), a tenured Princeton faculty member and former State Department officer, describes the difficulties of having it all for professional women—the unlikelihood that a woman can devote sufficient time to her family and her job. Using her own and others' experiences, Slaughter, like Wilson, attributes many of these difficulties to a system not designed to support women's choices; lack of child care, inflexible schedules, insufficient leave—these conditions contribute to women being less successful in their different roles and feeling anxious and guilty in the process. She is more realistic than pessimistic: "I still strongly believe that women can 'have it all' (and that men can too). I believe that we can 'have it all at the same time.' But not today, not with the way America's economy and society are currently structured" (2012). The current institutions and culture encourage doing more while limiting the support for doing so. And like Wilson, Slaughter limits the "all" women can have to professional and domestic duties.

One criticism of the having it all ideal/myth centers on professional women with children. Slaughter acknowledges this limitation, albeit briefly, noting many women have no choice but to take on multiple roles—and even multiple jobs—just to make ends meet, without the domestic assistance a more affluent woman can afford. But a belief that it's possible to have it all obscures more than just the flaws of a system designed for men who can have it all without doing it all; it also obscures structural inequities, highlighting opportunities and individual successes while directing attention away from those who lack opportunity and choice and face only responsibilities and pressures. The lower-income mother who must work to make ends meet, and who cannot say no to a change in her shift or increased duties, might exhibit the trappings of having it all—a job and a family. But she likely does so not because she's chosen to work outside the home for personal achievement but because she exists in an economic system that does not pay working-class people a living wage. And increasingly, this lack of choice applies to middle-class women, who find they can't afford a home and family unless they're part of a dual-income couple.

The idea of having it all reveals a complex web of opportunity, obligation, exploitation, choice, and systemic flaws. The belief in the ideal can open doors to ambitious goals, but it can also obscure the inequities and flaws in economic and domestic institutions insufficiently changed by women's participation in them. Moreover, these institutions often thrive on this participation and its attendant inequities. They get more labor for less money while lauding the laborers for "choosing" to take the opportunities—and blaming them when they struggle. Interrogation of the myth of having it all, though, can reveal what has been obscured.

WRITING FACULTY HAVING IT ALL

If we apply the idea of having it all to the movement of term faculty into university governance and service, we have a useful gendered metaphor—in the tradition of the mother or school marm—to help us understand the implications of that movement. The aptness of the metaphor is clear. Term faculty, and writing faculty in particular, are long marginalized and low status, just as women have historically been. They also, historically, comprise a high percentage of female faculty. At AU, for many years term faculty focused only on their teaching, not university service, partly because of a lack of opportunity and mentoring and partly because writing faculty's teaching obligations are labor intensive, with higher teaching loads and numbers of papers to respond to (adjunct faculty have lower teaching loads, of course, but many must work multiple jobs). Moreover, term faculty at AU are evaluated primarily on their teaching, not on their service to the university. Like many women throughout history, writing faculty have had institutionally determined, limited roles that have focused on more intimate work with young people (through their writing) and that have kept them to the sidelines of the institutional work of university faculty. So when those limits seemed to have been relaxed and doors opened via new policies, AU's writing faculty took advantage of the increased opportunities, just as women did in the second wave of feminism. They could teach writing and chair committees and direct programs and be leaders in faculty governance (and in some cases be research active); they could, it seemed, have it all.

The metaphor isn't a perfect match, of course. While one teaches writing for one's entire career, chairing a committee is a short-term obligation. One can avoid extensive service and focus on teaching without facing a consequence as severe as losing a source of income; on the other hand, taking on extra service duties does not usually bring in significant extra income, either. And tenure-line faculty at research institutions face similar pressures to balance teaching, research, and service—although pretenure faculty are often excused from service, and tenure-line faculty usually have lower teaching loads.

Despite these imperfections, it's instructive to look at some experiences of writing faculty with the gendered metaphor of having it all in mind. These experiences parallel many of the complexities revealed in the discourse around having it all, with faculty noting opportunities and choices along with obligations and pressures.

With one exception, the writing faculty at AU sought out the opportunity to engage in service beyond the writing program. For some long-time faculty, these were opportunities to reinvigorate their careers. Chuck Cox, director of the new first-year seminar program, Complex Problems, said that "after eighteen years, I wanted something new to do, to keep things fresh and challenging." The associate chair of the Department of Literature, Kate Wilson, applied for her position because she found herself wanting new work that would fulfill her ambitions. While they continued to find their classroom work meaningful, they also wanted the choice to do different kinds of work; this desire for change perhaps comes from the limited teaching opportunities for writing faculty, who, for the most part, only teach first-year writing.

These faculty also wanted to make a difference in the institution, beyond the influence they could exert in the classroom or the writing program. Cindy Bair Van Dam is the faculty chair of the faculty senate's AU Core Committee, which undertook a sweeping and often controversial overhaul of the general education program. She is the lone faculty member who did not apply for her position; she was asked to take it. But, she said, "I believe in the mission; I believe in what we're doing," and despite the pressures of her position, she has chosen to continue in it. Shelley Marion (a pseudonym), who has been with the university for four years, felt she could make "real contributions to campus-wide conversations" in her role as a university program director. Both Wilson and Cox, too, emphasized the desire to participate in and even effect change beyond the writing program. They sought not just new work but meaningful work.

And they have found rewards in these opportunities—although not material rewards. All expressed satisfaction with their work, largely in affective or emotional terms. Cox, for example, described "a sense of belonging to something bigger," and Marion explained she enjoyed working with faculty across the university "to do the real work, the hard intellectual, deep work" of developing a new curricular program. Bair Van Dam also pointed to the rewards of faculty engagement, as well as increased knowledge of the institution and greater faith in its mission. There is a sense in their remarks of satisfying greater social involvement—a kind of "getting out of the house" of the writing program.

While Marion, the most junior member of this group, expressed concern about vulnerability as a term-faculty member, others found their new duties didn't endanger them (in contrast, for example, to the sense of risk of expressed by Megan Boeshart-Buerelle and Elizabeth Vincelette in this volume), although their term status occasionally created some uncomfortable moments. Cox explained he felt somewhat "insulated because [he's] been here so long [with] multiple multiyear contracts." With twenty-five years at AU, Bair Van Dam also believed she had some protection from senior administrators—necessary because of the often-controversial general education changes. Sometimes, though, their NTT status did become salient. Wilson described the uncomfortable experience of being in meetings with other department chairs and associate deans, all of whom were tenured, and hearing them talk about term faculty in negative or dismissive ways. Bair Van Dam has found that her term status has been visible, especially when she first took her position: "I feel disrespected by tenure people who say, why is a term faculty member doing this?" In leading an initiative that wasn't universally welcomed, Bair Van Dam faced criticism and pushback, and her term status might have given tenured faculty one more way to undermine the programmatic changes.

These difficulties are largely social and relational, and to be sure, this work demands a level of emotional labor—what might be construed as traditionally women's work. In addition to the significant administrative work involved in developing an ambitious general education program, Bair Van Dam's duties are primarily relational: "My number-one job is to smile whenever I'm walking across campus"—to be a "goodwill ambassador, to be a good listener, to be a good problem solver, to try to be exceptionally kind and upbeat in an authentic way." Marion and Cox referred explicitly to the emotional labor involved in their positions, in part because both lead faculty training and help faculty develop courses.

All four positions require social and emotional interaction, not to mention political skill: addressing faculty and student complaints, soothing egos, quelling anxieties, "selling" new programs.

Because their duties encompass far more than being pleasant to colleagues, these faculty feel stretched thin. All have course releases and stipends, so they're not uncompensated, but managing the labor of teaching first-year writing along with performing significant service has proven difficult—a difficulty shared by women managing home and work duties. Wilson noted it's hard to be good at both administration and teaching, and she must, at times, put teaching "on the back burner" because of the pressing requirements of her position. Marion believes her "teaching is the most important thing," but she struggles to give it sufficient attention. Because he doesn't want to do a disservice to any component of his job, Cox felt that "one of the things that makes [him] most nervous is balancing [his] time"; he manages his work with "lots of to-do lists" and said that a long habit of being well organized benefits him: "I've always been very careful with my time; I have to regiment my time." For Bair Van Dam, "Teaching is compartmentalized," and other than in her teaching, she's "hanging on by [her] fingernails." She developed a complicated organizational system, with multiple to-do lists categorized with colored tabs, to keep her professional life in order.

As with writing-instruction labor, this service work isn't well compensated; it offers more emotional than material rewards. In these high-pressure, high-profile jobs, term faculty are almost inevitably compensated less than tenure-line faculty for systemic, not personal, reasons. First, even if they earn stipends for additional work, those stipends supplement salaries lower than tenure-line salaries. Second, term faculty start out with higher course loads, so even with course releases, their teaching loads are often higher than tenure-line faculty's in similar positions. And the new roles might incur additional costs, such as parking and child care if one must be on campus more frequently, as well as new clothing. The material inequities parallel those experienced by women in the workforce.

Term faculty's concerns about the quality of their teaching—their primary duty—involve more than the effects on their students; teaching is still at the heart of their evaluation and reappointment (similar to the writing center directors in Boeshart-Buerelle and Vincelette's chapter). Despite recent diminishment in the importance of student evaluations of teaching (SETs) in determining reappointment, especially in our writing program, the Department of Literature, and the College of Arts and Sciences, low SETs are a factor in a reappointment decisions.

As the junior faculty member in this group, Marion was the most concerned about the potential effect of both work positions on her SETs and reappointment, but the reality for all term faculty is that no matter how successful they might be in administrative roles, if their SETs drop too low, their jobs are endangered. This risk can be contrasted with research-active tenure-line faculty in administration, whose teaching plays a lesser role in evaluation and who are often expected to produce less scholarship while they're in administrative positions. As with women who are judged for their success or failures as mothers no matter what they accomplish in their professional lives, term faculty are bound to their traditional duties.

WHAT THE HAVING-IT-ALL METAPHOR REVEALS

The having-it-all metaphor can help NTTF, tenure-line faculty, and administrators understand the benefits and drawbacks that result from NTTF taking on additional roles in the institution: opportunity for new challenges, broader social engagement, chances to effect meaningful change, increased workload, questions about our qualifications, continued emotional labor, potential criticism of our primary identity (as teachers). But the metaphor also highlights the larger risk for NTTF: the institution has come to rely on lower-compensated, vulnerable, willing labor to accomplish both the teaching and service work of the university. In the thirty years the idea of having it all has been part of the feminist conversation, women have continued to bear much of the burden for maintaining home life, and they continue to earn lower pay than men. The economic system, writ large, has taken advantage of their labor in both areas, with insufficient support for working parents inadvertently made possible through the often-herculean efforts of women. That pattern is in the process of playing out similarly—and becoming as firmly established—in higher education.

But as I've discussed, the ideal of having it all has been frequently been exposed as a myth. The skepticism already built into the metaphor can be useful to faculty and administrators, a means of interrogating opportunity and resisting exploitation—and not perpetuating systemic exploitation. Research into having it all reinforces the necessity of skepticism, interrogation, and resistance. In her article "The Rhetoric of Choice and Twenty-First-Century Feminism," Virginia McCarver (2011) links feminist values to choice, with a goal of more opportunities and choices for women—the "more" Collins (2009) describes. But McCarver argues that this "rhetoric of choice" can contribute to an "obfuscation of oppression and patriarchy" (2011, 21); the risk is that success or failure seems to depend solely on individual choice and effort, absolving the larger social and economic systems of responsibility. The most successful women make the complicated balancing acts look easy, further obscuring the ways the system works against them. As a result, McCarver argues, the ways women have it all can help perpetuate, not change, a neoliberal system.

Similarly, Christine Everingham, Deborah Stevenson, and Penny Warner-Smith (2007), in their study of generational differences in women's perceptions of their choices for work and home life, found that older women (second-wave feminists) took opportunities to work outside the home but realized they weren't necessarily more equal as a result because the systemic inequality remained. Younger women (third-wave era) didn't see the choice to work outside the home as a gendered issue but still struggled to balance their home and professional obligations. They viewed this struggle as an additional matter of personal choice, not in gendered or systemic terms. Slaughter, too, issues a warning: "It is time for women in leadership positions to recognize that although we are still blazing trails and breaking ceilings, many of us are also reinforcing a falsehood: that 'having it all' is, more than anything, a function of personal determination" (2012). Recognizing the inherent falsehoods of having it all can help NTTF avoid the mistake of conflating opportunity with equity, assuming additional work equates to positive systemic changes, and believing all responsibility for success or failure lies with them.

An interrogation of having it all reveals, too, that "all" includes the traditional gendered labor of writing instruction, with its pressures and limitations. As I've noted, institutional policies mandate that our primary roles are writing teachers, with the emotional, relational labor those roles require—and with the gendered perceptions of what writing teachers do. The woman in the professional workforce must still, as Collins notes, maintain the home, care for children, and be appropriately feminine and attractive, in a system that "might remain pretty much the same as always" (2009, 304). Like these women, writing teachers know their traditional identity matters; even when they take on high-profile service work, they must still care deeply about their teaching. Having it all often means having the obligation to do it all well with little support.

CHOOSING WHAT TO HAVE WITH EYES WIDE OPEN

The metaphor of having it all, then, can help us see the opportunities, burdens, limitations, and potential exploitation of our expanded work duties. Such clear vision is essential; NTTF are already an established component of academic labor, and they will likely continue to participate in more of the work of the university, including leadership roles, as the recent *Chronicle* article describes (Field 2018). Some of this participation might be voluntary, some required—or NTTF might be "volun-told"—but no matter what, NTTF should understand what they're getting into. And even in institutions where NTTF service is limited and regulated (such as by a union contract), faculty should understand the potential dimensions of their labor—as should tenure-line faculty and administrators.

Despite my cautionary tone, though, I believe that for many NTTF, expansion of their roles can be challenging and fulfilling. My term colleagues and I have found significant rewards in our work. And as some of my colleagues note, these roles provide access to different levels of decision-making, as well as the ability to influence university policy and curriculum. While having it all might not alter the deeply established university structure, or its more current neoliberal tendencies, expanded participation affords opportunities to effect smaller changes—changes that can potentially make learning and labor conditions better.

I'm not advocating for all NTTF to take on more service; choice should function as an affordance, not a neoliberal constraint. Someone on a semester-to-semester contract quite likely—and naturally—feels less of an investment in the institution than a long-time faculty member on a multiyear contract; an adjunct faculty member might rightly feel no such obligation. Nor am I advocating for an uncritical stance of saying yes to each opportunity. Quite the opposite: I am arguing that NTTF should examine opportunities critically for their possible rewards and exploitation—and for their potential to change an inherently exploitative system.

Likewise, I am urging tenure-line faculty and administrators to critically examine the system within which we all work. There can be a tendency for self-congratulation when NTTF conditions are improved. Some of that is warranted: it is a good thing to start to treat one's colleagues as equals. But those good feelings shouldn't contribute to the obfuscation of neoliberal exploitation. NTTF's opportunities to be full participants in the university should not be part of the project to cut budgets while extracting more work from faculty. Moreover, tenure-line faculty and administrators should avoid using these opportunities to blame NTTF—the reasoning that says, "You have all these opportunities now, so it must be your fault if you still feel underpaid/marginalized/low status." Such blame placing feeds into a system that holds individuals responsible for their own oppression. Instead, I would like to see faculty and administrators engage in the critical solidarity that benefits all constituencies so they can freely choose to take opportunities that advance them materially, professionally, and personally.

At my institution, term faculty fought for access to these opportunities; we believed it was fair for us to have the same opportunities as our tenure-line colleagues. And as women have discovered over the years, more opportunity is better than less; having more choices is better than few or none. But as women have also discovered, opportunity and choice don't guarantee equality, and they can lead to exploitation and even reinforcement of oppressive systems. This is difficult terrain to navigate. But I believe we are compelled to navigate it, not blindly seeking to have it all but examining with eyes wide open the opportunities, choices, pressures, sacrifices, and exploitation. We can participate fully in the work of the university and perhaps not have it all—but still choose to have new roles and challenges that benefit us and our NTTF colleagues.

REFERENCES

Collins, Gail. 2009. *When Everything Changed: The Amazing Journey of American Women from 1960 to the Present.* New York: Little, Brown.

Everingham, Christine, Deborah Stevenson, and Penny Warner-Smith. 2007. "'Things Are Getting Better All the Time'?: Challenging the Narrative of Women's Progress from a Generational Perspective." *Sociology* 41 (3): 419–37.

Field, Andy Tabusa. 2018. "'We Are the Most At-Risk People on Campus:' Non-Tenured Instructors Can Now Serve in U. of Mississippi's Faculty Senate." *Chronicle of Higher Education, September 18.* https://www.chronicle.com/article/We-Are-the-Most-At-Risk/244557.

Holbrook, Sue Ellen. 1991. "Women's Work: The Feminizing of Composition." *Rhetoric Review* 9 (2): 201–29. https://doi.org/10.1080/07350199109388929.

McCarver, Virginia. 2011. "The Rhetoric of Choice and 21st-Century Feminism: Online Conversations about Work, Family, and Sarah Palin." *Women's Studies in Communication* 34 (1): 20–41. https://doi.org/10.1080/07491409.2011.566532.

Miller, Susan. 1991a. "The Feminization of Composition." In *The Politics of Writing Instruction: Postsecondary,* edited by Richard Bullock and John Trimbur, 39–54. Portsmouth, NH: Boynton/Cook.

Miller, Susan. 1991b. *Textual Carnivals: The Politics of Composition.* Carbondale: Southern Illinois University Press.

Morical, Lee. 1984. *Where's My Happy Ending?: Women and the Myth of Having It All.* Reading, MA: Addison-Wesley.

Moses, Barbara. 2006 *Women Confidential: Midlife Women Explode the Myths of Having It All.* New York: Marlowe.

Schell, Eileen. 1992. "The Feminization of Composition: Questioning the Metaphors That Bind Women Teachers." *Composition Studies* 20 (1): 55–61. https://www.uc.edu/journals/composition-studies.html.

Schell, Eileen. 1998. *Gypsy Academics and Mother-Teachers: Gender, Contingent Labor, and Writing Instruction.* Portsmouth, NH: Boynton/Cook.

Schell, Eileen. 2017. "Foreword: The New Faculty Majority in Writing Programs: Organizing for Change." In *Contingency, Solidarity, and Exploitation: Labor and Action in English Composition*, edited by Seth Kahn, William B. Lalicker, and Amy Lynch-Biniek, ix–xx. Fort Collins, CO: WAC Clearinghouse.

Slaughter, Anne Marie. 2012. "Why Women Still Can't Have It All." *Atlantic*, July/August. https://www.theatlantic.com/magazine/archive/2012/07/why-women-still-cant-have-it-all/309020/.

Strickland, Donna. 2011. *The Managerial Unconscious in the History of Composition Studies*. Carbondale: Southern Illinois University Press.

Wilson, Julia. 2009. "The Mommy Track versus Having It All: The Reality of the Modern Workplace." In *You've Come A Long Way, Baby: Women, Politics, and Popular Culture*, edited by Lilly J. Goren, 177–97. Lexington: University Press of Kentucky.

6
GHOSTS IN THE BUILDING
Investigating Contingent-Faculty Experiences

Brendan Hawkins and Julie Karaus

Our chapter documents both quantitative and qualitative data on North Carolina's public university and community college non-tenure-track faculty (NTTF), specifically part-time NTTF. Our data support what has been established, demonstrating a preponderance of reliance on contingent faculty to teach introductory courses such as first-year composition courses (e.g., Coalition of the Academic Workforce 2012; MLA 2008, 2014; US House of Representatives 2014). Indeed, the validity of proffering our contingent colleagues' narratives as data is also well documented (e.g., Everett and Hanganu-Bresch 2016; Fulwiler and Marlow 2014; Kahn, Lalicker, and Lynch-Biniek 2017; Schell 1998; Schell and Stock 2001). What our chapter contributes to these conversations is twofold: (1) we present survey and interview data concurrently to highlight the connections between faculty members' material realities and affective dispositions towards the institutional spaces offered or, more often, not granted to them, and (2) we discuss the usefulness of participatory action research (PAR) as a research lens because it emphasizes recursivity and an awareness of sociopolitical systems within which researcher and researched are operating (McTaggart 1997). We see this project as employing facets of PAR: "to improve [a person's] own work and the way it is understood (theorized)[;] . . . to collaborate with others engaged in the project (academics and workers) to help them improve their work; and . . . to collaborate with others in their own separate . . . institutional and cultural contexts to create . . . the material and political conditions necessary to sustain the common project and its work," namely solidarity for/with NTTF (31). For example, we had not predicted that fellow adjuncts would share so intimately their pain and worry, and we posit that sharing our positionality as fellow NTTF opened space for those feelings to be shared by all. The political bent inherent in PAR furthermore asks us to consider these narratives'

DOI: 10.7330/9781646420759.c006

confluence with broader narratives and metaphors of composition and higher education.

We were and to some degree still are contingent. At the outset and design phase of this project, we shared the same home institution but worked in multiple programs, departments, and other institutions to make ends meet. We navigated spaces as instructors, faculty consultants, and faculty-development leaders, yet we were also classified with titles such as nonstudent temporary, adjunct, NTTF, and/or interim (depending on which job we were doing at the time). As we return to this text to collaborate almost four years since completing the research, each of us has changed positions in hopes of securing more predictable and sustainable work, still neither of us is tenure track (TT). Even with the security of a full-time staff position or further graduate study, there is always the specter of impermanence. We hope that shedding light on these spaces and narratives of NTTF speaking for themselves (and with fellow NTTF) will help connect those involved in making local policies to the human cost that results from overdependence on contingent labor and the too-frequent limited opportunity for advancement or institutional voice. The research presented here was first inspired by our own meditations on the relative poverty of our own working conditions and later, in the drafting phase, we were emboldened by Seth Kahn's (2017) essay on speaking for adjuncts; furthermore, we would like to demonstrate the power of speaking for oneself, as we were in the unique position to act as both researcher and subject.

NTTF are increasing in number yet losing ground. College and university systems have reached a level of dependence on adjunct labor that is no longer sustainable. This is a national issue, and studies like Paul Umbach and Matthew Wawrzynski's (2005) depict quantifiable differences in contingent versus full-time tenured teacher performance, time commitment, and pay. Others, such as Helen O'Grady (2001), analyze gaps between institutional promise and practice. For instance, the MLA committee's report on professional employment (1997 and 2008) argued that the increasing reliance on adjunct or part-time work potentially undercut the mission of universities in areas such as advising and mentoring but also in maintaining the status quo defined by departments. Later, MLA (2011) gave additional recommendations for professional development and maintenance of a contingent workforce. We do not find these implemented frequently in North Carolina.

Given these struggles facing NTTF and their allies, we understand the need to consider not only numbers and narratives but also how those are physically represented and discussed. Nedra Reynolds (2007) and Michelle LaFrance and Anicca Cox's (2017) assessments of space and place urge readers to consider the ramifications of how space is conceptualized and how we play out that discourse in the university every day. Reynolds argues that it "is urgent for us to consider how spaces impact upon learning, reading, and writing" (3). Similarly, LaFrance and Cox employ a photo essay to demonstrate the spatial politics of their workspace and the material conditions therein, claiming that "space requires action. And movement and action require purpose. And so, our daily routines echo with dominant notions of our status, our value, our place" (291).

In agreement with Reynolds's (2007) assertion that places become meaningful when bodies occupy them, and in response to Kahn (2017), our chapter frames and presents our inquiry into the spaces of adjunct labor in North Carolina as they relate to college composition. We see our exigence in the lack of permanent professional homes we had as adjuncts, as well as the many other places adjuncts do not or cannot occupy. We are aware of the volumes of research that chronicle the adjunct crisis in higher education more generally and in composition programs more specifically. Rather than bemoan a lack of space, we aim to uncover the spaces adjuncts occupy and how they frame their relationships with those spaces. We call these *contingent spaces* for the ways NTTF in our interviews describe their relationships with institutional spaces. In these interviews we hear corroborations of O'Grady's "freeway fliers" as well as the disembodiment and ironic metaphor of one adjunct's ghostly "presence" on her campus (2001, 139). Our research also elucidates the difficulties of locating these spaces: adjuncts are hard to find because they are highly mobile. Their professional spaces lack fixed addresses—they occupy spaces only temporarily.

What we sought to accomplish with this research was a greater understanding of contingent faculty's relationships to their workspaces, not from a theoretical or anecdotal perspective but from a systematic, mixed-methods study. If the field understands NTTF do not have as much time for or cannot (for many reasons) participate in the institutional (re)structuring that may improve their lives, we must better understand ways adjuncts negotiate their liminal spaces. We were particularly interested in gauging those connections between what Eileen Schell (1998) terms "the psychic capital" of NTTF work and how that translates to effective pedagogy and enhanced interactions with students. (As Liliana Naydan and Lacey Wootton each address in this volume, composition work is highly gendered.) Our research rose from reflections on our own experiences in which access to safe spaces and adequate resources impacted our classroom performance, job satisfaction, and successful student interactions. Even in our desire to perform the role of researcher, we were unable to sever researcher from our simultaneous identities as subject and worker. Although real change may be best implemented at the local level down to institution, college, department, or even building or office suite, the local context for many NTTF is broader, as many traverse multiple locations seeking work yet ultimately belong to none. Contingent faculty piecemealing full-time workloads out of several positions become further alienated because they are not considered whole by any one entity. Adjunct space is by nature interinstitutional. Therefore, an examination of a contingent space had to include consideration of the state system in order to create a clearer definition of the workspaces we were interested in observing.

METHODS

This project was conceived in 2016 when the researchers, both working as adjuncts on more than one physical campus and in more than one program on their primary campus, began having conversations on the difficulty of finding and defining work space. That difficulty was aggravated by the realities of navigating multiple jobs, roles, and institutions, none of them feeling like home. Originally, we considered our physical (dis)placement; however, as our conversations evolved, we realized we could not isolate physical spaces from other influences, such as digital presence on department websites and emotional disaffection interviewees later described as a result of their interinstitutional work. The original research was designed to be mixed methods. We wanted to deploy surveys, solicit and conduct interviews, and collect actual images of how contingent faculty conceived of their work space. Our central research questions were, How are contingent faculty defining and navigating their work spaces? Are there general statements we can make about the state of contingent composition labor through this inquiry of space?

The first step in the research process was to find our target population. This proved to be no simple task. According to the US Bureau of Labor Statistics (2015), the total number of literature and language faculty in North Carolina for 2015 was 2,880. We hoped for an estimated 10 percent response rate, as many as 250 respondents to the survey. We relied only on publicly available information, meaning the way they are listed on the websites of the institutions they serve—a more difficult task than we envisioned. The North Carolina University system keeps few records on its adjunct instructors, and institutional websites are inconsistent and not always easy to navigate. We collected email addresses by searching through the departmental websites of all seventy-five North Carolina public two- and four-year colleges and universities. Some institutions listed all English and composition faculty by their titles on the website. Others listed only more permanent faculty, and in some places, the status of the listed individuals was unclear or out of date. Still others listed individuals by department or division rather than subject taught. Therefore, we were unable to access a firm number of individuals teaching as NTTF, nor can we be certain the survey and invitation to participate in the interview were as available to our target population as we hoped they could be. Preliminary data represent but a snapshot of the labor conditions faced by North Carolina's adjunct writing faculty, as there was and continues to be a notable lack of data kept on the target population.

We solicited interviews through the survey by asking individuals to contact us if they wanted to contribute further to the project. We also asked faculty we knew personally or with whom we worked for individual interviews. In total we interviewed eight individuals: two via email, four one-on-one, and two interviewed together due to scheduling constraints. The interviews were recorded for transcription. While we had a script of interview questions to guide the process, most of the interviews evolved into natural conversations that happen when people share common experiences. It is in the interview process that the location as both researcher and researched benefited our research goals. As we suggest in our results and discussion, the depth of discussion was reached because of the trust in us as researchers *with* as opposed to researchers *on*. With the rubric set by Robin McTaggart (1997), the power in this approach produced knowledge simultaneously developed by both academics and workers and shared by the larger group. Regarding further research by us or other groups interested in investigating issues surrounding contingent labor, we recommend beginning with PAR principles in the initial design.

RESULTS

Our survey results show a workforce that frequently fills multiple roles within institutions, such as writing center consultants, to make ends meet. These results correlate with scholarship in our "References" and this volume that represents the lack of financial stability for contingent faculty. While our qualitative data are far from conclusive, they offer a glimpse into contingent-faculty members' contexts. Our results vary widely in respondents' feelings towards the presence or lack of institutional support, and the interviews we conducted contextualized some of these feelings. Our interviews, presented below, correlate with our survey results that depict uneasiness about respondents' financial futures. Likewise, the "Methods" section depicts our difficulties locating contingent faculty based on outdated or absent institutional digital presence. Therefore, conclusions that can be drawn from our mixed-methods approach rely heavily on interviews to frame inconclusive survey data. In these interviews, we found ourselves becoming imbricated in the interview process, as fellow contingent faculty frequently framed their lack of institutional support as a need for validation.

Survey Responses

Our N population came from eighty-three survey responses from the more than seven hundred survey requests to faculty we could find listed on institutions' websites. From the responses we received, we understand our typical survey responder had been working any number of years in higher education, though slightly over 50 percent had been working in the field under ten years. Our respondents who did have a "home" institution ranged from across North Carolina, both universities and community colleges. The typical responder was adjunct or part-time faculty (48 percent), with only 33 percent of respondents having a full-time faculty position. Our survey allowed for an "other" option, and several responses wrote out "adjunct" or "part-time," suggesting the 48 percent may underrepresent the contingent faculty taking our survey. Many other responses about contingent working status included "professor" or "instructor," so we are not able to conclude what their full-time status would be. Thirty-four percent worked at more than one institution, and 15 percent claimed no home or main institution. Responses like "I go where there is work" clarified a typical "no" response.

Participants demonstrated consistent wariness about their financial future: 69 percent reported inhabiting uneasy financial spaces. This unease was reflected in responses that indicated 53 percent have had to work outside their academic institutions for extra income. The statement "I go where there is work" expresses not only the interinstitutional nature of many NTTF but also depicts those piecing together jobs through faculty and staff positions and a general lack of permanence or institutional commitment. The top two nonfaculty roles were writing center consultant at 67 percent and academic advisor at 38 percent, indicating that respondents have served or do serve multiple, concurrent roles.

When respondents indicated what their institution offered them in terms of physical space, they pointed towards less space to meet with students and fewer opportunities for out-of-class, in-person student contact. Forty-five percent of respondents reported having an office, and 55 percent had no office. Yet, of those who had an office, 60 percent shared that office with four or more people. These faculty reported they do not meet with students (16 percent), meet elsewhere (33 percent), or meet in their office (29 percent). A typical "other" response said, "If students wish to meet, I meet with them just before or just after class in the classroom. Email is the majority of 'meeting' with students. Meetings are uncompensated and not required by the adjunct contract."

In other areas the data are mixed. There's a positive skew towards feeling institutional support, academic freedom, and satisfaction with current employment, though all three questions elicited a range of responses. While the responses for satisfaction level in current access to technology and comfort using the virtual platforms on campus (i.e., Moodle, Blackboard, etc.) were slightly skewed positive, respondents wrote fifteen stories on the survey that depict hardships with technology, including mandatory unpaid training sessions or having to learn content-management systems alone.

Bleak Interviews

The statement "I plan to move on" lingered due to implied dejectedness. There was enthusiasm in initial email responses thanking us for surveying adjuncts and an eagerness to respond to an email interview within a few hours. However, the responses were bleak in tone. One respondent reported moving through several teaching arrangements and locations but failing in ten plus years to find more stable working conditions. The semester of this research, he reported having six classes to start but dropping two of them, realizing he was overburdened with so many commitments and so few resources. His responses indicated not an aversion to professionalization but to the logistical difficulty of teaching at three locations in a day, two of them back to back with scarcely enough travel time. He wrote "Professional space is irrelevant to me" and indicated he considered giving up teaching or "moving on" in some way.

While this response, as indicated, holds the least hope for the profession, it represents our findings. Another interviewee who taught in the evening called herself the "ghost" of her community college because she never saw or communicated with any colleagues. She reported walking by empty office spaces on her way to the classroom that served as the only professional space made available to her. When we asked her what she would like others to know about her as a professional she answered,

> It is important to understand that the people being hired as adjuncts are qualified, intelligent, educated, individuals, who are dedicated and driven, because why else would you do this? And they cannot perform as well under these circumstances, so if you want better students, you want better outcomes, they need better resources . . . that includes . . . being part of the actual department.

For another example of this sentiment, we can look at another highly qualified instructor's inability to get stable work. This instructor had been teaching for over twenty years in multiple states, both high school and community college, full- and part-time. Despite his obvious dissatisfaction with his current professional situation, it was clear this individual loved teaching and was concerned with the well-being of his students and their learning, as he spent more time bemoaning how the adjunctification of the profession was hampering his academic freedom in the classroom than he did discussing the material conditions of his classroom reality.

The desire to belong was often represented in conjunction with a desire for professional space. Often, these desires for professional space were simple gestures to share space, such as a chance to pass colleagues in the hallways or an invitation to sit in on department meetings. Most of our interviewees reported going to work, teaching their classes, and leaving. Most interviews were cynical, as many NTTF displayed resentment regarding their experiences. One woman even used a Dickens reference to elaborate on her feelings of dispensability:

> There's that one book by Charles Dickens where he keeps calling the people "hands" . . . he refers to the people working for industry as "hands" and he calls them "hands" because they're just people. . . . We're just people they found to fill an empty class, and we don't matter—we're expendable, they could get rid of us and replace us easily with someone else.

While new teachers still hold to the feeling that their hard work and dedication to their craft and their students will result in a position of stability and respect, those who have been in the game for a long time inevitably succumb to the reality that they are working too hard for the reciprocal material gains or institutional respect.

According to the American Academy of University Professors (2018), the number of folks employed on a contingent basis is now above 70 percent. This number is not sustainable on an institutional or an ethical level, and this project is concerned with the human cost of contingency. This cost is evidenced by quotes from interviews such as the following:

> I love what I do but as the year starts to get toward May, I start thinking about am I going to be able to do what I love to do, and I try really hard and I work really hard, but is trying hard and working hard enough?

As researchers and NTTF ourselves, we understand these moments are unique when shared in the safe space that exists between colleagues. Moreover, we understand these moments cannot exist in a space inhabited by administrators or faculty with greater degrees of institutional power. Nor can they exist in front of students, whose evaluations often underpin the bulk of a teacher's institutional assessment.

On an institutional level, classroom observations, when they are done, and student evaluations are the only measures of adjunct work. Movement toward standardized syllabi and module-based education only reinforces the lack of faith many have in our institutions of higher learning and the devaluation of critical-thinking habits that form the core goals of general education. Exhibiting his lack of faith, our veteran interviewee, in response to the standardized syllabus and preprogrammed Moodle site he was expected to use remarked, "If you want a unified product, don't hire cats; make us robots."

DISCUSSION AND IMPLICATIONS

What this research has uncovered is not groundbreaking, nor do we have reason to believe the stories here and the attitudes reflected are uncommon. Graduate schools continue to produce more degrees than the job market has positions. The situation—already problematic when Schell published *Gypsy Academics* in 1998, for example—has only been further aggravated by the 2008 recession, the burgeoning gig economy, competition for already scant resources on campuses, and hostile political attitudes toward labor organization and agitation.

Focusing on inclusion and solidarity is important, especially as new teachers are brought into the existing system. From our experience as both participants and researchers, part of a productive emotional culture of teaching is feeling an institution values both labor and laborer. While this is an important first step, we caution against the temptation to stop there. In places like North Carolina, an employment-at-will state, tenured faculty have the only positions of real power. Those individuals must be reminded that fighting for the rights of contingent faculty benefits them as well. Georgia Rhoades, Kim Gunter, and Elizabeth Carroll

(2017) exhibit that behavior by leveraging their tenure-track positions and research time to publish on labor issues. Their work efforts not only speak on behalf of, but also speak to and with NTTF. Rhoades, Gunter, and Carroll and others like them demonstrate collaborative spaces wherein contingent faculty are seen, known, and advocated for by their tenure-track colleagues. We see this work as socially responsible in that it capitalizes on what Danielle Lake and Joel Wendland call "the attempt to collaboratively generate knowledge . . . for the purpose of both using that knowledge (i.e., acting upon it) and sharing potentially valuable lessons with others" (2018, 12).

Lots of Bodies, Empty Space

Reynolds writes, "Places only become meaningful . . . when bodies occupy them" (2007, 145). In the final phases of this project, we scoured the faculty and EHRA budget records from the university where we were employed. We searched for mention of wages for part-time composition faculty in documents that were supposed to include all wage data for faculty from the 2016–17 academic year. The reality was that there was not even a single line dedicated to the wages of part-time faculty. In searching for email addresses, we discovered that individuals we knew to be teaching classes were not listed on departmental websites. This phenomenon of invisible labor permeated every aspect of this research, from the language used by the folks who participated to the difficulty reaching them and their desire to remain invisible as participants. Not keeping records is a form of labor erasure that reinforces a striking trend seen in US higher education.[1] We ask tenured faculty and administrative allies to take note and recognize the need for creating space for contingent faculty to be both seen and heard.

It is in PAR principles and methods that we see the most potential for filling these spaces. Reflecting upon the research contexts in which we found ourselves, we now more fully understand the functionality of our role as participant-actors. We see more clearly how PAR offers potent methods for recognizing vulnerable laborers and labor contexts, engaging them as coconstructors of research parameters and disseminating the research with the goal of social activism. Lake and Wendland suggest

> that community-engaged scholars pursue more transparent and self-reflexive methods of engagement around the risks and challenges of this work; operate as boundary spanners by pursuing intentional, ongoing dialogues across disciplinary and institutional divides; integrate transdisciplinary planning methods, tools, and assessment metrics designed to

reduce risk and assess power dynamics; and commit to more inclusive authorship and open-access publishing practices. (2018, 12)

In line with these guidelines, we have tried to be transparent about our positionality regarding our research. Furthermore, we seek here to advocate for the betterment of contingent faculty in any or all the parameters of our study (i.e., the physical, virtual, emotional, and economic labor conditions of NTTF).

Kahn (2017) writes about being an ally for adjunct faculty as a way of dispensing advice to other like-minded tenured faculty. As both researchers and as NTTF who found a platform for our voice in spaces created by dedicated allies, what resonates with us most is the call to listen first. Our addition to that call is to provide space for those voices and engage in a belief in the common good. As we attempt here to define it, we can see space can be defined in multiple ways. We ask that tenure-track faculty listen and look for the real physical bodies that inhabit the empty spaces around them.

Moving from Privilege to Action

The conversation regarding the human cost and real price of the university's overreliance on adjunct labor has begun, but the extent to which individuals working as contingent faculty have been actively involved in those conversations is limited. In an employment-at-will state like North Carolina, those conversations are especially tricky. Employment at will means that either the individual or the employer can terminate the employment relationship at any time. Labor laws and fiscally conservative politics in twenty-first-century North Carolina continue to foster an ecosystem that allows exploitative practices to grow by reducing budgets for hiring and salary and cultivating practices that erase laboring bodies from the spaces where they work. They also work to erase the natural partnerships that should and could exist among stakeholders within institutions.

The effects of those limited budgets and erasures are evident in our own professional journeys, yet we were privileged to work for allies and decided we should devote our energies to speaking up and speaking out in the only way we knew how at the time: recognizing the affective power of adjuncts researching adjuncts. While we acknowledged our privileged status in having emotional support from tenure-track allies, we knew our positionality as fellow adjuncts would affect the research context.

We firmly believe there is strength in shared experience. This strength is evident in the conversations we had during this project. But the conversation cannot stop there. Securing more reliable positions for contingent faculty is not impossible, but literature describing success stories points to collaboration in specific and localized contexts more than sweeping legislation. It is our belief that there are multiple layers to that context in North Carolina. There should be a visible community of laborers involved in the overarching struggle for educational resources in this state. However, the struggle for adequate working space must happen on and in individual campuses, buildings, and departments. For this, contingent faculty need allies, and those alliances must be able to listen, learn, and be capable of self-inventory.

In the effort to create more equitable work spaces where the opinions and needs of all members of a department are considered, we look to Peggy McIntosh's (1989) seminal article on the unpacking of (white) privilege, Lacey Wootton and Glenn Moomau's (2017) argument for self-advocacy, and the MLA Committee on Contingent Labor (Modern Language Association 2011) for ways to recognize academic privilege(s). In solidarity with those efforts, we invite TT and administrative allies to reflect on exactly what constitutes the privilege that comes with an institution's commitment to them. This privilege can be as small as access to supplies and space to safely meet with students, or it can be as large as advocating for departmental voting rights for NTTF. The way forward will require action from allies, trust among colleagues, and acceptance of the reality that in the current economic and political climate, no one stakeholder within the higher education community can thrive without the labor of the others being appropriately valued, recognized, supported, and compensated.

NOTE

1. The AACU called this trend the "unbundling of a traditional faculty role" (2018, 1).

REFERENCES

American Association of University Professors. 2018. "Data Snapshot: Contingent Faculty in U.S. Higher Education." October 11. https://www.aaup.org/news/data-snapshot-contingent-faculty-us-higher-ed#.Xin2-2hKjHo.

American Federation of Teachers Higher Education. 2010. "A National Survey of Part-time/Adjunct Faculty." *American Academic* 2 (March). https://www.aft.org/sites/default/files/aa_partimefaculty0310.pdf.

Coalition of the Academic Workforce. 2012. "A Portrait of Part-Time Faculty Members: A Summary of Findings on Part-Time Faculty Respondents to the Coalition on the Academic Workforce, Survey of Contingent Faculty Members and Instructors." www.academicworkforce.org/CAW_portrait_2012.pdf.

Everett, Justin, and Christina Hanganu-Bresch, eds. 2016. *A Minefield of Dreams: Promises and Perils of Independent Writing Programs.* WAC Clearinghouse & Colorado State University Open Press.

Fulwiler, Megan, and Jennifer Marlow. 2014. *Con Jobs: Stories of Adjunct and Contingent Labor.* Logan: Utah State University Press and Computers and Composition Digital Press. http://ccdigitalpress.org/conjob.

Kahn, Seth. 2017. "The Problem of Speaking for Adjuncts." In *Contingency, Exploitation, and Solidarity: Labor and Action in English Composition,* edited by Seth Kahn, William B. Lalicker, and Amy Lynch-Biniek, 259–70. Fort Collins, CO: WAC Clearinghouse.

Kahn, Seth, William B. Lalicker, and Amy Lynch-Biniek, eds. 2017. *Contingency, Exploitation, and Solidarity: Labor and Action in English Composition.* Fort Collins, CO: WAC Clearinghouse.

Lafrance, Michelle, and Anicca Cox. 2017. "Brutal(ist) Meditations: Space and Labor-Movement in a Writing Program." In *Contingency, Solidarity, and Exploitation: Labor and Action in English Composition,* edited by Seth Kahn, William B. Lalicker, and Amy Lynch-Biniek, 279–302. Fort Collins, CO: WAC Clearinghouse.

Lake, Danielle, and Joel Wendland. 2018. "Practical, Epistemological, and Ethical Challenges of Participatory Action Research: A Cross-Disciplinary Review of the Literature." *Journal of Higher Education Outreach & Engagement* 22 (3): 11–42. https://openjournals.libs.uga.edu/jheoe/article/view/1399/1396.

McIntosh, Peggy. 1989. "White Privilege: Unpacking the Invisible Knapsack." *Peace and Freedom* 49 (2). https://psychology.umbc.edu/files/2016/10/White-Privilege_McIntosh-1989.pdf.

McTaggart, Robin. 1997. *Participatory Action Research: International Contexts and Consequences.* Albany: SUNY Press.

Modern Language Association. 1997. "Final Report from the Committee on Professional Employment." Modern Language Association, December. https://www.mla.org/Resources/Research/Surveys-Reports-and-Other-Documents/Staffing-Salaries-and-Other-Professional-Issues/Final-Report-from-the-Committee-on-Professional-Employment.

Modern Language Association. 2014. English Departments in United States Insitutions of Higher Education: MLA Survey of Departmental Staffing, Fall 2014. https://www.mla.org/content/download/103529/2303971/2014-Staffing-Survey.pdf&sa=D&ust=1579796462566000&usg=AFQjCNGuOJnTgG2uswKR35iIYOzkCdL5hw. October 2018.

Modern Language Association and Association of Departments of English. 2008. "Education in the Balance: A Report on the Academic Workforce in English: A Report of the 2007 ADE Ad Hoc Committee on Staffing." December 10. https://Www.Mla.Org/Content/Download/3255/81374/Workforce_Rpt03.Pdf.

Modern Language Association Committee on Contingent Labor in the Profession. 2011. "Professional Employment Practices for Non-Tenure-Track Faculty Members: Recommendations and Evaluative Questions." June. https://apps.mla.org/pdf/clip_stmt_final_may11.pdf.

O'Grady, Helen. 2001. "Trafficking in Freeway Flyers: (Re)Viewing Literacy, Working Conditions, and Quality Instruction." In *Moving a Mountain: Transforming the Role of Contingent Faculty in Composition Studies and Higher Education,* edited by Eileen Schell and Patricia Lambert Stock, 132–58. Urbana, IL: NCTE.

Reynolds, Nedra. 2007. *Geographies of Writing: Inhabiting Places and Encountering Difference.* Carbondale, IL: Southern Illinois University Press.

Rhoades, Georgia, Kim Gunter, and Elizabeth Carroll. 2017. "Still Trying to Break Our Bonds: Contingent Faculty, Independence, and Rhetorics from Below and Above." In *Minefield of Dreams: Triumphs and Travails of Independent Writing Programs,* edited by Justin Everett and Cristina Hanganu-Bresch, 139–54. Fort Collins, CO: WAC Clearinghouse.

Schell, Eileen. 1998. *Gypsy Academics and Mother-Teachers: Gender, Contingent Labor, and Writing Instruction.* Portsmouth, NH: Boynton/Cook.

Schell, Eileen, and Patricia Lambert Stock. 2001. *Moving a Mountain: Transforming the Role of Contingent Faculty in Composition Studies and Higher Education.* Urbana, IL: National Council of Teachers of English.

Umbach, Paul, and Matthew Wawrzynski. 2005. "Faculty Do Matter: The Role of College Faculty in Student Learning and Engagement." *Research in Higher Education* 46 (2) 153–84. http://10.1007/s11162-004-1598-1.

US Bureau of Labor Statistics. 2015. "Occupational Employment and Wages May 2019: 25-1123 English Language and Literature Teachers, Postsecondary." http://www.bls.gov/oes/current/oes251123.htm#(2).

US House of Representatives House Committee on Education and the Workforce Democratic Staff. 2014. "The Just in Time Professor: A Staff Report Summarizing eForum Responses on the Working Conditions of Contingent Faculty in Higher Education." https://edlabor.house.gov/imo/media/doc/1.24.14-AdjunctEforumReport.pdf.

Wootton, Lacey, and Glenn Moomau. 2017. "Building Our Bridges: A Case Study in Contingent Faculty Self-Advocacy." In *Contingency, Solidarity, and Exploitation: Labor and Action in English Composition,* edited by Seth Kahn, William B. Lalicker, and Amy Lynch-Biniek, 199–211. Fort Collins, CO: WAC Clearinghouse.

PART III

Lived Experiences

7
AN INCONVENIENT TRUTH
Labels and Limits in Writing Center Directorship

Megan Boeshart Burelle and Elizabeth J. Vincelette

Twenty-eight years ago, Gary A. Olson and Evelyn Ashton-Jones claimed, "During the past decade, . . . the role of the writing center director has never been adequately defined, and center directors are thus experiencing a kind of identity crisis. The lack of consensus about the center director's role is unfortunate, since the WC is an essential complement to any comprehensive writing program" (1998, 19). Today, little has changed regarding the role of writing center directors (WCDs), most of whom are non-tenure-track faculty (NTTF) and many of whom have vague job descriptions, leaving their labor fraught with unclear boundaries.

Our chapter offers the reflections of two WCDs at the same institution; one has returned to the classroom full time (Beth), and the other has been hired to fulfill the directorship (Meg). Both NTTF, our status is far from unique in the writing center field, in which approximately 70 percent of directors are non-tenure-track (Isaacs and Knight 2014). As such, our positions are contingent, and although job loss is unlikely, our NTTF status inaccurately marks us as performing nonscholarly, administrative service work and not as writing professionals with knowledge grounded in writing center theory and practice. We focus both on the struggles with our positioning as NTTF and on the ways we have advocated for changes to be made for the position and for the WC that have made a considerable difference.

On our campus, we have seen increased awareness and demands on WC services from across the disciplines and have experienced major changes in WC location and larger departmental and university initiatives related to writing. Not only has our WC moved to a learning commons during Beth's directorship, the university also undertook a quality-enhancement plan (QEP) involving writing, which evolved into an initiative entitled Improving Disciplinary Writing. During the first year of Meg's directorship, the WC moved again to a different location; the university's Writing Sample Placement Test for incoming students and instruction for developmental writing both moved from an office outside the English department to English; and a job search began in English to hire a writing program administrator (WPA) to oversee the composition program (including the addition of developmental writing) and the writing center.

While increased awareness of writing on campus and institutional involvement can be seen as good problems to have, several years into these changes, the WC's funding (or lack thereof) remains the same, as does its structure and the structure of the WC director role. During Beth's time as WC director, we had ten graduate student tutors, all from English, who served twenty-eight thousand students. Appointments were full most of the time. Beth supervised ten tutors a semester who conduct approximately four thousand appointments a year, all while she taught between fifty-five and seventy students per semester. During Meg's second year in the position, the number of tutors has grown to seventeen a semester. The appointments have remained full even with the growth in tutoring hours available. While Meg's teaching load (per her contract) is smaller than Beth's was—she has nineteen students a semester—our WC remains full and continues to grow. And, despite this growth in both the number of tutors working in the writing center and the number of students using the WC, the budget has remained virtually nonexistent. The department pays for WCOnline and supplies the WC with basic office supplies like printer toner; however, the WC does not have its own operating budget. We give these numbers for context because the related administrative reporting problem involves what we call *blurred reporting lines*—how in addition to the work we've noted here, a WCD is open to tasking from outside their line of reporting—and the potential for job creep is theoretically endless, not to mention fraught with political landmines.

We organize our chapter around two interrelated strands of professional experience: our job descriptions and performance evaluations. The lack of clarity in our job descriptions has left the evaluation process of our work opaque, as a core part of our position as lecturers in our departments is our work as writing center directors, but our evaluation process is the same as other lecturers teaching a 4/4 load. For each strand, we each offer a narrative describing how we have individually responded to the challenges of what we see as necessary reform of fundamental and routine administrative matters.

JOB DESCRIPTION

Swathmore's National Census of Writing data on WCs shows that at four-year institutions, 35 percent of director positions are tenure track (when the WC director position is associated with a stand-alone position). Jill Gladstein, who heads up the census, argues that in a time during which NTT jobs are outpacing TT positions, "If we continue to use TT positions as the baseline, we will always come up short" (2014).

At our institution, the WCD by contract carries a 4/4 teaching load and directs the writing center for "course releases." Even in the job posting when Meg took over the position of director, the course releases were designated for "administrative duties." What exactly those duties are, however, has not been officially defined. There is no official position description, fostering a perpetual lack of clarity and transparency regarding the WCD's duties at the departmental and university levels, leading to unclear practices for performance evaluation and promotion.

The need for a clear position description connects to Jeanne Simpson's list calling for ethical working conditions for WCDs. Thirty-one years ago, Simpson authored a position statement that addresses professional concerns for WCDs, calling for the position to be "one that requires specialized preparation and administrative experience. It should be recognized as such and should carry the same rights and responsibilities as other professional faculty positions" (1985, 36). In particular, the need for a job description overlaps with Simpson's suggestion that the "demands of the position" should be taken into consideration and related to promotion. The demands, unfortunately, are often seen as service work alone, not research or intellectual work. This, in part, is one reason for the continuing use of NTT WCDs—because a number of English professionals outside the writing or comp/rhet field view WPA or WC work as service only. Margaret Marshall, regarding the evaluation of WCDs, argues that the two-part classification of administrative work as either service or teaching "regularly precludes submission of the very documents that would demonstrate the intellectual dimensions" of writing program administration, and in our case, writing center work (2001, 81). Pigeonholing WC work as service only diminishes research and scholarship in the field, particularly when many NTTF WCDs produce scholarship without recognition of their publications because their positions as NTTF do not require, and sometimes even discourage, publishing.

The lack of an official job description has meant it has fallen upon our shoulders to define our own goals and plans for our administrative duties. Much of the administrative work we have done in the WC has been unknown to most of our faculty, and the most documentation we are to create is a one-page report to the chair that is forwarded to the college's dean. While some of these duties may seem obvious—we train, supervise, and mentor the tutors who work in our WC—the relocation of the WC into the learning commons has meant an increase in committee work, new services for specialized populations such as veterans and international students, and data reporting. Within the home department of English, however, the committee work duties remain the same while the committee work outside the department not only grows with the expansion of tutoring services elsewhere on campus but also with ad hoc committees that request input.

For example, during Beth's time as WC director, she was serving on two special committees appointed by the vice provost's office, where she was invited to offer her insight regarding how to improve tutoring and writing at the university—again, all positive things here, yet a fellow writing NTTF member also on the committees expressed concerns when she asked Beth, "How open we should be? What are we allowed to say?" The answers were unclear; outside our home department (English), as NTTF without position descriptions, we are exposed to political tensions without a clear sense of what protections we have.

Beth

In her 1985 statement, Simpson included the position of the National WC Association (now the IWCA) against hiring part-time faculty as directors "unless they are given full access to the rights, privileges, and services available to regular faculty" (36). Simpson set an ideal many WCDs strive for, but unpacking her description reflects holes in what is otherwise a seeming match between what was my directorship and the ideal. Although I am now, for example, a full-time faculty member, as a senior lecturer I was a part-time WC director because I taught two classes a semester in addition to my WC duties. Furthermore, the "rights, privileges, and services available to regular faculty" means one thing to me, a NTTF member with a contract (renewable every year), another to a tenure-track or tenured faculty member, and yet another to a staff member, graduate student, or adjunct faculty member—all of whom can and do serve as WCDs at various institutions.

The protection for a WCD like myself should have arisen from a job description, and the position did not have one at the time. Without a job description, the role was open to interpretation. I was vulnerable, especially regarding the lack of clarity about reporting lines. Susan Mueller (director of the Norton WC and WAC coordinator at the St. Louis College of Pharmacy) posted on the IWCA listserv several years ago that she struggled with a reorganized reporting structure for her WC after its move to a Student Success Center: the it reflected a complete misunderstanding of her professional work as a WCD and the perception that her position was disposable or that the WCD was easily replaced. But it was the pressure of administrative reorganization that prompted what she described as "all hell break[ing] loose" (2015). Although for me the situation was not as extreme, the blurred reporting lines resulted in my receiving tasking from outside my reporting line (to English).

I'm one of many WCDs who is NTT with a PhD. My research training equipped me to create data-driven studies, but my split job and number of students did not permit the time needed to undertake such work. Furthermore, the WC directorship did not require or prefer a PhD from my department, but within an institution such as my own, the PhD letters behind the director's name lent me ethos, even though actual status within my department did not match the rest of the university's view of the position of WCD. I had little doubt that when I instructed faculty on best writing practices (including a large number of tenured faculty and even a few deans), the letters behind my name somehow mattered, yet the mismatch in actual work and the unclear expectations led me to feel shortchanged in status and pay.

Although being involved in many of the committees and initiatives I describe does suggest I'm viewed as a writing specialist on my campus, I worked without the limits imposed by a job description, limits needed for my protection.

Meg

The restructuring of the WCD job at our institution did change in a positive way when Beth stepped out of the position—only because she actively advocated for the position during the job-ad creation and hiring process, particularly the reduction of the teaching load and establishing clear reporting lines, which were necessary because the department decided to have the position remain an NTT line. Beth's work to restructure the position put me as the new director in a much more stable position, though the potential for job creep has not really changed. However, the clarification in reporting lines has meant I've received much more substantial support from my chair and dean when I come to them with various issues that may arise. As Jessica Cory and John McHone argue in chapter 8 of this collection, "A Tale of Two Pities," "We've learned that faculty and administrative support is incredibly helpful, not just through increased funding (though that's certainly welcome!) but also through simply understanding what it's like for NTT folks in our departments and on our campuses. Simply recognizing the inequalities that exist between TT and NTTF at different institutions is the first step in working toward a solution" (chapter 8). It is because of Beth's advocating for the WCD position during the hiring process that upper administration was much more cognizant of the support an NTTF member would need given the WCD's role across our campus.

For example, during my first year as director, I was invited by the vice provost and executive director for Academic Enhancement to discuss the movement of their Writing for College Success program into the English department. The clarification of the reporting lines made it easy for me to involve my department chair and dean in the conversation. Despite my position as an NTT lecturer, I was invited to the meeting and expected to contribute to the discussion of how this shift should happen. I took this particular moment and the conversations I had with my department chair following the meeting to articulate the need for the voice of someone who is a writing expert but who also shas the protection of tenure to advocate for our writing program's needs. I was not the first to voice this concern, and this was not the first time our chair had heard the concern that those of us in charge of various entities within our writing program need someone to advocate on our behalf, especially when our knowledge of pedagogy and research are at odds with what is being asked of us. Perhaps therein lies the key—we must continue to articulate our needs to upper administration who do listen to us. The ongoing discussion and articulation of needs has meant a drastic step in our department though—the creation of an associate chair who is focused on the writing program. Although it may not always be evident, the work our NTTF colleagues do before us, such as the work Beth did before I took over the role of WCD, paves the way for our jobs and makes our work more tenable and viable. Her advocating made it possible for the job to be reimagined with a more sustainable workload and with more clarity on how other administrators could support the work in the WC.

The university is beginning to recognize the writing support various populations of students on campus need, but they are not necessarily providing any kind of resource support. Despite the lack of budget or monetary support, I created a new type of writing support for graduate students this year. We now offer a weekly graduate student write-in to help graduate students create and sustain a writing habit as they work on large research projects, theses, and dissertations. The number of tutors I supervise has almost doubled, from eight to ten tutors per semester to sixteen to eighteen, as I've shown with our numbers how widely used our services are and how many more students we could serve with increased available tutoring hours. I'm asked to give presentations, information sessions, workshops, and more, though none of this appears in my job description or is included in how I am evaluated.

The difficulty, of course, is that we want the WC to be well known and respected on the campus so faculty, staff, and students feel comfortable recommending students use the service. We want to provide effective tutoring sessions to all our student populations and try to provide students with the most positive experience possible as we help them grow as writers. In terms of the job description, though, there is not a clear designation of what is and is not included as part of that job. Instead I'm left to make a lot of decisions about whether I should or should not pursue a particular project or initiative, carefully considering whether I have enough time to be able to create and sustain the project. While this freedom is in many ways positive, as Beth mentions, the lack of boundaries of the job (and administrative help) means the duties of my job often proliferate quickly. It is also difficult to deal with requests coming from faculty with tenure, especially tenured faculty who hold positions of upper administration and are asking for my input and labor. I'm left in a vulnerable position in which it is not always clear when I can say no. I mention the feelings of vulnerability in regard to whether I can say no, as well as the ever-growing demands of my position, as I think many NTTF may feel similarly as they juggle teaching, service, and scholarship expectations.

EVALUATIONS

As lecturers directing the writing center for course releases, our job is an anomaly in our department, and there is no method in place for evaluating our writing center work. The yearly performance portfolios we submit are supposed to emphasize teaching, with the bulk of interest placed on course evaluations by students. There is, then, little to no oversight of writing center labor. In addition, the department's annual report does not contain information about the WCD's role, accomplishments, or duties, so the work remains behind the scenes, administratively absent.

Especially critical are not only the methods used to evaluate the director, but, in turn, those used to evaluate the tutors. Like the assessment of the director's performance, the tutor assessment remained outdated. And, as the director's evaluation should be based more clearly in job description, the tutors' evaluations should be noted during hiring practices. In our current model, all graduate student tutors are assigned to the WC by their graduate-program directors and not by the WCD. As such, the selection of tutors results in some successful tutors and some who are unsuitable for writing center work. Without communication (and accountability) based on a tutor's job description, the director's job performance depends more on chance than it would were she directly involved in tutor selection.

Furthermore, with such lack of clarity for the director's evaluation, the promotion process is muddled. Our institution is working hard to develop better guidelines for the promotion of NTTF, yet those guidelines are still based entirely on teaching portfolios. For the WCD (and other "hybrid" instructor-administrators), the path up the promotion ladder appears less direct, at worst, and difficult to demonstrate on paper, at best.

Beth

Because my directorship consisted of half of my job, there was no method in place for evaluating 50 percent of my work. As a 4/4 lecturer, I turned in yearly materials that were designed to evaluate teaching only, with the most emphasis placed by the department on course evaluations filled out by students. There was little to no oversight of my WC duties.

To address this incomplete evaluation, I designed my own evaluation materials. In addition to my teaching evaluations, I turned in a copy of the WC yearly report sent to the dean in charge of my department; to that I added a copy of a writing center self-evaluation based on a copy of an old document recommended by the IWCA, as well as a reflection on my work and a suggested job description. After the evaluation cycle in the department ended, I was asked not to include the materials in the future because it was too much reading for the reappointment committee to sift through. Although my immediate reaction was disappointment and disbelief, I realized the committee simply had no model, no template, and no guidance regarding how to evaluate a job that didn't "fit" and that the solution was to have a job description on which an evaluation could be based.

I frequently found myself at ethical crossroads, vacillating between trying to find the time to complete what I believed were necessary actions towards improving writing tutoring (improved training, program assessments, outreach) and feeling stymied by lack of motivation due to my workload. At the same time I was overwhelmed, the title of being a WCD was motivating, a seemingly high-status position and a high-visibility role despite the blurry reporting lines and evaluation methods. Nevertheless, much of my work was invisible, not seen and unreported.

Meg

Despite the creation of the new position that restructured the directorship in some ways, the means of evaluation have remained the same for me as they were for Beth in this position. All the materials I am asked to submit are focused on my teaching, which in my case is only 25 percent of my work. Although I do not submit all the documentation of my work in the WC, I do submit the yearly report, as well as a two-page report detailing major initiatives the WC undertook and our numbers breakdown of students using our service. I share this with my colleagues who do the peer review of my materials, as well as with the evaluation committee.

I have been fortunate in that the colleagues I have asked to peer review my teaching portfolio are cognizant that most of my work is in the WC. I have tried to strategically choose colleagues I knew would also refer to my work in the WC in their peer-review letters submitted to the evaluation committee. Despite my best efforts to ensure that this information about what most of my job entails reaches the evaluation committee, I am left unsure as to what does or does not count in terms of evaluating me or renewing my contract because, as Beth mentions, there are not clear guidelines or templates for how the committee would evaluate a lecturer who is not teaching four classes each semester. Based on my previous evaluation, I know my chair discussed initiatives I had begun and my work in the WC in her letter for the evaluation committee. However, my concern is that while my chair is wonderfully supportive, there are not necessarily guidelines for a future chair to consider the work I do in the WC. The chair position will eventually transition to someone new, and there are not guidelines in place to help guide whoever fills that position next. The same thing applies to my colleagues who are aware of and recognize and value the work I do in the WC who wrote letters for the evaluation committee. Without these structures in place within the evaluation system, we rely on the relationships we develop with particular faculty members to ensure they understand and value the work we do.

TRANSFORMING HOW OUR WORK IS DESCRIBED AND EVALUATED

Our chapter ends with several suggestions for transformation, not only for ourselves but also for those writing center directors whose working conditions prohibit their professional and scholarly development and promotion. By extension, we argue for ethical standards for NTTF writing center professionals and for institutional change.

Such changes underscore the need to professionalize writing center directorships, with acknowledgment of writing center studies as a legitimate field grounded in research. Directorships should be staffed voluntarily through an official job search that requires applicants to demonstrate tutoring experience and knowledge of the field. When Beth agreed to the directorship, she did so with a great deal of experience teaching composition but no administrative experience and no practical understanding of writing centers, including everything from managing tutors to developing evaluation methods. When Meg took the role, she did so under conditions that reflect our institution's commitment to improving the WC overall. Meg had composition teaching experience, writing center administrative and tutoring experience, and was in the early stages of planning a dissertation devoted to writing centers. Her job description indicates that her labor is specifically designated as being 75 percent in the writing center and 25 percent teaching composition (with one class a semester at the general education level).

However, it has become clear that there is a need for a WC course for tutors, especially as expansion has become necessary. Even with the increase to seventeen tutors, the WC runs close to capacity all semester, and with the influx of undergraduate tutors in addition to our graduate student tutors, it is important they are provided with sufficient training before taking positions as tutors. The creation and acceptance of a writing-tutor course has proven difficult because the department is experiencing a major overhaul to curriculum and a shrinking number of English majors. Despite these challenges, Meg will continue to advocate for the creation of the class, carefully considering the ways the course can match up to other programming on campus. While an undergraduate class would be a significant step forward, many graduate students, especially those in our department's PhD program, would like a writing center course, primarily focused on administration, to be offered. Right now, as NTTF and a current graduate student, Meg would not be able to teach the course. Meg also tries to consistently take up the call to advocate for the writing center and the ways the labor is viewed and compensated. In other words, we encourage NTTF to consistently advocate on their own behalf and to take steps to make their labor as visible as possible to their colleagues. We think the movements we make forward are possible because of the advocating done by other NTTF before us.

To conclude, we offer a model that demonstrates the ways our evaluation should be conducted to reflect the WCD's responsibilities. As previously mentioned, the evaluation currently emphasizes teaching only, even for NTTF with administrative duties. For the WCD in particular, the percentage of space on the evaluation form devoted to nonteaching responsibilities should reflect the percentage of duties described for the directorship. For Meg, with 75 percent of her job in the WC and 25 percent of it in the classroom, 75 percent of what she reports for evaluation should reflect her achievements, grants, proposals, committee work, and more associated with the WC. The other 25 percent of her evaluation should follow the standard reporting in the department associated with teaching.

Currently, the evaluation system requires NTTF to submit peer-review letters from three other faculty members, a faculty information sheet, an up-to-date CV, and student opinion surveys for the classes taught in the past academic year. The policy for evaluating teaching effectiveness through the peer-review letters is shared through email. The policy states, "The function of Peer Review of Portfolio is to evaluate teaching effectiveness by an examination of the documents used in instruction" and is specifically focused on course-based instruction. We believe that since 75 percent of the WCD job is focused specifically on writing center duties, there should be space for the inclusion of documents beyond teaching and the two-page WC report.

We feel that even if the focus of the evaluation is on instruction, the process and materials submitted do not consider the types of instruction we do as WCDs outside the classroom. For instance, the inclusion of materials we create and use for tutor training during orientation and ongoing professional development, professional development and/or training during staff meetings, and tutor observations are all documented materials that could be considered as part of our evaluation. They would reflect the work we do more accurately than just our classroom materials and student evaluations. These documents do not even take into consideration workshop or presentation materials we have created based on current needs of faculty or students, but they at least do reflect a key component of our job: that we train, mentor, and support tutors and their professional development. We also feel the WC evaluation should ask for the yearly report, which may include the number and breakdown of students and student populations using the WC, new and sustained initiatives undertaken by the WC, and a list of presentations and workshops given by the director from across campus.

What we want to emphasize the most is that we think institutional change, including the ways our institutions view our position as WCDs, often have little to do with our actual job performance. Often, the ways our institution views us have everything to do with resources and funding, campus culture, upper administration, and the support within our particular divisions where our WCs are housed. Although our progress is slow, we want to put forth that our ongoing effort to articulate to various entities across campus the WC's needs, the needs of the director, the needs of our tutors, and the needs of the students using our services has slowly created changes. Perhaps not the level of the changes we know still need to happen, but positive changes nonetheless.

REFERENCES

Isaacs, Emily, and Melinda Knight. 2014. "A Bird's Eye View of Writing Centers: Institutional Infrastructure, Scope and Programmatic Issues, Reported Practices." *WPA: Writing Program Administration* 37 (2): 36–67.

Marshall, Margaret. 2001. "Sites for (Invisible) Intellectual Work." In *The Politics of Writing Centers*, edited by Jane Nelson and Kathy Evertz, 74–84. Portsmouth, NH: Heinemann.

Mueller, Susan. 2015. "[Wcenter] Reporting Structure Problem." WCenter Listserv. May 18, 2015. http://lyris.ttu.edu/read/messages?id=24645477#24645477.

Olson, Gary A., and Evelyn Ashton-Jones. 1988. "Writing Center Directors: The Search for Professional Status." *WPA: Writing Program Administration* 12 (1–2): 19–28.

Simpson, Jeanne. 1985. "What Lies Ahead for Writing Centers: Position Statement on Professional Concerns." *Writing Center Journal* 5 (6.1): 35–39.

8
A TALE OF TWO PITIES
An Inside Look at a Dual Non-Tenure-Track Household

Jessica Cory and John McHone

THEIRS: INTRO

We met in grad school, like many other academia couples. The benefits of meeting your future spouse in graduate school can be many: the potential for higher lifetime earnings, partnering with someone who shares your values regarding higher education, and even someone who understands all too well when you once again bemoan grading. However, if the couple are graduating from the same program, they are also likely to compete for the same jobs, and in composition, without a terminal degree (and often, even with one), jobs may not be in robust supply. Full-time positions as university lecturers are hot commodities with many applicants, and tenure-line positions at community colleges may not frequently open. Writing center administration may be another full-time option, but some of these positions prefer candidates with PhDs. Tutoring and adjunct work are often the only other options if someone with an MA in English wants to stay in academia.[1]

Our household is headed by two adults who both hold MA degrees in English. Jessica, who has an MA in creative writing, works full time as a lecturer at a four-year public, mostly undergraduate, institution. John, who has an MA in literature, is currently an adjunct at the same institution and at a nearby community college. Some of the difficulties that come with dual non-tenure-track household are balancing schedules, dealing with financial concerns, and reaching long-term goals, such as home ownership and retirement. Both of us are facing or on the cusp of professional decisions: Jessica is beginning a PhD program part time and will remain in her full-time NTTF position; John is considering leaving academia in favor of more robust fields such as marketing and graphic design, on the brink of burnout after working as an adjunct for nearly seven years.

Our stories are not unique. Throughout academia, NTTF face a host of difficulties that seemingly fly under the radar of tenure-track and

DOI: 10.7330/9781646420759.c008

tenured faculty, as well as some administration. Our stories are testaments to this truth, but so too are many of the stories collected in the documentary *Con Job: Stories of Adjunct and Contingent Labor* (Fulwiler and Marlow 2014). Numerous professionals interviewed echo how low-to-modest compensation, little opportunity for professional development, and limited options for growth fly in the face of publicly held notions that teaching at a university means termination is impossible and paychecks are inflated. Perhaps by raising awareness of the conditions and lives of NTTF, this perception may be altered, even if the challenges go underaddressed.

HIS: BACKGROUND

I come from a family of educators. My mother earned her master's degree in education and was a middle-school teacher for all of my childhood. Her parents were educators before her. My father wasn't a teacher, but as a first-generation college grad, he was a life-long learner. I started my college career as an art major but switched to English after three years. I felt an English degree was more prudent and would offer more job prospects, which were few and far between in eastern North Carolina. After two years without a full-time job and making ends meet by substitute teaching and doing odd jobs, I felt I would be more marketable with more education, so I decided to go back for my MA in English. In grad school, I concentrated on literature with particular focus on postmodern literature and science fiction, and my independent research often revolves around film and new media. For the past seven years, I have adjuncted and tutored my way across the state of North Carolina.

HERS: INSTITUTION LIFE

For someone without a terminal degree (yet), I am very fortunate to have full-time work as a lecturer, teaching first- and second-level composition classes. I was hired to teach four courses a semester (summers off but still paid) without any scholarship or service expectations. In addition to my regular compensation, my department has also been supportive of travel for scholarship and publication opportunities (despite these not being required), and I'm often able to teach summer courses for additional experience and income. I also receive compensation for interdepartmental service, such as sitting on committees. However, service to the university or college is often not compensated at an additional rate.

While I have been in my current position since August 2016, I am still categorized as temporary, meaning my contract is academic year to academic year. This classification initially was worrisome, particularly because moving is expensive and my initial salary would not have allowed any savings for a moving fund. Owning a home is often less expensive than renting in our area, but buying a home is a risky move if the buyer is on a one-year teaching contract. It does help to know I am not alone in these concerns, though. Our department relies almost entirely on full-time lecturers to teach the foundational composition courses, and many of my colleagues are considered temporary after being here several years. During the 2017–18 academic year, our faculty senate formed a Non-Tenure-Track Faculty Task Force to address the promotion of NTTF. After much discussion with NTTF on campus, they made their recommendations, which were quite similar to the lecturer to senior lecturer step described in chapter 9 in this collection, to administration, who agreed to implement promotion pathways for the institution's NTTF. These suggestions were put on the back burner following a series of administrative changes, including a search for our new chancellor. While we have now someone in that position, and were informed the new promotion pathways would start January 2020, many of the pathway details have yet to be worked out, including the potential pay increase and title changes for current NTTF, nearly all of whom are housed in the English Department, causing confusion for NTTF faculty, as Angie McKinnon, Christopher Lee, and Linda Shelton explain in the chapter 9 of this collection was the case at their institution as well.

My department head has also supported me by allaying my fears about the temporary status. He has assured me that unless enrollment drops dramatically, he intends to keep renewing my contract and does not see me as a temporary employee, so I feel a bit less nomadic. However, as the department head rotates every few years, this assurance only engenders so much confidence. I do find it encouraging that our institution was recently targeted for its continued growth and, as such, is a participant in the NC Promise Tuition Plan,[2] which helped bolster an already-growing student population, with a 5.5 percent increase from 2017 to 2018 and a 29 percent increase since 2008 (Studenc 2018). I am not terribly concerned about drastic decreases in student enrollment, particularly since the increase in enrollment is largely fueled by incoming first-year students, the exact demographic I teach. That said, with the rise in high-school students utilizing early-college high schools, which allow students to take courses for college credit at no cost while obtaining their high-school diplomas, we may see an increasing number of students who opt to transfer these credits rather than take them in our English Department at some point in the non-so-distant future. Then again, if the NC Promise Plan caters to traditionally underserved populations, we may see fewer of these transfers than other universities do. As with most facets of academia, particularly in the humanities, the future is difficult to predict.

While the focus on teaching and pedagogy is paramount, as I am employed at a mostly undergraduate institution, I wonder how the non-emphasis on scholarship and publication prepares my colleagues should our current positions no longer be available, especially since some of our lecturers have PhDs. Certainly, many positions want or require teaching experience, but many positions, particularly tenure-track ones, require publications as well. This uncertainty about the future is part of the reason I engage in scholarly conversations. Not only am I passionate about my specializations in the field, but I also understand the importance of visibility and networking. I recall hearing from older professors in the field that it was once possible to land a TT job shortly after graduating with one's doctorate. However, this hasn't been the case since the mid-1990s, perhaps even earlier.

It is my goal that by furthering my education and continuing to teach and research, I'll be better able to advance the research in my field but also care for my family and their piece of mind. A permanent position would be one way to accomplish this.

HIS: THE ADJUNCT HUSTLE

In recent years, the term *gig economy* has risen with the popularity of Airbnb, Uber, and Lyft. Low-wage workers found a way to supplement their income in their free time by offering their homes and cars to their neighbors. These industries go largely unregulated, and now we leave our sleeping arrangements and safe passage in the hands of strangers (and not just that, but amateur strangers). As scholars, you'd think we'd be smart enough to avoid this type of system in academia. Cue the adjuncts. The idea of hiring instructors to teach a couple of classes sounds like a good idea in theory. Enrollment changes every semester, and instead of laying off full-time instructors in times when enrollment is low, and overburdening them when enrollment is high, departments can have a base of teachers that will always be needed and then supplement those faculty with qualified people to handle the excess. This isn't how the system has come to work though. One of my schools has six full-time faculty on the spring 2019 schedule and thirteen adjuncts (with six unstaffed courses, meaning two more adjuncts will need to be hired). This issue has been a persistent within academia since the 2007 recession, and the job market has still not bounced back (Weissmann 2015). The full-time faculty teach five or six courses while adjuncts only teach two or three. If adjuncts were used supplementally instead of exploitatively, there would be an additional six full-time faculty members.

This account of my experience in this system is purely anecdotal but by no means unique to me. I've worked at community colleges, for-profit colleges, and private and public universities across North Carolina and have seen my former grad-school classmates go through similar realities. Fresh out of grad school in early 2011, I started working at a local community college.

Now, North Carolina has a pretty extensive community college system, with sixty-five schools spread over its one hundred counties, and pay scales and policies are fairly consistent across this system. At my first postgrad teaching job, I taught six classes as an adjunct. At most community colleges, this would be considered a full load (which in and of itself is criminal, but that's a topic for another book), and at most four-year colleges, this is 150 to 300 percent of a full load. Still, on paper, I worked eighteen hours a week. Thirty dollars an hour may sound like a lot. However, when one is only paid for fewer than half the hours actually worked, and those hours leave no time to work any other jobs, this pay barely amounts to a living wage. The fact that adjuncts were teaching full loads without benefits goes to show that the system was already flawed when I entered it in 2011. That problem was exacerbated when the Affordable Care Act was implemented (specifically the provision that employers must offer health insurance to employees working ten hours or more a week). Instead of offering health insurance, it became policy in the community college system that adjuncts could not teach more than nine credit hours in a semester, or three courses. By doing this, they ensured paying the same low wages with no benefits. However, this workaround leads many adjuncts into working additional jobs in retail, food service, and sex work (Gee, *Guardian*, September 28, 2017), or relying on food stamps (Patton 2012). This system had a brief stint in our national discourse back in September 2013 when the *Pittsburgh Post-Gazette*, in an article by Daniel Kovalik, covered the death of Margaret Mary Vojtko, a veteran adjunct who lived, and died, in extreme poverty, and whose story went viral, but the issue has largely been forgotten, though the system still remains unchanged (Harris 2019).

I, like much of my graduating class, cobbled together two or three classes here, two or three there, and supplemented my income with tutoring work in writing centers at community colleges. This has been the case for most of my teaching career, and every semester plays out in roughly the same way. I spend a good portion of my unpaid summer and semester breaks planning my courses, updating resources, and completing the online supplements for all my courses—all in addition to my regular summer job. When I was single, I was able to scrape by on tutoring for the maximum allowable twenty-five hours and austerity. For the last two years, I've been a line cook in a local restaurant. Usually department meetings over these breaks happen when I'm working my summer job or teaching elsewhere, but if I do get the chance to attend, I'm not compensated (beyond seeming like a go-getter to administration, which may prove useful in the off chance that a full-time gig does open up). I show up on the first day of class to teach. Sometimes my contract has been signed. More often than not, I haven't received it yet. I spend my week bouncing around multiple campuses. Hopefully I only have to visit one campus a day, but that isn't always the case. Hopefully there is an office for me between classes so I can grade in peace or meet with students, but that isn't always the case either. I juggle teaching duties with various school requirements, such as record keeping and progress reports. Student emails come directly to my phone late into the night, and I'm expected to respond to every last one of them. I rarely see my colleagues and am almost always unsupervised. The only interaction I have is with my students, aside from the rare observation (the last of which was over a year ago). This goes on until the end of the semester—wash, rinse, and repeat.

The biggest issue that arises in this system is that adjuncts don't feel valued as employees. They are compensated at a rate that is not equivalent to the amount of stress they must endure. I spend an hour or two commuting to multiple jobs five days a week where I barely get acknowledged as an employee, and at the end of the year I tally up my five or six W2s to find out I made $25,000. For the workforce bearing the brunt of teaching intro courses, this just isn't enough. It would be different if this job were to lead to something, but it doesn't. There is a misconception among adjuncts that you must pay your dues. However, when a full-time job does become available, hundreds of applicants apply, and adjuncts ultimately lose out to those with full-time experience. Opening the job search to other areas of academia such as advising or tutoring may provide some new opportunities, but ultimately direct experience is more appealing than tangentially related experience. The same holds true for the private sector. So now we have this group of highly educated people who are kept on the brink of financial ruin with skills that aren't transferable outside their current positions.

It may seem strange that a system with so many flaws could retain its workforce. The system actively holds back up to two-thirds of its faculty, so it's surprising the entire system hasn't collapsed but instead still remains the system used by many of our schools. In many cases, this avoided demise is because adjuncts have two things: passion and hope. For many, what initially attracts them to this job is that they want to teach, and adjuncting is viewed as a foot in that door. Community colleges are a perfect place for those who want to teach at a postsecondary institution with a master's degree. It also works well for those who are more passionate about teaching than research. Adjuncts also remain hopeful that the job they are doing will lead to something better. That light is always at the end of the tunnel, and with a foot in so many doors, it always seems that it's only a matter of time before the hard work pays off. It is idealistic, and for some it will work out, but the sheer numbers are just not in most adjuncts' favor. Even in defense of adjuncting, Rob Jenkins states, "As I scan our faculty roster, I can see that about a quarter of the full-timers began as adjuncts in our department" (2015). Full-time positions rarely become available, and when they do, there is no guarantee adjuncting is actually a stepping stone to a full-time career.

The biggest issue with this lifestyle is that there is no sense of normalcy. Every semester provides a new schedule and new challenges. Since we moved to western North Carolina two years ago, I've worked at five different institutions but never more than three at a time (online classes notwithstanding). It would be impossible to work at all five at the same time, but it has been important to keep these opportunities open in case my course load is lighter than our bills. Every semester, roughly a month into classes, I start getting emails from department chairs about scheduling preferences for the upcoming semester. While my classes for the immediate semester have been secured, I spend most of the semester worrying about the next one. I can request all Tuesday and Thursday classes for the first school that makes a schedule but pray the other schools have need for me on Mondays, Wednesdays, and Fridays. My wife and I chose our current residence based on the fact that it is within a convenient hour commute of a dozen different postsecondary schools where I can beg for work.

If scheduling around three different schools seems difficult, budgeting around them is even harder. A typical three-credit-hour class can pay anywhere from $1,400 to $2,700 before taxes, which is split into four or five monthly payments, and tutoring inevitably pays hourly and once a month. Budgeting means planning five or six months in advance to see how much one needs to save for those months without a paycheck. This stress was exacerbated in the fall of 2018 when I received a raise from one of my schools. I had planned on being paid in five installments of $750 after taxes. Due to the raise, the contract I had signed was tossed out by administration so I could sign a new contract that included the higher hourly rate. The problem was that the new contract wouldn't be processed in time to get paid for August, so now my five payments of $750 were replaced with four payments of $930. Administration lauded the pay raise for adjuncts while I put bills on credit cards because the $750 my initial contract stated was now postponed for a whole month. That pay raise equaled $12 a month.

It's also important to note that these are just the going rates in North Carolina. In early 2013, the *Chronicle of Higher Education* took over the Google document Joshua Boldt, an adjunct faculty member, created to allow adjuncts to search salaries and benefits for each state in the United States (Stratford 2012). In the introduction of their new resource, the *Chronicle*'s Audrey Williams June and Jonah Newman (2013) discuss the vast difference in adjunct pay based on the type of institution, degree held by the adjunct, cost of living, and the state. Their article follows one adjunct, Margaret Hanzimanolis, who adjuncted in Vermont "teaching six courses for about $24,000 a year, without health insurance" and then moved to California, where she taught "13 classes year-round and earned $88,000" while qualifying for health insurance after eighteen months (June and Newman 2013). "So why don't all of the adjuncts just move to places that pay better, or offer benefits?" some might wonder. Part of this answer is, of course, that if everyone moved to strike it rich in California, supply would exceed demand and result in joblessness. However, a much simpler answer is that interstate moves are quite costly and present an economic impossibility for adjuncts who are barely scraping by, especially with a family.

HERS: THE MENTAL LOAD

One of the biggest challenges of heading an NTT household is having a schedule that changes each semester. As NTTF, I do not have much of a say in what times and on what days I teach. My department head has been very accommodating and my schedule has been the same since January 2017. However, there is no guarantee it will remain the same. Because John teaches and tutors at different schools each semester, his schedule is completely unpredictable, often up until a month or even a couple of weeks before classes begin. While this precarity might be difficult for two adults cohabiting, we also have a young son who attends a child-development center every day while we work. Each semester, we have to figure out who will take him to the center and who will be responsible for picking him up. I teach until 5:15 p.m. most semesters, so John must often decline late-afternoon or evening courses so he is available to pick up our son by 5:30 p.m. While it would be nice for John to teach more classes and maximize income—and quite important, as saving up is essential when adjuncts are generally only paid four times a semester—in order to take on more classes, we would have to pay a babysitter. Given adjunct wages, paying someone $10 an hour to watch our son hardly seems worth it.

As two NTTF, another battle we face is who is responsible for which domestic and household tasks. As we both have to grade in our "downtime," loading and unloading the dishwasher; washing, drying, and putting away laundry; and planning and cooking meals are generally not split evenly. John and I both grew up with mothers who worked outside the home. In my home, my mother not only had her career but also managed the majority of the domestic duties. Sure, my father folded clothes or washed dishes sometimes (this was in the day before dishwashers, though my parents still don't have one), but generally his helpfulness was related to making pancakes on Saturdays or performing much-needed car repairs. This was largely due to the fact that he worked longer hours than my mother did and had a lengthy commute, not because he was unwilling or unable, so expecting him to do a larger share may not have made sense to them. This division of labor though meant I grew up watching a woman balance it all, and I normalized her behavior, eventually taking on just as much myself because that's just what women do. My mother used to tell me women had failed to gain equality, as "all they did was make more work for themselves" with the expectation that a patriarchal society would change to believe women belonged in the home and at work. Many recent articles on the mental load being carried primarily by women discuss the reality of my mother's perspective.

While I may be guilty of taking on traditional gender roles in my household, I do challenge the notion of the man as the breadwinner in a hetero, cisgender partnership, as my job provides us with a year-round income higher than John's and supplies my medical insurance, which keeps me healthy enough to continue being the breadwinner. I should note that John and our son have non-employer-sponsored coverage, as the family option offered through the UNC system is not affordable on a lecturer's salary. I am fortunate that John's masculinity is not threatened by the fact that I make a higher salary than he does. Although I am currently the main breadwinner, I do not see this as a position of power. If John was the breadwinner, I would be completely supportive of his new role. Fortunately, we view the main breadwinner as a position from which to support our family, not control the family dynamic.

HIS: GENDER ROLES AT HOME

Thankfully, I've never felt men should be the primary breadwinners in the family unit. There may be some subconscious part of me that has been influenced by the social construction of the nuclear family at play, but on a conscious level, I understand this issue does not negatively affect my masculinity. I've always based my ideas of masculinity on care and support. The self-constructed man is one who takes care of his family. One who is self-reliant and a problem solver. While I may not bring as much to my family financially, I bring other tangible benefits. I'm good at keeping a car running. I'm good at repairing things around the house. These skills are traditionally thought of as masculine, but my value of a man is defined by the support I provide, financial or not. The problem then arises that the "adjunct hustle" is so time consuming it leaves me less time to take care of things at home. Now I'm in a position in which I don't bring in more financially and I do less housework and child rearing. This hasn't led to me questioning my masculinity but to an existential dread that has me questioning my value as a person.

This semester, I have roughly nine hours per week of time at home without a toddler, which is the most productive time I have available. Doing housework or grading after I've picked him up from daycare is difficult. It's like sending in the cleanup crew before the hurricane has run its course. Sure, you can get things accomplished, but it's going to take twice as long and be four times as difficult. Certain tasks like dishes, laundry, and straightening up that must be done daily take most of the two hours I have on Mondays and Wednesdays. Fridays provide me with a little more time, and they're devoted to doing the floors so that job doesn't fall on Jess every week. Since it is my shortest day in terms of course load, Friday is also the day I devote to errands and tasks like car maintenance (which, with a thirteen-year-old car, is fairly frequent). The huge time commitment involved with commuting and working multiple teaching positions leaves little time for much else. Since I utilize these nine hours for home and car maintenance, as well as errands, it can be easy to fall behind on grading and lesson planning. In short, the adjunct hustle can do a disservice to students.

So, where does this leave me? With crippling anxiety and depression! Okay, maybe not crippling, but the negative effects of this vocational choice have made their presence known. Every semester is filled with worries about whether next semester will have enough work, and if there is work, will it pay enough to make the bills? A hopelessness creeps in when one realizes the extra mile many of us go has no bearing on advancement. Publishing in the field, attending faculty meetings, or even wearing a tie to work start to seem like feeble attempts at a lost cause. I've begun to realize I could make more as a line cook (my summer job) and I wouldn't have to bring home my work. I could have hobbies again, and read things I'm passionate about, and help more around the house. Many adjuncts hold on because of hope and passion, but after six years, I can safely say that once that hope is gone, the passion is soon to follow.

THE TAKEAWAY(S)

In juggling the NTT lifestyle for a few years now, we've learned that faculty and administrative support is incredibly helpful, not just through increased funding (though that's certainly welcome!) but also through simply understanding what it's like for NTT folks in our departments and on our campuses. Simply recognizing the inequalities that exist between TT and NTTF at different institutions is the first step in working toward a solution. Administration should also be aware that by not supporting NTTF, you're showing your students how much you care about them. Giving an adjunct an office within which to work and meet with students allows that faculty member to be more productive and is a visible way to tell the instructor's students that their instructor is valued. Having to meet with students in a hallway or the library doesn't send the same message. It's also our hope that this chapter, and indeed collection, will serve as a reminder to other NTTF that you're not alone in the struggle, and perhaps the sense of solidarity will spark real change.

NOTES

1. We use the term *contingent* in a manner similar to Schell (2017) and Seth Kahn, William Lalicker, and Amy Lynch-Biniek (2017), who refer to contingency as those faculty teaching without the benefits of a long-term contract. Our study sought to better understand those with semester-to-semester appointments as well as those who might have year-to-year appointments.
2. The revising process of *Contingency, Exploitation, and Solidarity* ran concurrent to our initial 2016 study but was available to us during the data-interpretation and article-drafting phase.

REFERENCES

Fulwiler, Megan, and Jennifer Marlow. 2014. *Con Jobs: Stories of Adjunct and Contingent Labor*. Logan: Utah State University Press and Computers and Composition Digital Press. http://ccdigitalpress.org/conjob.

Jenkins, Rob. 2015. "Is Adjuncting the 'Kiss of Death'?" *Chronicle Vitae*, July 1. https://beta.chroniclevitae.com/news/1051-is-adjuncting-the-kiss-of-death.

June, Audrey Williams, and Jonah Newman. 2013. "Adjunct Project Reveals Wide Range in Pay." *Chronicle of Higher Education*, January 4. https://www.chronicle.com/article/Adjunct-Project-Shows-Wide/136439.

Harris, Adam. 2019. "The Death of an Adjunct." *Atlantic*, April 8. https://www.theatlantic.com/education/archive/2019/04/adjunct-professors-higher-education-thea-hunter/586168/.

Patton, Stacey. 2012. "The Ph.D. Now Comes with Food Stamps." *Chronicle of Higher Education*. May 6. https://www.chronicle.com/article/the-ph-d-now-comes-with-food-stamps/.

Stratford, Michael. 2012. "A Simple Spreadsheet Strikes a Nerve among Adjuncts." *Chronicle of Higher Education, February 19*. https://www.chronicle.com/article/Accidental-Activist-Collects/130854.

Studenc, Bill. 2018. "It's Official: WCU Experiences Third Consecutive Year of Record Enrollment; Student GPA Soars." Western Carolina University, August 31. https://www.wcu.edu/stories/posts/News/2018/08/its-official-wcu-experiences-third-consecutive-year-of-record-enrollment-freshman-gpa-soars/index.aspx.

Weissmann, Jordan. 2015. "Update: The Job Market for Academics Is Still Terrifying." *Slate*, March 23. https://slate.com/business/2015/03/academic-job-market-still-terrifying.

9
THE SOUND OF SILENCE
Negotiating Non-Tenure-Track Invisibility within the Institution

Angie McKinnon Carter, Christopher Lee, and Linda Shelton

"What should lecturers be voting on?" The question—posed by a tenured professor—punctuated the awkward tension in the room, discernible to even the most aloof faculty member occasionally glancing up from a phone or laptop. This unanticipated question had stalled a previous monthly faculty meeting. Since lecturers (full-time, non-tenure-track instructors) had more than doubled within a year, the question was unavoidable. Policy related to lecturer voting was invoked, but the details remained forgotten and ambiguous. Clearly, our department was unprepared to account for lecturers' roles in department decision-making. Since the increased number of lecturers comprised a significant and potentially powerful voting block, unprecedented in the department, the discussion sparked by the question seemed particularly sticky. An otherwise invisible issue was becoming visible.

A faculty meeting a few months previous serves as a noteworthy juxtaposition. After our dean announced for the first time that lecturers were to exclusively teach and avoid participation in scholarship and service, our colleagues' response was encouraging and validating. Our department collectively pushed against the administrative edict to deny lecturers, who most likely wouldn't remain in their current position forever, the opportunity for professional development. Restrictions on professional development, among restrictions on communication, pay, and contact with students (Gallant 2018; Kezar 2013; Kezar and Sam 2014), contribute to contingent faculty feeling like laborers rather than professionals (Kezar and Sam 2014), to their feeling voiceless and invisible.

Notably, our tenured colleagues overwhelmingly rallied to support our engagement in scholarship and service. They intuitively recognized Adrianna Kezar and Cecile Sam's point that participating in professional development is a "fundamental component" of being a

DOI: 10.7330/9781646420759.c009

professional (2014, 451). It was as if tenured faculty wanted to represent the silent majority of lecturers. Beyond that, their support signaled they saw us as colleagues. The department chair also clearly supported us, vocally criticizing the new policy, which remains nebulous even today. This support set us apart from NTTF elsewhere who, Kezar and Sam report (and Jessica Cory and John McHone's chapter in this volume illustrates), are not viewed as professionals or colleagues by tenure-track coworkers.

In this sense, we recognize we hold an in-between position in the field, what John Levin and Genevieve Shaker call "hybrid and dualistic identities" (2011, 1462). We are neither contingent, defined by Tricia Gallant (2018) as part-time, non-benefits-eligible faculty, nor are we tenure-track faculty. As Kezar (2013) and Eileen Schell (2016) have noted, part-time contingent faculty have little voice in their working conditions. This is definitely true across many institutions, including ours—adjuncts work without any way to change their working conditions. Our position, however, is different. While we contribute in faculty meetings, we cannot serve on official venues of shared governance such as the faculty senate. In this sense, we occupy an in-between position: neither as fully disenfranchised as our part-time associates nor as fully empowered as our tenure-track colleagues. That in-between status often prevents us from speaking because we don't know whether we are allowed to speak.

Further, the threat of an additional course for lecturers (from four to five), also a point of interest in our meeting, was firmly rejected by most faculty. The chair actively defended us, even forming a committee to present evidence to upper administration against increasing our workload. Certainly, the drive for lecturers to teach more classes for the same pay is not unique to Utah Valley University (UVU). In fact, debates over class-size increases, the push for composition lecturers to teach five classes instead of four, and a teaching load increasingly born by adjuncts evidence the neoliberal push in higher education to restrict resources (Scott and Welch 2016). Yet our department seems sufficiently in tune with the national context to resist this agenda.

Our administrators misunderstood what good teaching requires. Tony Scott and Nancy Welch have noted, "As the neoliberal reordering of higher education deepens and widens, composition still lacks a developed understanding of how labor conditions shape pedagogy, scholarship, and the production of literacy and students' writing" (2016, 6). In fact, Kezar's (2013) case study of three four-year Master's Carnegie schools notes how several departmental policies can negatively impact teacher performance and student learning. Among these policies and practices are limiting NTTF's professional development and input into their curriculum or book options, scheduling courses within weeks of classes beginning, and their working at multiple institutions. Gallant (2018), picking up Scott and Welch's (2016) argument, contends that no one seems to connect teachers' working conditions to some at-risk community college students' lower success.

In fact, although our part-time colleagues experience these policies, as FT NTTF, we do not. In this sense, our department's recognition that full-time instructors promote student success pushes against cost-cutting trends that adjunctify faculty, particularly in composition, yet the dean's pronouncement about lecturer workload worried us. Could a more restrictive environment eliminate these gains? For instance, while we currently control our own curriculum, there could eventually be a push for tenure-track faculty to control our pedagogy.

Although tenure-track faculty supported us, their support varies with the context. What factors influence these decisions? Did the threat of external intervention facilitate cohesive support for us lecturers? If faculty support lecturers' research interests, despite current administrative caution, how far does this support extend when lecturers request limited funding? Which committees are appropriate for lecturers to serve on, and who decides?

It's within these seemingly contradictory circumstances that we find ourselves, circumstances that prompt complicated questions and produce few answers. In this chapter, we—three full-time lecturers with renewable contracts—describe our individual and shared experiences navigating the ambiguous waters of NTTF. We find Cheryl Glenn's book *Unspoken: A Rhetoric of Silence* a useful frame for interrogating our own negotiations between silence and speech. As Glenn notes, "Whether to speak or remain silent (who gets to speak; who should remain silent) always depends on the rhetorical situation" (2004, 5). Moreover, Glenn argues that language and silence are symbiotic, having "complementary rhetorical significance" (7). In our case, as perhaps in other NTTF experience, the rhetorical situation is constantly shifting. As we discuss in this chapter, we struggle to know when we should speak or remain silent. Our silence helps us remain invisible and do our work without undue constraints, yet maintaining our favorable work conditions sometimes requires us to speak. To that end, we pose the questions above and offer our experiences in hopes that readers may reflect on their own navigations between silence and speech and what that negotiation means.

LINDA

I thought only my department chair treated adjuncts as less than professionals, such as requiring us, without pay, to sit at a table, imitating office hours, so we would be more available for students. Equally insulting was when she forbade adjuncts to use any handouts unless she approved them first. Gradually, I realized that lack of respect for adjuncts was a problem across our campus and many others. I saw the magnitude of a nationwide college labor crisis with more low-paid, part-time instructors than tenured faculty (Hoeller 2014; Jacobsohn 2001).

A major part of this labor crisis was from rising enrollments and decreasing funds. Utah was challenged by both. Our community college was not just growing: it was exploding. We first became a four-year college, and then, in 2008, a university. During my career at UVU, enrollment has more than quadrupled. The number of adjuncts at UVU has been as high as 60 percent. While accreditors frown at that ratio, they don't view full-time NTTF as negatively (AAUP 2019).

So, UVU began hiring full-time, non-tenure-track lecturers in 2000, and I was one of the first hired. Maybe the role of a lecturer focusing on teaching helps our students. As an open-enrollment college, UVU admits students with diverse levels of preparation. Though now a university, we still try to fill a community college mission. Administrators call this a "dual-mission model"—"the practicality and accessibility of a community college, combined with the rigor and seriousness of a four-year teaching institution" (Shumway 2018). This mission seems clear to administrator, who stress that UVU is a teaching university. The mission is less clear to recently hired tenure-track faculty working toward tenure, which still requires research. In addition, faculty must help many underprepared students. Perhaps non-tenure-track instructors who don't feel the pressure to conduct research are better positioned to assist less prepared students. It's not fair to make hasty generalizations, especially with scant anecdotal evidence, but this question about focusing on teaching is part of the conundrum surrounding lecturers. Kezar emphasizes, "The NTTF are often experienced teachers as it is their focus, and their knowledge is also overlooked—particularly those long-time NTTF who have been on campus longer than many tenure track faculty" (2013, 584).

Even after being a lecturer for twenty years and watching UVU's growth, I still feel conflicted about how I fit into the department and the university. I'm grateful for a full-time contract, benefits, and an office. My conflict is rooted in a dilemma: Do I want my job description defined in more detail or not? Will a more carefully defined role actually restrict my opportunities? Even after twenty years, I still don't have the answers to these questions.

When I was the only lecturer in our department, the tenure-track group greeted me with different reactions. Some were welcoming and warm; others seemed resentful and annoyed. I was bewildered until a kind colleague explained that some saw me as a threat to the strength and protection of tenure. If the college continued to create a two-tiered system, would non-tenure-track lecturers eventually outnumber tenure-track faculty? I vividly remember the department voting on whether lecturers should be able to vote in department meetings. I felt conspicuous sitting there, and I wondered whether I was the only one who noticed the irony that a group of college professors who taught students about marginalized voices, social justice, and equity in the workplace were deciding whether I would have a voice in making departmental decisions. The vote was close, but lecturers retained voting privileges. Although some tenured faculty periodically challenge it, that right to vote in department meetings has continued for twenty years. I was glad to find I was not alone in my discomfort. Elizabeth Hoffman and John Hess report that "a full-time tenure-track faculty leader shouted in a union meeting, 'Throw the lecturers out of the union!'" The authors note the axiom that no contingent faculty member is "ever more than fifteen seconds away from total [professional] humiliation" (2014, 9).

Having a vote in the department and across campus is key to improving NTTF working conditions. After extensive interviews on thirty campuses, Kezar and Sam concluded that voting rights support and validate NTTF voices, prove they are effective faculty members, encourage flow of information, and "empower . . . them as an important part of the decision-making process who cannot be dismissed" (2014, 444).

Along with having a voice, questions of promotion and pay raises have added to the mystery of being a lecturer. UVU uses the term *senior lecturer*. After teaching for seven years, I was able to apply for that rank, one of the first to go through this process. I followed the model of those applying for tenure. I put together huge binders of documentation showing strong supervisor evaluations, high scores on student evaluations, conference presentations, publications, and extensive service. I was promoted to senior lecturer, which included no pay raise. I remember the next faculty meeting, where the chair announced my rank advancement, and someone asked if it meant a pay raise. The chair said "No," and someone said, "Well, can we at least give her a brownie?" Several words came to my mind: condescending, patronizing, demeaning, and, yet again, irony.

Christopher Morphew, Kelly Ward, and Lisa Wolf-Wendel (2017) confirm the need for respect and courtesy. They suggest that because tenure-track faculty and NTTF do not interact enough, they can't share information or bond as a faculty. Departments could use orientation and professional-development time to help all faculty participate in activities that build and inform. They also report that NTTF have less access to institutional resources "ranging from office space and computer access to involvement in shared governance that might result in the faculty being less likely to be engaged with their colleagues or to participate in student learning experiences outside the classroom" (77). So the need for integration among different types of faculty is about more than just being polite; it's about getting what we need to be excellent teachers.

I know my research has improved my teaching and helped me stay current. Working on committees helps me keep a voice in decisions that affect my students and me. However, the question of whether lecturers should even be allowed to serve on committees came up recently, proving Sean Gehrke and Kezar's (2015) point that the work lecturers can do is often restricted. New administrators were advised that legal action could be taken if lecturers ended up doing the same work as tenure-track folks. The fear of litigation is a powerful force. So, in fall 2017, the dean told us no more committee work. We should be grateful because we weren't getting paid for it anyway, right? But then we have no say in policies that affect us. Interestingly, we haven't heard a whisper about that proposed ban since. We follow the primary rule for lecturers: fly under the radar.

Perhaps those faculty members who were resentful and annoyed when I was hired were right after all. We now have forty-eight full-time faculty in our English Department, and fifteen of us are lecturers. I don't have the answers to these difficult questions surrounding the two-tiered system in higher education. I have only tried to present some questions from my perspective. I do know we can't act like dogs fighting under the table for scraps dropped off the state legislature's table. Certainly, educated people, even if they are on different pay levels, can treat each other as valued and appreciated colleagues while we all find solutions.

ANGIE

I entered the faculty meeting following my promotion to senior lecturer feeling neither valued nor appreciated. Determined to remain uncharacteristically silent, I half-listened as a tenured colleague explained updates to the department's rank, tenure, and promotion guidelines as I perused the changes. I landed at the lecturer section just as he did.

Listening to this discussion was bound to be painful, given Chris's and my different outcomes to seeking our promotions to senior lecturer. About three weeks earlier, over a year after submitting our applications, we had learned Chris's promotion had been denied because he had not been a lecturer for at least seven years, a policy we learned about in Chris's rejection letter. One might think I would find this faculty-meeting discussion less painful because my application had been approved. One would be wrong. We had been so certain we would be promoted together that his rejection strained our relationship and, I felt, my relationship with other colleagues. One tenure-track colleague called my promotion "lucky." Apparently, my promotion was viewed negatively because Chris had not also received one. Certainly, Chris's promotion was denied on a technicality. I never quite understood the logic of assuming my promotion was an unearned technicality. The implication stung.

My colleague's summary of the revised guidelines made the situation even more painful. The guidelines not only provided less clarity for lecturers, they perpetuated the erroneous six-year requirement for attaining senior-lecturer status. Although I would have preferred to remain silent, I knew I couldn't let what had happened to Chris happen again. "____, did you know that UVU policy requires lecturers to be employed at that level for seven years before they are eligible to become senior lecturers?" Predictably, my comment was marked (Glenn 2004). He didn't know those policies, which I forwarded to him at his request.

Yet I couldn't help feeling . . . what? Insignificant? Erased? Five years earlier, a balanced committee of lecturers and tenure-track faculty, including Linda and me, had crafted the lecturer policy now being subsumed into RTP guidelines intended mainly for tenure-track faculty. Watching it happen felt symbolic of our life in the department—buried on page 5, a footnote to tenure-track needs. That we lecturers might need clarity on how our promotion process differed remained unaddressed.

The tension surrounding the RTP document amplified my angst during my recently completed promotion process. Compiling my lecturer binder had been a frustrating ordeal. At three inches thick, and despite three-quarters being devoted to teaching rather than equally dividing the materials among scholarship, service, and teaching, my binder represented a failed attempt to negotiate the tightrope of not working above my paygrade while valuing our department's culture of excellence. Don't act like a tenure-track hire, but do aspire to a culture of excellence. Don't include too much scholarship lest upper administration think you have time on your hands, but demonstrate continued currency and relevance in the field. Don't spend too much time on the binder, but make it look thorough and professional. My frustration increased with the binder's size. I complained to one colleague that my binder looked like a tenure binder. Yet I had no guidance on how to navigate this thorny rhetorical situation. Lacking formal mentors (a way both Gehrke and Kezar [2015] and Kezar [2013] have noted departments can support NTTF) and relevant examples, we modeled our binders on a tenure-track colleague's binder for promotion to full professor. No wonder the process caused anxiety and frustration.

Chris and I were aware of several unspoken departmental tensions between lecturers and tenure-track faculty but not how our binders would create a focal point for them. Our binders were still being reviewed when our dean made the startling announcement regarding lecturer service. Our scholarship-and-service-filled binders were still MIA. Our worry shifted from attaining senior-lecturer status to fearing our binders could be construed as subversive.

But I had another concern. At the time, I was finishing my dissertation, intending to enter the job market the following year. When I informed my graduate school's job-placement coordinator about the dean's new rule, she insisted, "You have to publish. You have to do service." Lacking those CV lines would doom my tenure-track search. I felt trapped between my team-player, stay-invisible instincts and my desire to be a serious candidate for future tenure-track positions. My agency over my working conditions was shrinking, a condition Schell (2016) notes as common among contingent faculty, yet trying to improve my situation in this environment felt risky.

The silence surrounding our binders dragged on for months. After six months of waiting (midsemester of fall 2017), we started asking. Our chair was baffled by the delay. Then around December we learned that the vice president of Academic Affairs (VPAA) had them. What? Neither Chris nor I had considered upper administration as a potential audience. Only the dean had reviewed our three-year binders. What would the VPAA think of our scholarship and service, especially given the recent edict that lecturers should do neither?

Three more months passed. Inquiring outside the department was out of the question, but no one in the department had news either. I asked the RTP chair for more details about the timeline. "I finished your binders and sent them to the chair. My part is finished." But he had told Chris that the RTP committee had recommended him for promotion. His not offering me the same assurance troubled me. What if Chris were promoted but I wasn't? What would that mean for my standing in the department? Would I be able to renew my three-year appointment? And if there was a problem, what was the nature of it: a problem with my teaching or too much emphasis on scholarship and service? The waiting and lack of answers was agonizing.

Finally, in January 2018, Chris and I learned that the dean had recommended we both be promoted. Clearing the dean's recommendation seemed to be the biggest hurdle. When I read the letter from the VPAA's office in late March 2018, over a year after submitting our binders, informing me that my promotion had been approved, I reasonably thought Chris's letter contained similar news.

I never imagined that my being promoted instead of, rather than with, Chris would undermine my standing in the department. While Chris faced reapplying for the promotion, I endured some tenure-track colleagues' implied criticism that my promotion was unearned. My rank's legitimacy seemed to hinge on Chris's attaining senior lecturer at the same time.

Yet this narrative obscures the fact that I love my job. I love teaching composition and seeing students realize they can write. And my department's policies for FT NTTF are among the best in composition: we have offices, good salaries with benefits, and multiyear contracts (Gehrke and Kezar 2015); we determine our own curriculum and textbooks; and we receive travel funding to attend conferences and workshops (Kezar 2013). I thought this job security was what I loved. Yet this experience made me realize collegiality is as important as those other benefits. Liz Gumm's narrative in chapter 10 of this collection mirrors my feelings of isolation during this time: "Community is also a necessity, not a luxury, for contingent faculty" (chapter 10). In this sense, the sound of silence resonates loudly—without community, we lose our voices because we lack places to share what we learn, what we experience, and what confuses us.

I realize now that complaining about my binder's size was a call for help: How do I justify a promotion without implying I deserve tenure? That day, my colleague saw me as a threat, evidence of the dean's concern: another uppity lecturer grabbing an unearned tenure-track position. Had I kept my concerns unvoiced, would my rank advancement be viewed as legitimate now? Ironically, my promotion makes my job standing feel more tenuous rather than less.

CHRIS

A three-ring binder rests on my desk, waiting—for the second time—to be sent up the channels of the academic hierarchy, leaving me with what I can only describe as contradicting feelings of accomplishment and anxiety. Seven years of work comprise the contents of this binder, a record of my time serving my university as an NTT renewable lecturer. In an institutional environment that discourages lecturers from engaging in university service and scholarship, my portfolio serves as a reminder, a symbol, of the complex waters NTTF like myself must navigate when renewal or promotion forces an emergence from the shadows of invisibility.

I was in good company; Angie and I were on the same track and shared these concerns. We'd grown accustomed to our liminal position as lecturers. We both have engaged in scholarship and service, which our department generally supports, and we both have received the same rather indefinite admonition from upper administration to refrain from participation in activities perceived as only relevant to tenure-track faculty. We understood our portfolios would only go as high up as the dean, which mitigated the fear of any administrative retaliation for transcending our primary roles as instructors. Still, since we were among the first in our department to apply for promotion to senior lecturer, we recognized the precedent we might set for future lecturers seeking promotion, and we came to recognize the difference between policy and practice, the latter being much more interpretive. After talking with an RTP committee member, we concluded that setting a high bar for department lecturers would be a positive reflection on the commitment to employing and retaining excellent faculty and that the dean would agree.

Our department policy stipulated that portfolios be submitted in March. As months passed, we received no information regarding our status. Three years previous, I had submitted an application for renewal, which also required a teaching portfolio. That time, I received confirmation of renewal in June, directly from the RTP committee. Since this was my only frame of reference regarding an expected timeline, I followed up with our department chair midsummer, who indicated my application for promotion to senior lecturer had been approved by himself and the RTP committee; based on that approval, he had forwarded the recommendation for promotion to the dean. I received no official word until January of the following year, when the dean forwarded me his recommendation to the Office of the Vice President that I be promoted. The excitement of the dean's endorsement was dampened by my realization that my portfolio was being sent to the vice president and induced distress because I had submitted what resembled a tenure binder. Would I confirm upper administration's suspicions that lecturer entitlement would culminate in a lawsuit for tenure benefits? I asked the RTP committee chair if he knew our binders made it all the way to the VP's office. As I thought, he was unaware our files would go beyond the dean's office, indicating that he couldn't think of a precedent and that this procedure was certainly not stated in department lecturer promotion policy. The confusion of the situation was compounded when the chair also indicated that the current situation didn't align with his knowledge but explained the extended time delay. Angie and I were assured that the recommendations from the RTP, the department chair, and the dean would positively influence the VP's decision.

In March, a full year after my submission, I learned my application for promotion to senior lecturer had been denied. Although I had six years' experience as a lecturer, university policy stipulated a minimum requirement of seven. My anxiety over being completely ignorant of this policy was only slightly alleviated by the knowledge that university policy directly conflicted with department policy and that the RTP committee, the department chair, and the dean were also unaware of the seven-year requirement. Bureaucratic miscommunication isn't unique to NTTF, but it's hard not to view this disconnect as a reflection of the ambiguous nature of the full-time-lecturer position at our institution.

Clearer mentoring practices, then, are crucial regarding renewal and promotion. In a study examining how environmental supports influence NTTF well-being, Matthew Seipel and Lisa Larson discuss communicative barriers and propose that "deans and upper-level administrators need to be reminded that in addition to the policies they implement, the manner in which they are implemented and communicated down the institutional hierarchy" (2018, 167) impact NTTF.

The disconnects among department, college, and administration in my experience reflect the struggles faced by NTTF at other institutions. Gehrke and Kezar argue that among the many factors influencing NTTF working conditions and supportive policies (mentoring, promotion, professional development), deans' values play a crucial role, particularly as they bridge the gap between NTTF and upper administration. In citing factors that shape their decisions regarding NTTF policies, many deans identify attitudes of upper administration. Specifically, "lack of priority from senior leadership and an institutional belief that certain supports are not important are reasons also given frequently for not providing support for NTTF" (2015, 950). I imagine my situation is indicative of this kind of low prioritization. Do administrators, deans, and faculty members view us as professionals or simply as laborers who help alleviate enrollment pressures? As one dean in Gehrke and Kezar's study puts it, "NTTF are hired to teach here not to develop their scholarship" (951).

As I place the final piece into my portfolio for its second submission, I must accept that the shifting landscape within my institution, which seems to represent similar changes occurring nationwide, poses complicated questions that lack clear and definitive answers. Does my portfolio represent an accurate and compelling reflection of teaching excellence, or does it subversively challenge administrative restrictions on activities deemed outside the direct purview of teaching? In a sense, I could say I get a "do over." I now know my portfolio will make its way to the Office of the Vice President and ultimately be reviewed by the Board of Regents. I could perform an appendectomy of sorts on my binder, leaving in student and peer evaluations, indications of professional development, and other generally recognized measures of teaching. But I choose to walk the rhetorical tightrope, explicitly connecting all scholarly and service activities to teaching.

Becoming more visible as a lecturer has had some positive outcomes. Our department is becoming more deliberate in making sure our guidelines align with university policy, although codification seems to be contingent on vigilant NTTF. Lecturers in line for renewal and promotion should have clearer expectations and be informed of the pros and cons of including additional scholarship and service content in their portfolios. Still, uncertainty remains. It's been over a year since upper administration announced the lecturer service and scholarship prohibition. I haven't been denied opportunities within the department and was even solicited by the associate dean to serve on a college-wide teaching committee. In these cases, I wonder if it's better to ask if I'm violating university policy before committing or simply go along with it and worry about potential fallout later. Should I feel guilty about receiving department funds for conference travel and registration? Do I have to keep this funding from other lecturers—friends and colleagues—in order to ensure future funding for myself, or should I be helping them with strategies to secure funding for their projects? Ultimately, I have to think that at least being aware of the complicated feelings and questions that seem to plague NTTF like myself is a step in the right direction, even if the answers, at the moment, remain nebulous.

LESSONS LEARNED

As we conclude our narratives, we feel it is necessary to make the implicit explicit. Although writing this narrative has been therapeutic and insightful, publishing it is politically risky. As Glenn notes, "Those who feel silenced fear that if they tell, if they speak, if they so much as discuss a bad situation, they will be harmed in some way—if not immediately, then eventually" (2004, 42). Before writing this chapter, the three of us discussed potential implications. On the one hand, improving ourselves professionally is impeded by institutional tensions between honoring our professional expertise and keeping some crucial distinctions between tenured and non-tenure-track faculty. On the other hand, having renewable lecture lines provides us more money, benefits, and autonomy in teaching (see Gehrke and Kezar 2015). As Kezar (2013) notes, few departments within our institution and other institutions have created such positions for NTTF. We felt as if we risked these benefits by speaking out. Ultimately, we decided that articulating our experiences, making invisible tensions visible, and giving ourselves permission to speak was more important to our profession's long-term health than remaining silent.

Yet while writing our narratives, we learned our journey had implications beyond NTTF's experiences. Chris's and Angie's rank-promotion narratives occurred simultaneously with discussions to make the RTP guidelines for tenure-track faculty more explicit, to reduce the uncertainty surrounding that process. Viewed in this light, our struggles may be explained, in part, as the growing pains of a thriving institution. In fact, our positions, and the benefits that occur with them, exist because of this growth, which is uncharacteristic by most comparisons.

Nevertheless, our relatively powerless position impedes our ability to navigate the tensions that arise with that growth. Invisibility hurt us—personally and professionally. We argue that it hurt, and continues to hurt, the institution in multiple ways. Mainly, it made us question each other, to view each other as potential adversaries instead of allies, undermining cooperation and collaboration, creating a more competitive environment that only feeds the increasing corporatization of US higher education (Scott and Welch 2016). Those tendencies are real but are often hard to detect. Now that we are beginning to recognize them, we can address them. Thus, while speaking out and making ourselves visible is risky, we seem to have reached a point at which silence and its inherent invisibility have become riskier, particularly as NTTF ranks within and outside the institution grow (see Kezar and Sam 2014).

Our experiences navigating the blurry line between adjuncts and tenure-track faculty pose complicated questions that, we admit, have no definitive answers. However, we offer our narratives and the questions they pose in hopes that they may serve as useful comparison points for other NTTF and help facilitate a broader conversation.

REFERENCES

AAUP: American Association of University Professors n.d. "Looking the Other Way? Accreditation Standards and Part-time Faculty." July 1, 2018. https://www.aaup.org/report/looking-other-way-accreditation-standards-and-part-time-faculty.

Gallant, Tricia Bertram. 2018. "Part-Time Integrity? Contingent Faculty and Academic Integrity." *New Directions for Community Colleges* 2018 (183): 45–54.

Gehrke, Sean J., and Adrianna Kezar. 2015. "Supporting Non-Tenure-Track Faculty at 4-year Colleges and Universities: A National Study of Deans' Values and Decisions." *Educational Policy* 29 (6): 926–60.

Glenn, Cheryl. 2004. *Unspoken: A Rhetoric of Silence.* Carbondale: Southern Illinois University Press.

Hoffman, Elizabeth, and John Hess. 2014. "Organizing for Equality within the Two-Tier System: The Experience of the California Faculty Association." In *Equality for Contingent Faculty: Overcoming the Two-Tier System*, edited by Keith Hoeller, 9–27. Nashville, TN: Vanderbilt University Press.

Jacobsohn, Walter. 2001. "The Real Scandal in Higher Education." In *Moving a Mountain: Transforming the Role of Contingent Faculty in Composition Studies and Higher Education*, edited by Eileen E. Schell and Patricia L. Stock. Urbana, IL: NCTE.

Kezar, Adrianna. 2013. "Examining Non-Tenure Track Faculty Perceptions of How Departmental Policies and Practices Shape Their Performance and Ability to Create Student Learning at Four-Year Institutions." *Research in Higher Education* 54 (5): 571–98.

Kezar, Adrianna, and Cecile Sam. 2014. "Governance as a Catalyst for Policy Change: Creating a Contingent Faculty Friendly Academy." *Educational Policy* 28 (3): 425–62.

Levin, John S., and Genevieve G. Shaker. 2011. "The Hybrid and Dualistic Identity of Full-Time Non-Tenure-Track Faculty." *American Behavioral Scientist* 55 (11): 1461–84.

Morphew, Christopher, Kelly Ward, and Lisa Wolf-Wendel. 2017. "Contingent Faculty Composition and Utilization: Perspectives from Independent Colleges and Universities." *New Directions for Institutional Research* 2017 (176): 67–81.

Schell, Eileen. 2016. "Austerity, Contingency, and Administrative Bloat: Writing Programs and Universities in an Age of Feast and Famine." In *Composition in the Age of Austerity*, edited by Nancy Welch and Tony Scott, 177–90. Logan: Utah State University Press.

Scott, Tony, and Nancy Welch. 2016. Introduction to *Composition in the Age of Austerity*, edited by Nancy Welch and Tony Scott, 3–15. Logan: Utah State University Press.

Seipel, Matthew T., and Lisa M. Larson. 2018. "Supporting Non-Tenure-Track Faculty Well-Being." *Journal of Career Assessment* 26 (1): 154–71.

Shumway, Layton. 2018. "The Dual Mission Model." *UVU Magazine* 10 (1): 48–51. https://www.uvu.edu/magazine/spring2018/spring2018_dualmission.html.

10
DISUNITY IN A WRITING COMMUNITY
A Post-PhD Memoir of Professional Transitions

Liz Gumm

I'd just finished my first year as a full-time writing instructor at Inland Empire University, and I was in a summer limbo. The summer course I taught at a nearby community college was complete, but my new position at another southern California university didn't begin for another six weeks. I felt a little like a teenager packed and ready for college, still living in my parents' house but everyone continuing on with everyday life around me. Without a schedule, I was hopeless to write anything for this very project you are reading.

I didn't just work one year full time at Inland Empire University; I had recently graduated from there, too, with a PhD in English. Effectively, I'd worked for this university for the last six years, teaching the same four composition classes. When I became a lecturer, my job didn't really change except to expand my set of students each term. I still go to the same coffee shop, trying to get some work done.

As a writing teacher, I do believe part of my job is to maintain my own writing practice, whether or not I am published. But a writing practice is easier to nurture as a graduate student in English than as a full-time lecturer in the university writing program. Normally, I met up with academic friends and we at together a few times a week and wrote. But, alas, within the year of my graduation, all my writing partners have moved away for postdocs or full-time positions in other cities. Anyone left—like me, working for our former graduate institution—expresses variations of apathy regarding writing. After all, neither publication nor professional development is a requirement of non-tenure-track work, at least at IEU. I thought in continuing on at my graduate institution, I'd have easy and established access to some of the structure and community that made my graduate work productive. Indeed, my experience working as a full-time adjunct instructor at Kansas State, where I earned my

DOI: 10.7330/9781646420759.c010

masters in English, provided precisely such support as I worked on my PhD applications. But enduring community has become another thing to add to the list of how the PhD differs from the MA.

Intellectually lonely, I seek out the public privacy of the local coffee shop to write.

As I park my car, I look up and notice someone familiar. A baby-faced, white-haired man, whose signs of age and youth make his age impossible to tell, walks intently past my car and into the coffee shop. Beau Thomas is another lecturer at IEU, and for the last year, my office has been just two doors down from his. Before that, when I was a graduate student, my office was just around the corner from his. And during my graduate-teacher training, I actually observed him teach; we've sat in grade-norming sessions together; we've attended the same program functions; we've exchanged greeting in the empty morning hallways; he also graduated from IEU. In many ways, I know this man and have known him for almost a decade. I know he knows me.

I walk into the coffee shop and prepare to say "Hi." But, before I can say anything, he briefly glances at me and quickly drops his eyes to the floor. Okay, I think, maybe he didn't register that he knows me yet. I walk past him, take up a table with my stuff, and set my intentions on smiling at him when he turns around. But his avoidance of eye contact is almost too deliberate as he turns away from me and briskly makes his way to a table far behind me. I give up and stop trying to make a connection.

I believe there is a professional identity crisis (Chernoff 2018) unique to contingent faculty whose careers begin at the institution from which they graduated. Far more than merely a lack of necessary mentorship Angie Carter, Christopher Lee, and Linda Shelton highlight in the chapter 9 of this collection, Beau's refusal to acknowledge me is a symptom of larger emotional-health issues among NTTF in composition. Professional stasis, along with depression and disconnection within academia, is often attributed to the corporatization of the university and its subsequent adjunctification of faculty ("How to Fix" 2018; Youn 2005), but I felt there was more going on in Beau's and my mutual agreement to pretend unawareness of each other. A community of alumni might be assumed to combat workplace morale issues among NTTF, but I believe staying at my graduate institution made my crisis of professionalism worse. Unlike problems of compensation and workload, problems of community have few tangible material effects, much less ones that can be quantified. In parsing my sudden lack of community in a place I had assumed to be a foundational professional network, I came to realize that my difficulty in transitioning into my professional career was significant to larger debates in our writing studies discipline. As Denise Comer states so eloquently in the chapter 11 of this collection, "Our local, personal experiences are always, inevitably, connected to larger landscapes."

A GENERATION GAP

Over a plate of fries and a couple of beers, my former graduate-teaching mentor and I sit outside in the hot California afternoon. Charles Westin is also an alum of the English PhD program and is now a senior lecturer in the university writing program. I often mistake him for being much younger than he is. Charles has been a consistent resource for me over the last few years, both in my final years of graduate teaching and during my year as a lecturer. He has been one of the few resources that survived my graduation and one of the only people to treat me as an equal contributor to the rigor of the writing program. I think he had an easier time embracing my professional identity shift from graduate student to faculty than I did. We've met up so I can interview him for this chapter—seeking insights into my awkward coffee-shop moment, among other feelings. Our conversation provided me not only with new awareness and context to my experiences but also a new appreciation for the emotional effects of the academic job market.

"So, what I think I've noticed is that there is a generational divide among the lecturers," I say, trying to tiptoe around a vague lecturer stereotype that governed my time as a graduate student. "Those who've worked for the program for a long time come across as disgruntled and sometimes even like they hate teaching. I know my perspective is limited, but all I hear from lecturers when I'm in orientation meetings or grade norming are complaints about students, and complaints that seem disconnected from the realities of our mostly first-generation student population," I explain. "I feel like those of us who were hired the last two years from among the recent graduates are really invested in the social importance of teaching composition, but that value seems incredibly unpopular among the older lecturers. I feel alienated by their pedagogical visions that seem so focused on student behavior." I take a pause before I come clean with the stereotype I've been talking around.

"You do know the stereotype among the graduate students is that the lecturers, most of them older, are ultraconservative, right? I'm not sure if that makes sense to you."

With unshakable good cheer, Charles takes my point. "Well, certainly we have some conservative instructors, but I wouldn't say they are representative of the lecturers in the program. But I get the disgruntled stereotype," he says. "You have to understand; when we were graduate students in the nineties, we were told that there would be an abundance of English-professor jobs waiting for us." He goes on to explain how professors didn't "gray out" as they were expected to, which left his cohort scrambling for jobs. IEU hired them on as contracted instructors for the writing program, which, despite its titular housing in the English Department, was limited in its opportunities to teach literature. Charles estimates that at least one third of the lecturers are former IEU English PhDs, spanning a decade or two.

"So, you see, lots of us didn't end up where we wanted or where we expected we would."

This is the first time I have heard about the Bowen Report. The literature on the Bowen Report details a generation of academics betrayed. The study anticipated a great demand for faculty positions, especially in the humanities, at the turn of the millennium. But such needs to hire more teachers with an expanding student population only seemed to generate a wide range of contingent positions (Conn 2010; Patel 2018; Youn 2005). Recently, *the Chronicle of Higher Education* published "How a Famous Academic Job-Market Study Got It All Wrong—and Why It Still Matters," arguing that the study, which many people knew of but had not actually read in full, effectively "changed institutional and personal behavior to such an extent that it overcorrected the problem it foretold" (Patel 2018). Throughout my research into this study, I felt I was encountering some hidden family secret. Suddenly, the inexplicable morale issue among composition instructors had something of a source. I could trace an origin to the professional Plan B (Bérubé 2013) for English PhDs.

DISCIPLINARY HIERARCHIES

I didn't go into earning an English degree with any more forethought than that I loved literature and I wanted to teach. I never really saw myself as an academic writer or someone who would write books for a living, much less scholarly ones. But in the process of getting a degree, I inevitably found myself amidst brilliant minds who were either accomplishing great things academically or who had visions to do so. Especially within the PhD program in English, I began to feel the pressure of priorities and values of a discipline that thrives on publication. Being a good writing teacher wasn't what (most of) my tenured English professors hoped for me in my academic career. I understood I needed to aim my professional goals "higher" than teaching composition.

Michael Bérubé's 2013 article "Humanities Unraveled" characterizes "Plan B" as the nonacademic career path many humanities PhDs take when the academic job market does not pan out, and "the rhetoric of 'alternative' careers leads students to internalize the values of tradition-minded faculty who regard nonacademic careers with disdain" (2013). But within English and literature disciplines, Plan B has more complicated layers. It is not simply that "the 'best' students will be professors" (Anthony Grafton and James Grossman quoted in Bérubé 2013), taking positions within the university, but that those who take their PhDs to community colleges or to non-tenured work—who become composition rather than literature teachers—have fallen short of the career path idealized by our disciplines. While such a values system was, of course, never explicit in my graduate classrooms, it was strongly implied. Graduate professionalization courses were centered around academic publication and the four-year university tenure-track job search; alt-ac workshops became more frequent, and nonacademic careers took on a romantic rogue character; even the department listserv that always announced recently hired graduate students never mentioned lectureship work. My own full-time lectureship at IEU passed unnoticed except with those who hired me, but my current position as a program administrator made it into the listserv. At this point, a career outside academia may be Plan B, but within English, non-tenured work is definitely Plan C.

Despite increased encouragement to explore careers outside the university, the fantasy of the tenure-track literature position still animates departments that, more often than not, train writing teachers. In her practical guide to academic job hunting, *The Professor Is In*, Karen Kelsky begins by painting the picture many imagine waits for them at the end of the PhD. At a professor's retirement party, she "ponder[s] the event through the eyes of graduate students in the crowd. It looks beautiful and soothing, a vision of a career and a life lived at a peaceful, gracious pace, filled with teaching and leisure, colleagues and family. [She] wonder[s] if they know that the life being feted here this evening is already a relic of the past" (2015, 3). While many humanities graduate students may serve as teaching assistants within their discipline, English graduate students serve a bifurcated profession. We take classes with assistant, associate, and full professors but make our living working in writing programs with lecturers who must reapply for their jobs, at best, every three years. How could we not internalize the value system that offers "literature experts" tenure and "teaching-writing experts" tenuous employment?

This hierarchy of literature over composition takes a particular toll on those of us who stay on at our graduate institutions. As graduate students, we may see a department's architectural spaces as neutral, but if we return as full-time non-tenured instructors, the spatial rhetoric contributes to a sense that we are not really disciplinary professionals. At my master's institution, the basement houses the offices of both non-tenured faculty and English graduate students. At IEU, the shared hallways make for awkward confrontations with faculty who were my mentors just six months earlier. My own lecturer office at IEU was directly across the hall from one of my advisors, and in the beginning of my year as a lecturer, I would stop by to chat with her. But I always felt the unspoken pressure to leave. At the time, such awkwardness felt personal, but I believe now that she didn't see any overlap in our respective work. In the pauses between meetings with my own students, I felt waves of homesickness as I overheard enthusiastic conversations about dissertations and research. I used to have these conversations with her—conversations that inspired me and reassured me about the good my work would do. But I had stayed in the same space, so the conversations didn't go anywhere either.

For Anna Reed, the experience with an advisor was even more uncomfortable. Anna graduated with me and also became a full-time lecturer at IEU. Her own advisor's office was down the hall.

"What are you doing here?" Anna's advisor asked in surprise upon seeing Anna in the fall after graduation.

"I work here," Anna said.

Anna describes to me the brief shade of disappointment on her advisor's face before it quickly turned into a cheerful smile. The advisor reassured Anna that she would find something better her next time on the market. Anna doesn't believe her advisor meant to be demeaning, but the professor's comment is revealing. The image of the successful path for the English PhD is full of good intentions. Anna reflects on how no one in her academic circle—advisors, current and former graduate students—seems to understand she wants to teach composition; she has no interest in becoming tenured research faculty. Even as Anna continues to publish in her area of study, she believes her most valuable work is in the composition classroom, not in the literature lecture hall. Anna says she regularly entertains people's surprise that her publications are not intended as a means out of a lectureship, especially given that the workload for most non-tenured faculty uses up the time and energy necessary to continue scholarly work. As a result, composition instruction and literary scholarship are assumed to be mutually exclusive. Our training as graduate students (i.e., writing literary scholarship) seems to have no outlet in non-tenured teaching, so to our mentors, we might be seen as abandoning our profession. As accidental expats, non-tenured faculty often develop into a cluster of disparate individuals rather than an organized community of professionals.

STARTING FROM SUSPICION

For graduate students at IEU, the first, and possibly only, interaction with full-time lecturers in the writing program occurs in the context of teacher training and being mentored through the first term of teaching by selected senior lecturers. Unfortunately, these lecturers, at least for me and my teacher training, were teachers whose perspectives of undergraduate students often did not reflect an investment in equity and at times bordered on contemptuous. My cohort and I struggled with the image of our writing program as one, despite good intentions, complicit in many of the systemic structures that often work against those students already disenfranchised. From the beginning, the weary disgruntled lecturers were positioned in stark opposition to the energetic bright-eyed and social justice-oriented English graduate students.

For the most part, I expected I would be employed full time at IEU. Early on in my graduate career, I accepted that the academic market was saturated, and since what I really loved was teaching, I set my sights on the practical position of teaching writing rather than literature. Despite first impressions and my uncertainties about the pedagogical visions of the lecturer pool, I believed in my ability to build bridges and make meaningful connections once I was a part of that group. I spent my final two years of graduate school integrating myself into the administration of the writing program. My positive relationships with program coordinators and teaching mentors signaled to me that my contributions were greatly appreciated and I would be a welcomed addition to the full-time faculty. But there were signs that I should have anticipated a more ambivalent reception.

During my final writing program orientation as a graduate student, I was asked to participate on a panel about teaching strategies for our developmental composition course. The coordinators of the orientation chose me to present not only to graduate students but also to the larger group of lecturers because I had expressed interest in administration and program responsibilities. I was clearly being groomed by program coordinators to become a colleague. At the time, I felt I was a legitimate part of a professional community, especially since I was joined on the panel by two senior and well-respected male lecturers. I felt my professional career in academia had started. But as much as graduate students may feel suspicion towards lecturers, I didn't anticipate lecturers might also feel suspicion towards graduate students.

During my presentation, I offered up a new grading strategy I had implemented over the last two years, which had significantly improved the relationship between students and assessment.

"You're just a GSI, right?" a male lecturer in the audience barked at me in a room of thirty lecturers and graduate students.

"GSI?" I asked. I stuffed down my panic at being confronted as I urgently searched for the meaning of the acronym.

"Graduate student instructor," he said impatiently, his brows pinching closer together under his glasses. His use of this title rather than the conventional TA or AD seemed intended to be pejorative.

"Yes, that's true. I am," I said, feeling angry and small all at the same time.

"So then, you have only one class to teach. Your process of grading isn't really practical for those of us who have triple the students you do."

Oh, I see, I thought. I'm not really a part of this teaching community.

"Well, actually," I emphasized with as much diplomacy as I could muster with my rising anxiety, "I haven't noticed that I spend any more time on grading or with students than I usually do."

The lecturer sat back, crossed his arms, and rolled his eyes. No discussion. No question about whether I'd ever taught full time before (I had). No exploration of how we might try to balance workload and meaningful praxis. I was simply an annoying graduate student who had no conception of the "real world" of teaching. I had the "luxury" to try new things with my students.

Quickly, I was defended by the two male lecturers on my panel. My brief sense of professional identity faded into the crowd as the session broke for lunch. Later, throughout the day, the story was told and retold among those at orientation. I was approached by several program coordinators and the other graduate students, who apologized to me on behalf of this lecturer, which at the time helped reassure me there was a community into which I was integrated. While I felt vindicated at the time, as I write this chapter, I wonder whether such gestures of support were in defense of me as a future full-time colleague or as a female graduate student whose sweetness deserved to be buffered from mansplaining. Staying on at IEU made the change in my professional identity difficult to ascertain. Whether or not my colleagues liked me, I felt stuck in my graduate-school identity.

I know graduate students and junior faculty, regardless of status, all experience some form of a professional identity crisis. We exist in a liminal space being more than students but less than experts. It never occurred to me, though, that the "Dr." preceding my name wouldn't be well known among my new lecturer colleagues. I was too familiar as a graduate student. Within these conditions of lost dreams, undervalued professional paths, and surface-level familiarity, I can see how the community of a writing program might fester into something unpleasant.

Suspicion that lecturers do not value students and suspicion that graduate students are too idealistic are only reinforced by other systemic elements at IEU. For example, only tenure-track faculty and graduate students can receive teaching awards, so the important work of lecturers often goes underappreciated, if not unnoticed, at a campus level. To the uninformed, it may seem like lecturers are not good teachers. Additionally, of the three required writing courses at IEU, only one allows for an instructor to teach a more literature-focused course, but often English graduate students are given priority to teach these classes so as to provide them experience teaching literature and therefore improve their job opportunities to teach literature. Within a discipline that privileges literature, graduate students can develop a sense of entitlement with these course assignments.

WRITING DRAMA

The entitlement at IEU manifested in a melodramatic fight between graduate students and the writing program. Under the guidance of the director of Graduate Studies in English, some graduate students filed a grievance against the program, citing racism and transphobia as fundamental to the curricula. Such critiques are not without some merit, but the organization of such complaints squarely within literature tellingly reveals that while we all may teach classes with course codes for English, we are definitely not a part of the same academic community. Further, in the absence of any lecturer voices in the grievance, the complaint points to, at best, the institutional insignificance of non-tenured faculty, and at worst, a complete disrespect for their expertise.

Indeed, the only time a lecturer was consulted regarding the grievance occurred when the director of Graduate Studies pulled me into her office to get "dirt" on the writing program's assumed conservative politics. Although my joint identity as a literature and writing studies scholar was finally acknowledged by someone in power, such recognition was muted by institutional theatrics. As a lecturer, I had come to understand how reductive the political stereotypes of the writing program and its lecturers were, but my attempts to explain complexities, while conceding deficits, were dismissed.

Depending on who I talk to and their perspective of graduate students, my expertise is characterized as idealistic or complicit with oppressive forces. I'm always a student.

But while graduate students have the support of tenured literature professors, non-tenured faculty have no organizational means to express critique. As a result, I can't even champion the points of a grievance that do have merit. For example, I once overheard a troubling instruction from a senior lecturer who was teaching in the room before me. As I waited for his class to end, I listened to him disparage the use of a singular *they* pronoun. Of course, grammar generally doesn't keep up with the evolution of language, but I was very concerned about this instructor's complete erasure of an identity—possibly of one of his own students. But my concern over his inequitable teaching on pronouns had no outlet. As a brand-new lecturer, and one who was often mistaken for a graduate student since I recently was one, there was no forum for my voice to be taken seriously. My concerns would not be taken as professional feedback but rather as personal criticism given the way most ideas floated around the program as rumor. I might find a sympathetic ear in another lecturer, but ultimately the general feeling was to mind your own business when it came to teaching.

It is true that the shift in the humanities to strengthen diversity, include more voices, and expand more into social justice has brought about a wealth of writing, either advocating more integration of gender, race, sexuality studies, and so forth into the academy (Bérubé 2013) or bemoaning how such issues unnecessarily politicize the university or distract students from developing the knowledge they need for the workplace (Teller 2016). But in the end, what is most significant is that these arguments almost exclusively occur in the public sphere of articles or social media rants, where their impact is diffuse, or the arguments do not occur at all. At IEU, they just seem to exist in the ether of the department hallways and periodic meetings about grading, informing tensions but never being worked through in an emotionally articulate way. Composition classrooms are generally the spaces where these educational values collide since such classes are typically small and required. A laissez-faire attitude that allows non-tenured instructors to avoid broader conversations about writing pedagogy and educational philosophy, particularly with colleagues who have different views, can make for a disjointed experience among students. If teachers don't communicate with each other, students can easily feel their writing courses do not build on each other. Further, without on-going professional discussion, I knew I was never going to get out of my graduate student identity.

WHERE DO I BELONG?

But the onus is on the individual instructor to build relationships. Whereas graduate students have classes and regularly organized events, non-tenured lecturers rarely meet with one another under conditions that would foster productive communication. (Grade-norming meetings are difficult enough but much harder when instructors don't know each other.) Even though I saw people I knew every day, as a lecturer, I was shut off from the structures of graduate student life and still viewed as a graduate student by my coworkers. I knew that if I was going to save my sanity, I needed to try to establish myself with other lecturers as a fellow lecturer.

I got more involved with the few external opportunities there were for lecturers so I could get to know this new community. I signed up for a high-school outreach program and a pilot first-year reading event. On the surface, these programs looked as if they would integrate professional and social engagement. But ultimately, my involvement yielded very little new understanding or deeper relations. I left the hour-long training for the high-school outreach program confused by the leadership's tunnel vision. The lecturers and organizers of this program were so narrowly focused on teaching the five-paragraph-essay exam that I wasn't certain how we were "reaching out" to students, particularly in the context of California's trending move away from essay entrance exams. I asked questions but was met with obtuse answers and slight impatience. The pilot first-year reading event was a complete failure, but there was no official gathering to discuss the event—a chance to work with other contingent faculty on creating a specific culture for the program. Rather, I was casually consulted by the organizer for five minutes in passing. Without structured social interaction among contingent faculty or forums for administration to take lecturer feedback seriously, many decisions are made, and experiments are tried, but there is little growth or movement. There is also no opportunity for someone like me to remake her image among her colleagues.

Recently, at his keynote talk for a writing program conference, Juan Guerra (2018) stated "writing teachers are writers, too." YES!, I think, and scribble down the sentence in my conference-provided notepad. As a graduate student, I had to write. As a lecturer, I can get away with never writing again if I want. Indeed, many full-time contingent lecturers opt to teach unsanctioned overload courses at different institutions rather than write and publish or otherwise engage with the philosophy of our discipline. But I believe such a choice would be dishonest. Teaching can very easily find a way to occupy all our professional energy, but how can

I create conditions for students to become their best writing selves if I am divorced from my own practice? I teach then only from memory and not my lived experience.

I believe that sometimes the difficulty in building a writing community among teachers of different statuses, especially the contingent, oftentimes allows for the romantic fantasy of the solitary writer to take over. Eric Muller explains that "for academic writers, some of the urge to isolation . . . comes from a faintly macho spirit in the traditional scholarly enterprise" (2014, 20). Certainly, keeping to oneself within program debates or a fluctuating pool of instructors can seem less stressful, especially when teaching is already so demanding. But in truth, writers know meaningful writing is a combination of community, brute force, and self-care. Otherwise, teaching something like peer review really is a selfish practice of "taking a break" in the classroom, not a method of guiding students towards self-sufficiency and learning to integrate alternative perspectives. When non-tenured faculty do not feel some sense of responsibility to each other, I think they can come dangerously close to not feeling responsibility to their students.

FINAL REFLECTION

Ultimately, I approached my experience of isolation in my home institution with the same methods I take to other areas of my life: I asked questions and I talked openly; I sought out trusted mentors; I wrote and revised; I ate frozen yogurt; I wrote and revised again. As much as I advocated for more communal writing practices as a graduate student, I didn't truly appreciate the necessity of a professional community until I was hired to teach writing full time in a place I thought I already had community. I have no doubt that had I stayed at IEU, I would have worked to make community in some way. But I think I needed to leave the nest. The distance of a new job provided me with the perspective necessary to articulate my professional needs, as well as the momentum to build community in a new place.

I've been at my current position away from my graduate institution for almost two years now. I believe I've grown out of my graduate student persona and more into a professional one, primarily because no one here knows me otherwise. Additionally, being new encouraged clear mentorship from both tenured and non-tenured faculty and administrators. Space for my contributions was already being created for me. Only time will tell whether my experience of a stronger contingent community (that has no memory of me as just some grad student) will address structural and philosophical problems more effectively than the fragmentation and disconnection at my graduate institution. But I can say that having formalized mentorship and more consistent discussion with fellow lecturers about teaching and program goals has made me less anxious that I've hit a standstill at the beginning of my career.

There are many, many problems non-tenured faculty encounter that are far more urgent than the experience of isolation: fair compensation, equitable hiring practices, and secure employment, to name a few (Conn 2010; "How to Fix" 2018). But community is also a necessity, not a luxury, for contingent faculty. It affects the well-being of not only non-tenure-track instructors but also students and writing program strength and versatility. Without a community, we undermine our own work in classrooms and in our culture at large.

REFERENCES

Bérubé, Michael. 2013. "The Humanities, Unraveled." *Chronicle of Higher Education*, February 18. https://www.chronicle.com/article/Humanties-Unraveled/137291.

Chernoff, Carolyn. 2018. "Tenure-Track Faculty Should Support Other Academics in More Precarious Career Situations (Opinion)." *Inside Higher Ed*, August 10, 2018. https://www.insidehighered.com/advice/2018/08/10/tenure-track-faculty-should-support-other-academics-more-precarious-career.

Conn, Peter. 2010. "We Need to Acknowledge the Realities of Employment in the Humanities." *Chronicle of Higher Education*, April 4, 2018. https://www.chronicle.com/article/We-Need-to-Acknowledge-the/64885.

Guerra, Juan. 2018. "An Embodied History of Translingualism." Keynote Address, Annual UC Writing Programs Conference, Merced, CA, November 2018.

"How to Fix the Adjunct Crisis." 2018. *Chronicle of Higher Education*, May 30, 2018. https://www.chronicle.com/article/How-to-Fix-Adjunct-Crisis/243535.

Kelsky, Karen. 2015. *The Professor Is In: The Essential Guide to Turning Your PhD into a Job*. New York: Three Rivers.

Muller, Eric. 2014. "Developing the Faculty as a Writing Community." *Academe* 100 (6): 20–23.

Patel, Vimal. 2018. "How a Famous Academic Job-Market Study Got It All Wrong—and Why It Still Matters." *Chronicle of Higher Education*, September 9, 2018. https://www.chronicle.com/article/How-a-Famous-Academic/244458.

Teller, Joseph. 2016. "Are We Teaching Composition All Wrong?" *Chronicle of Higher Education*, October 3, 2018. https://www.chronicle.com/article/Are-We-Teaching-Composition/237969.

Youn, Ted I. K. 2005. "The Academic Job Market Is Bad for All of Us." *Academe* 19 (6): 27–30.

11
COLLECTIVE BARGAINING, HETEROGENEITY, AND NON-TENURE-TRACK WRITING FACULTY

Denise Comer

"Why do you find us disposable? Why are you pushing us off a cliff?"

These were the refrains I encountered during summer 2017 from newly unionized non-tenure-track (NTT) writing faculty amidst collective-bargaining-agreement (CBA) negotiations. It bears noting that I myself am NTTF. However, as a writing program administrator (WPA) (director of first-year writing), I am classified under National Labor Relations Act (NLRA) Section 2.3 as a supervisor and am therefore excluded from union eligibility (National Labor Relations Board n.d.). Still, as someone who considers herself generally left leaning, I found myself in the remarkable position of paradoxically empathizing with unionization and proposed CBA terms for one cohort of NTT writing faculty while experiencing surprise and reluctance over the same potential terms for another cohort of NTT writing faculty.

From whence did my contradictory attitudes emerge? Do not *all* people deserve the job securities and rights unions promise? Perhaps I had been brainwashed to become an operative against my writing program colleagues. Perhaps my paradoxical position signaled an underlying hypocrisy: maybe I only valued equity in theory, just not in *my* backyard. Or, perhaps, as a midcareer WPA, I had just become completely out of touch, with my experience as contingent faculty several decades ago fading whilst I had morphed, unaware, into an antiunion bossman.

Amidst such self-doubt and disorientation, this chapter tells the story of a fierce battle for union representation and CBA terms involving three different cohorts of NTT faculty in the Duke University Thompson Writing Program (TWP): NTT adjunct faculty, NTT postdoctoral fellows, and NTT WPAs.

DOI: 10.7330/9781646420759.c011

At its core, this story explores two important ideas.

First, the lived experiences of NTT writing faculty vary immensely, with heterogeneity operating not only across but also within institutions, and even within one writing program. Such heterogeneity may seem somewhat self-evident. The Conference on College Composition and Communication (CCCC) offers a deliberately expansive definition of NTT: "all faculty who are not protected by tenure" (2016). Still, the range of heterogeneity emphasizes the complex and varied systems that impact NTT labor and may even contribute to the inequities themselves.

The second important idea involves how our local, personal experiences are always, inevitably, connected to larger landscapes. Here, intersections among writing program labor, institutional context, academic employment, and economic tides coalesced to influence unionization at what was, arguably, an improbable institution and, also arguably, an improbable writing program. This case, therefore, reinforces the need for significant reforms in the employment paradigms governing higher education and writing program labor, even as it also may serve as a harbinger, signaling that such reforms are seemingly (hopefully?) already in motion.

But, before proceeding, a caveat: many people were and remain involved with the events in this story, including, but not limited to, contingent and noncontingent faculty across Duke, WPAs and staff, union representatives, undergraduates, graduate students, attorneys, and administrators. I neither attempt nor presume to speak for others, nor do I speak for my institution, nor do I suggest my experience offers a comprehensive, objective rendering. Rather, my perspective is informed by my own biases and limited perspective.

"DUKE ADJUNCT FACULTY VOTE FOR UNION REPRESENTATION" ("DUKE ADJUNCT FACULTY" 2016)

On March 28, 2016, non-regular-rank[1] Duke faculty entered union representation by the Service Employees International Union (SEIU), Workers United Southern Region Local 26. The initial three-year CBA, ratified in July 2017, covers between 250 and 275 non-regular-rank faculty across Duke (Duke Faculty Union 2018a; Gronberg 2017c).

Non-regular-rank faculty in Duke's writing program were leaders during unionization and CBA negotiations. The Duke Faculty Union's first president, for instance, was a non-regular-rank writing faculty member (Gronberg 2017c). Twenty-three of the forty-one signatories from a June 2017 open letter to Duke provost Sally Kornbluth, criticizing the stalled

CBA negotiations, were non-regular-rank writing faculty (Cummings 2017; Gronberg 2017a). And, the banner for the official Duke Faculty Union twitter feed prominently features non-regular-rank writing faculty. The image depicts non-regular-rank writing faculty holding pro-union signs such as "Duke: (Spare Some) Change," with one person grasping a tin cup, connoting the Great Depression (Duke Faculty Union n.d.). The image has become somewhat iconic in this context, disseminated across several sites promoting the Duke Faculty Union or SEIU (Cummings 2017; SEIU 2017). At the time, non-regular-rank writing faculty numbered approximately twenty-five, and they now constitute the highest concentration of unionized faculty in any unit at Duke.

Here are the NLRB docket-activity facts for Case 10-RC 169472:

- 02/11/2016: Date filed
- 02/22/2016: Notice of Election
- 03/22/2016: Tally of Ballots:
    - Number of Eligible Voters: 296
    - Votes for Labor Union: 174
    - Votes Against: 29
    - Total Ballots: 217
- 03/28/2016: Certification of Representative
- 03/28/2016: Status: Closed (NLRB 2016)

Succinct as they may be, docket facts do not capture lived experiences, particularly with time. Belying this seemingly forty-five-day process, an SEIU union representative visited me at least one year prior to the vote to discuss writing program labor conditions, and CBA negotiations took over sixteen months following the vote. As I write this, nearly three years postvote, negotiations, grievances, and transitions are still actively in process.

Docket activity also does not reflect the remarkable context surrounding events. Case 10-RC-169472 was significant because Duke has two defining characteristics that made it, at the time, an unlikely site for a faculty union: it is private, and it is in the south. SEIU described the Duke faculty union as a milestone: "the first faculty union contract at a major private university in the South" (2017).

The American South has long been a bastion of union resistance. According to the Bureau of Labor Statistics, southern states have the lowest percentages of unionized employees (Brown 2018). Higher education faculty in the South, likewise, are comparatively less unionized than those in the West and Northeast (Sproul, Bucklew, and Houghton 2014).

Private institutions, located in the South or otherwise, are also comparatively less unionized. In 2014, private, four-year institutions had the lowest percentage of faculty unionization (7 percent) compared to two-year public institutions (42 percent) and four-year public institutions (25 percent) (Sproul, Bucklew, and Houghton 2014). According to 2012 data from the National Center for the Study of Collective Bargaining in Higher Education and the Professions, 93 percent of organized faculty were employed in public institutions (2002). Legal precedent had largely dictated these circumstances until the NLRB's December 16, 2014, *Pacific Lutheran University* (PLU) decision opened more pathways for unionization at private institutions (Scott 2015).[2] Coming on the heels of this PLU decision, the Duke Faculty Union signaled a turning point: "Emblematic of the changes in faculty unionization was the certification of SEIU as the representative of a [non-regular-rank] faculty unit at Duke University, the first new private sector faculty bargaining unit in a right-to-work state in a quarter of a century" (Herbert 2016).

In addition to this remarkable context, yet another aspect of Case 10-RC-169472 also merits attention: the resulting CBA converted the writing program's shorter-term postdoctoral fellowships in teaching writing into ongoing, renewable positions. This change marked a tectonic shift in Duke's writing program, which had been operating for more than fifteen years as a nationally recognized site for an innovative, multidisciplinary postdoctoral fellowship in teaching writing.

MAKING WRITING VISIBLE AT DUKE UNIVERSITY

Duke's independent Thompson Writing Program (TWP) offers a one-semester, theme-based, first-year writing course required of all Duke undergraduates. Since its founding in 2000, TWP has employed a cohort of twenty-five to thirty recent PhDs from across disciplines on three- to five-year contracts who design and teach theme-based writing seminars through their disciplinary perspectives under the auspices of a postdoctoral fellowship.

These fellowships, funded for a time by the Andrew W. Mellon Foundation, were designed to be developmental. Fellows could develop their writing pedagogy in a supportive environment, with time to advance their research agendas, strengthen their qualifications, and reorient their career interests. For some, the position enhanced their marketability through affiliation with Duke. The fellowship was designed to seed the academy with individuals who valued and had experience with teaching writing through their disciplines. Each year, as current TWP postdoctoral fellows found subsequent jobs, TWP would run a competitive, national search for more fellows.

Fellowship positions were structured to be materially fair, "not tenure-track positions but neither are they dead-end jobs" (Hillard and Harris 2003). Joseph Harris (founding director) and Van Hillard (then director of first-year writing) described the fellowship:

> Sections of "Academic Writing" are capped at twelve students, for a total of only sixty students taught per year by each fellow in the program. . . . We support their work through a series of symposia . . . as well as through an ongoing process of class visits, reviews of materials, and informal conversations about teaching.
> . . . The salary is reasonable . . . the support for research strong, the environment for teaching excellent, and the collegial support of the other fellows extraordinary. Fellows are offered an initial three-year contract. In the second semester of their second year at Duke, they undergo a rigorous review of their work based on a teaching portfolio that they have assembled. If this review is positive, their contract is extended to five years.

These postdoctoral fellows, however, constituted only the most visible cohort of TWP writing faculty. Other TWP faculty cohorts included several program directors (all regular rank, though not tenure stream) and a small number of graduate students from across disciplines who taught on a one-semester, one-course basis. Together, these cohorts, along with the fellows, ostensibly enabled full staffing for first-year writing. Every year, though, TWP had a small percentage of unstaffed sections, perhaps due to a larger-than-expected entering class size, or as a result of fellows taking leave, or because a fellow accepted a job offer after TWP had already concluded the search for new fellows. And, thus, TWP also regularly hired a cohort of non-regular-rank adjunct instructors.

According to the Center for Labor Research and Education at UC Berkeley, "One in four families of part-time college faculty are enrolled in at least one public assistance program, like food stamps, Medicaid or the Earned Income Tax Credit" (Wessler 2015). Nationally, first-year writing has exceptionally high rates of contingent labor; surveys conducted by MLA in 1996 and 2006 show that at doctoral institutions, 96 percent of first-year writing courses are taught by non-tenure-track faculty, and at master's and baccalaureate institutions, 78 percent and 57 percent, respectively, of first-year writing courses are taught by non-tenure-track faculty (Jaschik 2008). As a result, writing-studies faculty have long advocated for improving adjunct labor conditions, from the Wyoming Resolution of 1986 through the Indianapolis Resolution of 2016 and beyond (Cox et al. 2016; McDonald and Schell 2011). The deplorable working conditions of adjunct faculty have been well documented, notably consisting of poor wages, lack of health and dental insurance, limited or absent retirement and leave options, as well as job insecurity, institutional marginalization, and the prospect of becoming "freeway flyers" in order to barely (or not) make ends meet (Kahn 2017).

These imperiled conditions also largely afflicted TWP's adjunct faculty. Job security was virtually absent. Some semesters, adjunct faculty learned of a section opening only a few weeks prior to the term. Office space was also uncertain. Adjunct faculty did not receive laptop computers or research funds and were, for the most part, ineligible for medical and dental benefits or retirement unless they taught enough sections in a given semester to be considered full time. This rarely occurred.

Moreover, the adjunct experience teaching writing differed culturally from that of other faculty cohorts in the TWP. Liz Gumm, in chapter 10 of this book, "Disunity in a Writing Community: A Post-PhD Memoir of Professional Transition," emphasizes the critical importance of community for adjunct faculty, which impacts faculty at all ranks, student experiences, and programmatic strength. While TWP's adjuncts were included in some faculty meetings and professional-development opportunities, they were excluded from many as well. Without a formal review process, they had only sporadic class visits and little occasion for feedback on or interaction around their teaching.

While TWP adjunct faculty did earn a per-course rate higher than that offered by nearby institutions, and higher than the $2,700 national average for adjunct writing faculty (Kahn 2017), the compensation would have made it challenging to support oneself, let alone a family, especially without benefits and job security.

Some TWP adjuncts had been working for nearly a decade under these conditions. For them, TWP replicated the very structural inequities Harris was working against in 2000 as he and others designed the TWP's postdoctoral fellowships. Harris, at the time, called for "bosses and workers in composition to form a new class consciousness centered on the issue of good teaching for fair pay" (2000, 43). Yet, in retrospect, the TWP's laudable postdoctoral fellowships masked, and perhaps even instantiated, ongoing inequities for the TWP's adjuncts.

Remarking on this paradox is not meant to call out Harris; he, as with all of us, bosses and workers alike, is embedded within larger, more powerful systems that govern material labor conditions. Power structures always outpace individual intentions. As director of first-year writing, I wanted to offer adjuncts better compensation, earlier teaching contracts, office space, and more programmatic inclusion, but these good intentions were hampered by institutional structures. My point, then, is not to place blame on Harris, myself, or others, but to underscore the limitations of individuals—even well-meaning, capable, and thoughtful people—against institutional structures designed to maintain hierarchies of privilege.

The heterogeneity of non-tenure-track positions in TWP—whereby NTT postdoctoral fellows enjoyed stature and benefits unavailable to NTT adjuncts—constitutes an instance of "interest convergence" (Delgado and Stefancic 2001), in which structures enable the elite to maintain privilege, even unwittingly and through unexpected means. As Derrick Bell (1980) has argued with regard to *Brown v. Board of Education*, sometimes that which seems an advancement is actually an illusory structural intervention that, paradoxically, facilitates maintenance of (or exacerbates) systemic inequities.

Interest convergence emerges to an even greater degree when considering TWP's NTT WPAs. Over the years, select fellows had become program directors. I, for instance, started out in TWP in 2000 as a fellow. After a few years, I moved to regular rank, with the title of lecturer and with administrative responsibilities that eventually became the directorship of first-year writing. My new rank, though still NTT, carried longer-term job security and voting rights, although it still held less stature than tenure-stream faculty.

Others have identified the limits of authority for NTT WPAs, noting NTT status can hamper relationships between WPAs and writing faculty, as well as the longer-term success of a writing program (Mirtz and Cullen 2002; Rose, Mastrangelo, and L'Eplattenier 2013). In TWP, the highly limited opportunity for advancement to regular rank created an illusion of mobility for the fellows and deeper inequities among the three NTTF cohorts (NTT program administrators, NTT postdoctoral fellows, and NTT adjuncts), instantiating the worst conditions for those of lowest rank: TWP's adjuncts.

IT'S LIKE FINALLY BEING WELCOMED TO THE TABLE

Given the poor labor conditions for TWP's adjuncts, I largely supported their unionization and CBA terms. For them, SEIU held the promise of better wages, multiyear contracts, and more transparent and regulated discipline and dismissal processes (Yates 2009; Rhoads and Rhoades 2005). However, the prospect of unionization for TWP's postdoctoral fellows was, for me, somewhat of a surprise. To my thinking—limited as it was in retrospect—TWP fellows had reasonable wages, excellent benefits, and three- to five-year contracts wherein they gained valuable writing-pedagogy experience, which they could then take back to tenure-stream positions in their home disciplines. Fellows had applied for these positions under the aegis of continuing their research and building their skills teaching writing through their disciplinary lenses. I was surprised they wanted to become more permanent writing faculty, and I was concerned about their preparation for such a move—and the impact on the writing program—given that their disciplinary training and research interests were mostly from non-writing-studies fields. In hindsight, my surprise emerged from my own failure to take into account the structures of postdoctoral positions more broadly and the changes in the academic and jobs landscapes that had taken place over the past two decades.

Since 2000, postdoctoral positions have grown dramatically (AAU 2005; Flaherty 2017). In kind, postdoctoral fellowships in teaching writing now exist at a number of institutions, such as Stanford, Tulane, Notre Dame, Johns Hopkins, and Georgia Tech, among others. Similar positions also appear by other names, such as an opening at Smith College for five Mellon Visiting Assistant Professors in Public Discourse in the Disciplines who will work on three-year term limits (HigherEdJobs 2018).

Postdoctoral positions can advance careers, especially in some disciplines (Faupel-Badger et al. 2015; Lin and Chiu 2016). However, postdoctoral positions also have widely divergent terms of employment and have been charged with reaffirming globalized oppression, conferring unfair advantages on predominately white males, and symptomizing the more endemic problem of clogged employment pipelines across academia due to outdated tenure systems and overenrollment in graduate programs (Eisen and Eaton 2018; Lin and Chiu 2016; Patton 2014). Some critics maintain that postdoctoral positions offer universities a means to secure cheap labor that advances research for tenured faculty at the expense of the health, prospects, and well-being of the postdocs themselves (Flaherty 2017).

Postdoctoral positions have become especially problematic in the humanities, where they emerged in the early 2000s to address a lack of job openings (Ogden 2001). Now, as employment opportunities in the humanities continue to dwindle, people find themselves in serial, ongoing postdocs (Dunn 2014).

Given these concerns, postdoctoral unions are an important area for union growth (Flaherty 2017). Postdoctoral researchers in the University of California system, for example, claim that unionizing provided better wages, guaranteed salary increases, and offered affordable, quality benefits (Cain et al. 2014).

The University of California postdoctoral union, however, did not provide renewable contracts, as Duke's TWP for postdoctoral fellows did. Moreover, unlike many of the challenges that saturate postdoctoral positions more generally, the TWP fellowships largely satisfied many of the dimensions by which higher education labor (postdoctoral or not) tends to be evaluated: "course loads, compensation . . . professional support . . . multi-year contracts . . . teaching loads . . . and [job satisfaction]" (Melonçon, England, and Ilyasova 2016). TWP fellows received funding for relocating to Duke, laptops, office space, and research accounts with funds added annually. They were also eligible for additional research funding through competitive summer research grants. TWP fellows could take unpaid leave for up to two years to explore a different opportunity. And, they chose from among the same dental and medical benefits available to all Duke full-time faculty and staff, as well as the same retirement programs.

TWP fellows had no TWP summer obligations, and most designed one course per year and so had one course prep. With twelve-student caps per section, and a five-section load per academic year, fellows taught a total of sixty students per year. Since the fellowship was based on teaching, there were no research or scholarship expectations. Other than a monthly faculty meeting, service expectations were low, although fellows were asked to serve on a relatively time-consuming search committee during year two or three of their fellowship. Otherwise, fellows were invited to participate in ad hoc committees, though they were not obligated to do so.

Postfellowship placement and faculty development included professional-development speakers and workshops, as well as support for job searches through practice job talks and job-material workshops. Most TWP fellows secured subsequent, longer-term employment within the first four years of their fellowships. From 2000 to 2016, only a few from the more than 130 total TWP fellows were unable to find full-time, more secure employment after their TWP fellowship (Comer and Rego 2017). Granted, several position flaws did exist. The fellowship salary, characterized in 2003 by Hillard and Harris as "reasonable," had not grown accordingly. TWP fellows were also ineligible for the parental-leave benefits granted regular-rank Duke faculty (Comer 2009). Perhaps most significantly, however, was that TWP's fellowships did not have longer-term, renewable contracts and did not have the possibility of advancement at Duke. Nor was there any real structural cushion in place in the event that a fellow could not find a job, or the job they wanted, before the end of their five-year contract.

The prospect of overhauling the TWP structure, changing the vast majority of faculty positions from multidisciplinary postdoctoral fellowships to renewable writing positions, when the faculty were trained in disciplines outside writing studies, led to a sticking point during CBA negotiations. The question became, Were these fellowships a mechanism for cheap labor, rendering the people occupying the positions "disposable"? Was TWP pushing people off a cliff? Or, were these fellowships developmental, providing comparatively fair labor conditions while training postdoctoral scholars from across disciplines to teach writing, thereby improving their skills and marketability, and then seeding the academy writ large with writing-based expertise across disciplines?

During these antagonistic CBA negotiations, TWP fellows maintained that the larger impact of a rotating cohort of fellows who carried writing-pedagogy expertise across the academy was neither so important nor so valid as to be worth releasing strong-performing, well-trained people back into the abysmal job market.

WE FELT WE HAD NO VOICE IN THE UNIVERSITY, THAT NOBODY WAS LISTENING TO US

According to the Bureau of Labor Statistics, in 2017, 37.2 percent of US employees in "education, training, and library" occupations were unionized (2018). The specific number of unionized faculty in higher education is harder to specify, though one recent study estimates that 17.1 percent of all postsecondary teachers are unionized (Sproul, Bucklew, and Houghton 2014).

Arguments promoting faculty unions across higher education point to the increasing corporatization of universities and argue that faculty unions provide increased wages and better benefits (Edwards and Tolley 2018). Those opposing faculty unions in higher education claim unions lead to inefficiency, negative climate, and decreased performance and do not actually increase faculty job satisfaction (Cain 2017).

TWP's NTT adjuncts had much to gain from unionization, and little to lose. TWP's NTT postdoctoral fellows, though, made a decision through unionization to deidentify from their disciplines and their pursuit of tenure-stream positions in their disciplines. While most TWP adjuncts had an MFA or MA as their highest degree, all TWP postdoctoral fellows had earned a PhD and nearly all had entered the TWP indicating they wanted to use this fellowship to strengthen their teaching of writing in preparation for a tenure-stream position in their discipline. Granted, career aspirations are fluid, and renewable contracts do not preclude ongoing tenure-track job searches, but converting from a term-limited, developmental fellowship to a renewable lecturing position does amount to a significant shift in professional identity.

As it happens, several structural systems likely influenced the TWP fellows' decision to unionize: the socioeconomic context of Duke, the vulnerability of TWP within institutional structures, and the continuing impacts of the 2008 economic collapse. These influences are important to consider because, despite comparatively reasonable wages, benefits, and terms, TWP's fellows nevertheless identified with the disempowerment and voicelessness Anderson names above and that characterized NTT adjunct experiences at Duke.

Duke's endowment is estimated to be $7.9 billion, rendering it one of the twenty wealthiest institutions in the world (Barham and Rich 2018). Its tuition is among the twenty highest in the United States; for 2018–19, undergraduate tuition is $53,760, with a total cost of $70,873 when including tuition, room, board, and fees ("Duke Trustees" 2018). Granted, 52 percent of Duke undergraduates do not pay full cost (Duke University 2018). But many undergraduates do hail from privilege. Duke has been undergraduate home to a Qatari princess, children of celebrities, fashion designers, and the grandson of President Carter (Booher 2002; Setrakian 2009; Wilson 2004). According to the article "Economic Diversity and Student Outcomes" in *the New York Times*, the median family income for Duke undergraduates, based on data for the class of 2013, is $186,700 (2017).

Duke tenure-stream faculty are also comparatively well off. Former Duke president Richard Brodhead received $1,257,980 in salary in 2015, making him the thirty-third highest-paid private-university president (Stancill 2017). Duke full professors, according to ChronicleData, earn on average $188,199, considerably higher than the national average of $123,495 for similar faculty at four-year private institutions (2016). Also, according to ChronicleData, the average salary for Duke assistant professors is $84,987, again higher than the national average of $68,501 for assistant professors at four-year private institutions (2016). By contrast, according to ChronicleData, Duke lecturers make less than their peers, earning $53,244 as opposed to the national average of $63,928 (2016). Duke postdocs fare even worse, according to Glassdoor, averaging $45,263 per year (2018).

Data are malleable and depend on what figures are included or excluded, as well as how formulas are calculated. But it is also fair to say that complexities of class and privilege are woven into the fabric of Duke and certainly permeate the experiences of Duke's writing program faculty, who collectively teach every first-year undergraduate at Duke. Within this larger socioeconomic context of income and wealth disparity, TWP's fellows likely felt considerably underpaid, underrecognized, underrepresented, and underprivileged, particularly amidst the considerable privilege defining so many students, faculty, and administrators across Duke.

Such disempowerment became even more apparent in 2014 during a three-year initiative to revise Duke's undergraduate curriculum (Mock 2014). As a freestanding program without any majors, minors, or degree credentialing, and with an entirely NTT faculty (with the exception of a part-time chair position occupied by a tenure-stream faculty member from a different unit), TWP is disempowered compared to other Duke units. TWP only received voting privileges on Duke's Arts and Sciences Council in 2015 (Sarachek 2015). Perhaps partly due to this institutional vulnerability, the possibility emerged during the curriculum-revision process to eliminate first-year writing and replace it with a multidisciplinary, team-taught seminar (Xie 2016). This was, perhaps coincidentally (or not), also when SEIU representatives were actively pursuing TWP's NTT adjuncts and fellows.

Ultimately, TWP gained representation on the curriculum-revision committee, the curriculum revision retained first-year writing, and the proposed curriculum was eventually withdrawn from consideration altogether (Ashby and Broverman 2017; Trinity Administration 2018). Still, the curriculum-revision efforts, which occupied three years and overlapped with unionization, likely exacerbated the institutional vulnerability facing TWP's fellows, who had little to no voice throughout the process.

A third factor that may have influenced TWP's fellows to unionize involved the ripple impacts of the 2008 economic collapse. This generated negative emotional impacts worldwide on overall happiness and social well-being, which shaped subsequent behaviors (Aytaç, Rankin, and İbikoğlu 2015; Schooley and Worden 2016). A ten-year journalistic impact survey of college graduates from 2008 found that, in comparison to preceding peer cohorts, these individuals in 2018 have fewer children (or no children), less wealth, less inclination to invest in the stock market, less home ownership, and greater mistrust of people and structures (Gittleson 2018).

The majority of TWP fellows in 2016 had graduated college in or proximal to 2008. Perhaps, then, immediate long-term job security—even within the context of a fellowship—was a particularly valuable commodity for these individuals amidst less confidence in job-market prospects and having experienced global economic collapse in their early adult lives.

Given these circumstances, my surprise at the TWP fellows' desire to convert term-limited fellowships to permanently renewable contracts was, in retrospect, itself surprising. TWP's fellows were generally disenfranchised as faculty at Duke, working short term in a writing program with considerable institutional vulnerability and perpetually confronted with extreme privilege among students and other faculty, all along with reverberating impacts from having graduated college during the worst economic crisis of our time. Situate these circumstances within the gloomy picture of academic employment across disciplines and it makes considerable sense that these NTT fellows would seek to convert their fellowships into permanent employment.

SOLIDARITY, Y'ALL!

The rhetoric of collective bargaining promotes solidarity—and divisiveness. It turns on *kairos, ethos, logos,* and *pathos.* It breeds empathy, compassion, joy, anger, fear, and mistrust. It embodies the lived experiences of very diverse bodies in a labor force, moving along in currents among individuation, differentiation, and collectivism. It relies on narrative.

Over several years, I have learned new-to-me concepts: CBA . . . transition committee . . . grievance. I have also come to recognize the force with which institutional structures maintain power and the profound impact of larger socioeconomic contexts on local politics and experiences. Situated as I am now, a nonunionized NTT WPA who directs a unionized first-year writing faculty, individual interactions between unionized TWP faculty and me seem cordial, though strained. I sense increased tension among writing program staff, who are adapting to new processes in a more fraught climate that indirectly involves them but directly impacts them on a daily basis. Programmatically, fractures are palpable. Distrust abounds: I guard my words across stilted silences. Even in my words here I worry I am airing too much dirty laundry, that my writing will oppress or my words will be misinterpreted or misused. I ponder: Is it possible for union members and management to move from an adversarial relationship toward a cooperative model (Kleinhenz and Smith 2011; Ostrowsky 2005)? I take Zantac before faculty meetings. I breathe.

The narrative I had constructed about TWP fellowships was not a shared narrative. My version featured a multidisciplinary writing faculty who enjoyed fair working conditions and were engaged with the intellectual project of learning how to teach writing so they could go back to their home disciplines at other institutions and spread the impact of strong writing pedagogy. Although I understood that finding a subsequent job was undoubtedly stressful, I believed, based on the programmatic track record, that fellows would find jobs they wanted. I saw the impermanence of the fellowships as a necessary component of the position's developmental nature, one that benefited the academy across disciplines by opening opportunities for new cohorts of TWP fellows and creating pathways of impact for writing pedagogy across disciplines and institutions.

Fellows held a different narrative about these positions, one featuring solidarity against exploitative, elitist, and uncaring university structures and administrators. In this story, highly competent, caring individuals were systemically denied job security, and the corporatized university continued to benefit from expendable, affordable writing program labor. In this story, I, as a WPA, regardless of my own NTT status, was part of the privileged elite, striving to maintain the status quo and sustain oppression and injustice from my comfortable position with a longer-term contract and relatively more institutional privilege.

Solidarity can also mask fissures. NTTF are no more universal in their beliefs, strategies, attitudes, and aims than are individual members of management. Yet, I often find myself feeling an outsider, watching a collective, strengthening bond unite TWP's unionized faculty. I watch how they smile at one another, their body language as they greet one another, the ways their eyes meet in mutual understanding, unspoken agreement, and shared interpretations. Around me, I sense stiffness, suspicion . . . shadows of anger. I am NTT, but I am management. A line has been drawn, and I have been placed across it.

Undoubtedly, the most underprivileged people involved with the Duke non-regular-rank unionization efforts were the adjuncts (in the writing program and across Duke), who for years lacked basic job security, reasonable compensation, benefits, and inclusivity. Unionizing provided them with fairer labor conditions. Although the solidarity between the NTT adjuncts and the NTT fellows initially surprised me, given the differentiation in employment terms between the two positions, such solidarity may have been an important part of what ultimately helped accomplish some of that redistribution of power. In hindsight, the structures undergirding the writing program's NTT administrators and NTT fellows reinforced and exacerbated inequities, creating gradations of NTT writing labor that largely perpetuated the unsustainable labor conditions experienced by TWP's NTT adjuncts.

And now, sitting with that last sentence is really uncomfortable. I feel shame and regret. I was part of the machine of oppression that creates and sustains unfair working conditions for contingent first-year writing faculty. As an NTT WPA, I could have, should have, done more. Still, I am also aware that, self-proclaimed good intentions notwithstanding, institutional inequities are systemic, and NTTF across and within writing programs, heterogeneous as our positions may be, are all swept up in these structures and the larger socioeconomic tides that govern the lived experiences of individual faculty in writing programs. Because structural changes inevitably redistribute resources, power structures rarely change without compulsion. Likewise, those in power rarely discover with fuller awareness their own privilege unless and until they are confronted by the very structural inequities conferring those privileges.

NOTES

1. I use the term *non-regular-rank*, rather than NTT. Duke differentiates NTT faculty into non-regular-rank faculty, positions most similar to adjunct or contingent, and regular-rank faculty, positions that generally carry better wages, voting rights, and greater job security and stature.
2. Faculty unionization at private institutions became more feasible after the December 16, 2014, NLRB decision (Pacific Lutheran University, NLRB Case 19-RC-102521), which modified the standards used to determine who is "managerial" at private institutions (Scott 2015). Prior standards had largely prevented faculty unions at private institutions through the 1980 Supreme Court ruling in Yeshiva (Lieberwitz and Nisenson 2014).

REFERENCES

Ashby, Valerie, and Sherryl Broverman. 2017. "Briefing: Update on the New Curriculum Work." Trinity Administration, May 8. https://admin.trinity.duke.edu/dean/memos/4-8-2017-update-curriculum.

Association of American Universities Graduate and Posdoctoral Committee. 2005. *Postdoctoral Education Survey, Summary of Results*. https://www.aau.edu/sites/default/files/AAU%20Files/Education%20and%20Service/05-PostDocSumm101705.pdf.

Aytaç, Isik A., Bruce H. Rankin, and Arda İbikoğlu. 2015. "The Social Impact of the 2008 Global Economic Crisis on Neighborhoods, Households, and Individuals in Turkey." *Social Indicators Research* 124 (1): 1–19.

Barham, James A., and Bobby Rich. 2018. "The 100 Richest Universities: Their Generosity and Commitment to Research 2018." *The Best Schools*, September 13. https://thebestschools.org/features/richest-universities-endowments-generosity-research/.

Bell, Derrick A. 1980. "*Brown v. Board of Education* and the Interest-Convergence Dilemma." *Harvard Law Review* 93 (3): 518–33.

Booher, Bridget. 2002. "The Power of Privilege." *Duke Magazine, October 1*. https://alumni.duke.edu/magazine/articles/power-privilege.

Brown, Megan. 2018. "The $15 Wage Movement Moves South: Politics of Region in Labor Union Campaigns." *Antipode* 50 (4): 846–63.

Bureau of Labor Statistics, US Department of Labor. 2018. "Union Members 2017." Economic News Releases. January 19, 2018. Accessed November 26, 2018. https://www.bls.gov/news.release/archives/union2_01192018.pdf.

Cain, Benjamin, Jessica M. Budke, Kelsey J. Wood, Neal T. Sweeney, and Benjamin Schwessinger. 2014. "How Postdocs Benefit from Building a Union." *elife* 3. https://www.ncbi.nlm.nih.gov/pmc/articles/PMC4238050/.

Cain, Timothy Reese. 2017. "Campus Unions: Organized Faculty and Graduate Students in U.S. Higher Education." *ASHE Higher Education Report* 43 (3): 7–163.

ChronicleData. Duke University. 2016. https://data.chronicle.com/198419/Duke-University/faculty-salaries/. Accessed November 26, 2018.

Comer, Denise. 2009. "Changing Tables and Changing Culture: Pregnancy, Parenting, and First-Year Writing." *Composition Studies* 37 (2): 91–113.

Comer, Denise, and Márcia Rego. 2017. "Postdoctoral Writing Fellows: Cultivating Multidisciplinarity, Seeding Transfer." Paper presented at the meeting of the Conference on College Composition and Communication, Portland, OR. March 15–18, 2017.

Conference on College Composition and Communication. 2016. "CCCC Statement on Working Conditions for Non-Tenure-Track Writing Faculty." Urbana, IL: NCTE. https://cccc.ncte.org/cccc/resources/positions/working-conditions-ntt.

Cox, Anicca R., Timothy R. Dougherty, Seth Kahn, Michelle LaFrance, and Amy Lynch-Biniek. 2016. "The Indianapolis Resolution: Responding to Twenty-First-Century Exigencies/Political Economies of Composition Labor." *College Composition and Communication* 68 (1): 38–67.

Cummings, Alex S. 2017. "Duke Contingent Faculty Speak Out for Fair Wages in Open Letter." Tropics of Meta, June 16. https://tropicsofmeta.com/2017/06/16/duke-contingent-faculty-speak-out-for-fair-wages-in-open-letter/.

Delgado, Richard, and Jean Stefancic. 2001. "Introduction." In *Critical Race Theory: An Introduction*, by Richard Delgado and Jean Stefancic, 1–14. New York: New York University Press, 2011.

"Duke Adjunct Faculty Vote for Union Representation." 2016. Duke Today, March 18. https://today.duke.edu/2016/03/unionelection.

Duke Faculty Union. 2018a. "Facts about Our Collective Bargaining Agreement." Accessed November 19, 2020. http://www.dukefacultyunion.org/contract-facts/.

Duke Faculty Union (@teachdukeunion). 2018b. "Solidarity, y'all. A group of faculty at Loyola University Chicago (@loyolaforus) went on strike Wednesday after two years of negotiations with the Jesuit school over job security, wages and benefits failed to produce a contract." Twitter, April 6, 2:16 p.m. https://twitter.com/teachdukeunion/status/982336355257737217.

Duke Faculty Union (@teachdukeunion). n.d. https://twitter.com/teachdukeunion. Accessed April 27, 2017.

"Duke Trustees Approve New Tuition Rates for 2018–19." 2018. Duke Today, February 23. https://today.duke.edu/2018/02/duke-trustees-approve-new-tuition-rates-2018-19.

Duke University, Pratt School of Engineering. 2018. "Duke Launches Engineering Scholars Program with $15M Gift." April 2. https://pratt.duke.edu/about/news/clark-scholars.

Dunn, Sydni. 2014. "The Rise of the Post-Post-Postdoc." *Chronicle of Higher Education*, August 12. https://community.chronicle.com/news/655-the-rise-of-the-post-post-postdoc.

Eisen, Arri, and Douglas C. Eaton. 2018. "A Model for Postdoctoral Education That Promotes Minority and Majority Success in the Biomedical Sciences." *CBE Life Sciences Education* 16 (4): ar65.

Edwards, Kristen, and Kim Tolley, 2018. "Do Unions Help Adjuncts? What Dozens of Collective-Bargaining Agreements Can Tell Us." *Chronicle of Higher Education*, June 3.

Faupel-Badger, Jessica M., David E. Yahia, Izmirlian Grant, Katherine H. Ross, Kimberly Raue, Sophia Tsakraklides, Myaoka Atushi, and Maura Spiegelman. 2015. "Indepen-

dent Association of Postdoctoral Training with Subsequent Careers in Cancer Prevention." *PloS One* 10 (12).
Flaherty, Collen. 2017. "The (Possible) Postdoc Union Boom." *Inside Higher Ed*, October 31. https://www.insidehighered.com/news/2017/10/31/could-postdoc-unions-be-next-big-thing-collective-bargaining-among-academics.
Gittleson, Kim. 2018. "Lehman Anniversary: The Five Most Surprising Consequences." BBC News, September 13. https://www.bbc.com/news/business-45478670.
Glassdoor. 2018. Duke University salaries. Accessed November 26, 2018. https://www.glassdoor.com/Salary/Duke-University-Salaries-E2775.htm.
Gronberg, Ray. 2017a. "After Nine Months of Talks, Duke and its Adjunct-Faculty Union are Split on Two Issues." *Herald Sun.* June 22, 2017. https://www.heraldsun.com/news/local/counties/durham-county/article157493194.html.
Gronberg, Ray. 2017b. "With Contract Ratified, Duke Adjunct Professors Gain 'Freedom to Teach,' Union Says." *Herald Sun.* August 9, 2017. https://www.heraldsun.com/news/local/counties/durham-county/article166332512.html.
Gronberg, Ray. 2017c. "Unionization Leaves Duke Faculty with Questions—and Assurances—Going Forward." *Herald Sun.* October 17, 2017. https://www.heraldsun.com/news/local/counties/durham-county/article179030431.html.
Harris, Joseph. 2000. "Meet the New Boss, Same as the Old Boss: Class Consciousness in Composition." *College Composition and Communication* 52 (1): 43–68.
Herbert, William A. 2016. "The Winds of Changes Shift: An Analysis of Recent Growth in Bargaining Units and Representation Efforts in Higher Education." *Journal of Collective Bargaining in the Academy* 8 (1): 1–24. https://thekeep.eiu.edu/cgi/viewcontent.cgi?article=1647&context=jcba.
Hillard, Van, and Joseph Harris. 2003. "Making Writing Visible at Duke University." *Peer Review* 6 (1). https://www.questia.com/library/journal/1P3-592166021/making-writing-visible-at-duke-university. Accessed November 26, 2018.
Jaschik, Scott. 2008. "The Adjunctification of English." *Inside Higher Ed*, December 11, 2008. https://www.insidehighered.com/news/2008/12/11/adjunctification-english. Accessed November 20, 2020.
Kahn, Seth. 2017. "Redux: Contingency Is Still Worse." *Here Comes Trouble*, May 12. https://sethkahn.wordpress.com/2017/05/12/redux-contingency-is-still-worse/.
Kleinhenz, Jack, and Russ Smith. 2011. "Regional Competitiveness: Labor-Management Relations, Workplace Practices, and Workforce Quality." *Business Economics* 46 (2): 111–24.
Lieberwitz, Risa, and Aaron Nisenson. 2014. "NLRB Decision Strengthens Organizing Rights of Private-Sector Faculty Members." AAUP. December 22, 2014. https://www.aaup.org/news/nlrb-decision-strengthens-organizing-rights-private-sector-faculty-members#.X7c-JtNKhao.
Lin, Eric S., and Shih-Yung Chiu. 2016. "Does Holding a Postdoctoral Position Bring Benefits for Advancing to Academia?" *Research in Higher Education* 57 (3): 335–62.
McDonald, James C., and Eileen Schell. 2011. "The Spirit and Influence of the Wyoming Resolution: Looking Back to Look Forward." *College English* 73 (4): 360–78.
"Mellon Visiting Assistant Professor in Public Discourse in the Disciplines." 2018. HigherEdJobs. Accessed April 26, 2018. https://www.higheredjobs.com/institution/details.cfm?JobCode=176858832&Title=Mellon Visiting Assistant Professor in Public Discourse in the Disciplines.
Melonçon, Lisa, Peter England, and Alex Ilyasova. 2016. "A Portrait of Non-Tenure-Track Faculty in Technical and Professional Communication: Results of a Pilot Study." *Journal of Technical Writing and Communication* 46 (2): 206–35.
Mirtz, Ruth M., and Roxanne M. Cullen. 2002. "Beyond Postmodernism: Leadership Theories and Writing Program Administration." In *Writing Program Administrator as Theorist*, edited by Shirley Rose and Irwin Weiser, 90–102. Portsmouth, NH: Boynton/Cook.

Mock, Geoffrey. 2014. "Imagining an Undergraduate Curriculum." *Duke Today*, November 14. https://today.duke.edu/2014/11/curriculum.

National Center for the Study of Collective Bargaining in Higher Education and the Professions. 2002. "Directory Highlights." http://www.hunter.cuny.edu/ncscbhep/assets/files/Directory%20Highlights.pdf.

National Labor Relations Board. 2016. "Duke University." Accessed November 26, 2018. https://www.nlrb.gov/case/10-RC-169472.

National Labor Relations Board. n.d. "National Labor Relations Act." https://www.nlrb.gov/how-we-work/national-labor-relations-act.

Ogden, Daryl. 2001. "Beyond the Adjunct Principle: Envisioning a Future for Postdoctoral Fellowships in Language and Literature." *Journal of the Midwest Modern Language Association* 34 (3): 26–37.

Ostrowsky, Jane. 2005. "Union-Management Cooperation: Can a Company Move from an Adversarial Relationship to a Cooperative Relationship and Is Interest-Based Bargaining a Necessary Condition to Do So?" Seminar Research Paper Series Paper 12, Schmidt Labor Research Center. https://digitalcommons.uri.edu/cgi/viewcontent.cgi?referer=https://www.google.com/&httpsredir=1&article=1010&context=lrc_paper_series.

Patton, Stacey. 2014. "Between Postdoc and Job, a Whole Lot of Questions." *Chronicle Vitae*, July 30. https://community.chronicle.com/news/632-between-postdoc-and-job-a-whole-lot-of-questions.

Rhoads, Robert, and Gary Rhoades. 2005. "Graduate Employee Unionization as Symbol of and Challenge to the Corporatization of U.S. Research Universities." *Journal of Higher Education* 76 (3): 243–75.

Rose, Shirley, Lisa S. Mastrangelo, and Barbara L'Eplattenier. 2013. "Directing First-Year Writing: The New Limits of Authority." *College Composition and Communication* 65 (1): 43–66.

Sarachek, Sydney. 2015. "Arts and Sciences Council Makes Thompson Writing Program a Represented Department, Adds New Certificate Thursday." *Chronicle*, November 12. https://www.dukechronicle.com/article/2015/11/arts-and-sciences-council-makes-thompson-writing-program-a-represented-department-adds-new-certificate-Thursday.

Schooley, Diane K., and Debra Drecnik Worden. 2016. "Perceived and Realized Risk Tolerance: Changes During the 2008 Financial Crisis." *Journal of Financial Counseling and Planning* 27 (2): 265–76.

Scott, Judy. 2015. "PLU Decision on Faculty Unions Will Reverberate across the Country." *The Hill*, January 27. https://thehill.com/blogs/congress-blog/labor/230763-plu-decision-on-faculty-unions-will-reverberate-across-the-country.

SEIU Faculty Forward. 2017. "Transforming Higher Education. Movement Milestones and Victories: 2017 Victories." December 5. https://victories.seiufacultyforward.org/index.php/2017/.

Setrakian, Lara. 2009. "Flush with Cash, Arab Royals Pave Path of Modernity." ABC News, January 27. https://abcnews.go.com/International/AroundTheWorld/story?id=6383651.

Sproul, Curtis, Neil Bucklew, and Jeffrey Houghton. 2014. "Academic Collective Bargaining: Patterns and Trends." *Journal of Collective Bargaining in the Academy* 6 (1): 1–10.

Stancill, Jane. 2017a. "Duke Faculty Members Win Big Raises in Historic Union Agreement." *News&Observer*, July 12. https://www.newsobserver.com/news/local/education/article160915224.html#storylink=cp.

Stancill, Jane. 2017b. "N.C. College President was the Highest Paid in the Country." *News&Observer*, December 10. https://www.newsobserver.com/news/local/education/article189077639.html.

Trinity Administration. 2018. "Imagining the Duke Curriculum Committee." Accessed April 26, 2018. https://admin.trinity.duke.edu/arts-sciences-council/imagining-duke-curriculum.

Wessler, Seth Freed. 2015. "Your College Professor Could Be on Public Assistance." NBC News, April 6. https://www.nbcnews.com/feature/in-plain-sight/poverty-u-many-adjunct-professors-food-stamps-n336596.

Wilson, David McKay. 2004. "Dylan Lauren '96. Sweet Inspiration." *Duke Magazine*, January 31. https://alumni.duke.edu/magazine/articles/dylan-lauren-96.

Yates, M. D. 2009. "Why Unions Still Matter." *Monthly Review* 60 (9): 18–28.

Xie, Abigail. 2016. "Proposed New Curriculum Features Duke Experience Seminar, 'Credit/No Credit Option.'" *Chronicle*, November 8. https://www.dukechronicle.com/article/2016/11/proposed-new-curriculum-features-Duke-experience-seminar-credit-no-credit-option.

12
OFF TRACK AND SIDETRACKED

Seth Myers

I miss grad school. A friend of mine—we are NTT instructors, full time on renewable contracts—shares this sentiment, so we've formed an informal, irregular, beer-soaked reading group. Our first book, *The Nonhuman Turn*, edited by Richard Grusin (2015), represents a conference that brought together philosophers reworking ancient questions from a perspective that seeks to decenter or subvert human supremacy. The prose is by turns painfully, academically abstruse and radically playful. Our conversations about this book ranged from expositions on current hip-hop, my dog, his cat, teaching, gossip, food, family, friends, and places. There are—as posthumanism demonstrates—a lot of ways to be in the world and, by extension, a lot of ways to read and write and teach and talk.

The fundamental premise, as I see it, of the contemporary theories that inform the disciplines of composition and rhetoric is that simple distinctions between epistemological and ontological categories often serve the interests of institutions of power. The linguistic and social and posthuman turns explode, primarily, the ways Cartesian binaries hegemonically justify human institutions and by extension suggest that other oppositions might be just as specious. This is, I realize, such a broad generalization of some of the most complex writing produced by humankind that it ceases to be meaningful in any academic sense. And yet I offer this generalization because I continue to so powerfully feel the destructive pull of the old enlightenment binaries. No matter how happy I am in my teaching career, I still feel the institutional power afforded to the tenure track and the distance between it and me. As Liz Gumm eloquently narrates in this volume, the subtle and social hierarchies that exist between literature and rhetoric and composition, and the caste system of job titles, are more immediately obvious than any other aspect of this life. Our job titles make us feel lesser or ambitious or alone for reasons I'd guess are related to the histories of power in European colonial culture.

Ian Bogost writes in Grusin's collection, "Ideas become professionally valid only if written down. And when published, they are printed and bound not *to be read* but merely *to have been written*" (2015, 85). My purpose in this essay, simply put, is to narrate the way I've come to understand my career path as a lifeway, to make the writing and reading of the thing the thing itself. I want to let go of the idea that teaching is subordinate to research, that work is somehow outside life, in order to celebrate my experience and in that celebration argue for the importance and beauty of the work of literacy education. I want to offer my young NTT career as a far-from-perfect example of one that allows the intellectual, physical, and emotional space in which I can, paradoxically, more fully understand and put into practice contemporary theories of the body and affect.

Thus, this essay follows the formal leads of the posthumanists, especially Gilles Deleuze and Félix Guattari's *A Thousand Plateaus* (1987). The following is a collection of anecdote, quotation, autobiography, and cooking tips as an offer to you, dear reader, to have an experience of a set of thoughts to do with as you wish because with these words we will become what we already are: inevitably, perpetually, and holistically connected in mysterious and obvious, invisible, and practical ways for the rest of our lives.

THESIS

> Re-examine all you have been told at school or church or in any book, dismiss whatever insults your own soul; and your very flesh shall be a great poem and have the richest fluency not only in its words but in the silent lines of its lips and face and between the lashes of your eyes and in every motion and joint of your body. (Walt Whitman 1855, 622)

CAVEAT

Without citing the voluminous research on the topic, I want to recognize the huge discrepancies in workload, remuneration, and workplace respect I've personally experienced in my various academic communities. Although I am NTT faculty, I am a white, cisgender, heterosexual man, and among my many privileges, one is to witness the tangible and intangible inequities applied to certain intersections of race, gender, class, cultural background, and job title. This essay represents my recognition and acceptance of my experiences but does not apologize for or accept the unconscionable realities so many of us face. The fight must continue, and it must continue from a place of self-love and recognition of strength.

ANECDOTES

The aggrieved voice came from the back of the room: "What is the *telos* of a *writing* curriculum if it does *not* include the consistent and *microscopic* attention to the *sentence*?" The room shifted and psychically groaned, and I sensed I was witnessing the latest salvo in a likely decades-old debate. This was my first faculty meeting, and I was enthusiastically and confusingly both as sure and unsure of myself and my work as I have ever been. I was full-time faculty. I had had a PhD for about two months. I had been an adjunct lecturer at two community colleges, full-time staff in a support program at a small state school, a graduate student instructor and administrator, and now here I was at a large, flagship, R1 university in the Rocky Mountains in one of the most beautiful places on earth. And yet the pain of the job search and tenure-track rejection still throbbed.

The director of the writing program moved to change the subject. Introducing that year's cohort of new hires at all ranks, he referred to me, collegially, as Mr. Myers. I corrected him (the memory of my mortifying "Ahem, *Doctor* Myers" still feels like biting into grit in an imperfectly washed salad). The psychic groan grew. And then I was in; I was who I am.

But, oh, my dreams of the tenure track! Deep into the grind of grad school, I often had to scream the words of a text in my mind in order to maintain focus. I graded and planned my classes on the weekends between marathons of reading and writing. But those dreams kept me going. I could see so clearly my first book, the second job, negotiating teaching load, contributing to the body of teaching scholarship I was working so hard to consume. I imagined dinner parties and introducing myself as a professor of rhetoric and making everyone around me unreservedly, and without qualification, proud.

By my last year of graduate school, I gained a bunch of weight, I was drinking more than I should, and I was a bit of an emotional wreck. The spring in southern New Mexico is the most difficult time of year. The relative ease of the winter months gives way to relentless wind and a sun whose growing intensity desiccates the country. Dust and sand from the desert collect on interior window sills. I woke up with dirt in my hair and teeth. And that spring I was drafting chapters and on the job market and traveling for job interviews. I lived in a cheap apartment near the university, and it was fine except that you could see blue sky through the busted bathroom ceiling vent and one of my neighbors kept shitting in the shared laundry facility. I've always struggled with anxiety, but after the difficult end of a relationship and the suicide of a close friend, I was really in a rough place. I was inching closer, though, to those TT dreams of my ivory tower.

I interviewed for a TT job in New Jersey first and sweat through my three-piece suit while trying to figure out how much sushi to order and how to balance my conversation between collegiality and theory performance. I was rejected.

Then one in Iowa, where one of the tenured faculty (a lovely woman, kind and intensely smart) ordered a glass of milk at an upscale steak house. I laughed nervously and waved away the siren song of that third beer. I was rejected.

I had another TT interview in Utah, where I was told Mormons typically greet their new neighbors with canned goods to fortify basement reserves of nonperishables.

And then Lebanon. I left my cheap apartment, drove down to the airport in my crappy Corolla, trying to stay in the zone between 66 and 70 mph where it didn't shake too much, and took a plane to New York, and then Frankfurt, and then Beirut.

On arrival I saw signs of the civil war, of course, but the city is a tropical paradise. The streets heaved with cars and mopeds and pedestrians. I saw a man riding a Vespa, smoking a cigarette and talking on his phone driving the wrong way on a tight one-way street, swerving onto the sidewalk when he needed to avoid oncoming traffic. I walked the city's beautiful seaside promenade, and I bought coffee from a man squatting before a coal-fired samovar. There were Israeli warships on the horizon, and as the sun set, I heard the call to prayer. The next morning I began two days of interviews.

The campus visit went well, I thought. I talked about philosophy over endless plates of *mezze*, and I gave a teaching presentation in a room lit by a Mediterranean sun. I met with the provost in his office overlooking the sea. I took a tour of the campus museum and considered ancient Phoenician writing. I touched Roman ruins. I enjoyed my time.

And I made the mistake of checking my email before the last day's meetings and my flight back to the occidental desert. I'd been rejected by Utah, which aside from Beirut, was my last and best hope for a job. I struggled to swallow. My hotel room got hotter and smaller. I catalogued all the work, all the suffering, all the doubt.

On the red eye from Frankfurt to New York, I covered my face and wept for hours. Living in Beirut would be an adventure, but I was lonely, and after a life spent in search of my place in academia, I needed to find a home, and as wonderful as Lebanon was—and it really was—I could barely stand the thought of that now being my only option for employment and for my life. I lost it again when I got back in the Corolla, still hot from the scorching March day, to drive back to my empty apartment to have a drink and sleep in a dusty bed.

AUTOBIOGRAPHY

My parents are both academics now but have taught at every level throughout the course of my life. There's a photograph of mother, fit to bust with me inside, saying goodbye to her sixth-grade French class in London before my folks and I headed back to Colorado where they were from. That was, of course, before my parents took a job teaching in Japan when I was five. And before we moved to Texas for my mom's PhD in literacy education. And before her first job in southern California, and her second in upstate New York, and my dad's various spousal hires as an NTT writing instructor. We followed my mother's TT career around the country because we all believed in the goodness and potential of reading and writing and teaching.

I had a lot of practice moving boxes of books, and I began to feel more comfortable in classrooms—islands of refuge—than in the shifting landscapes around me. I began to feel like we existed outside time and place.

Philosophy

> The wisdom of the plants: even when they have roots, there is always an outside where they form a rhizome with something else—with the wind, an animal, human beings. . . . "Drunkenness as a triumphant irruption of the plant in us." (Deleuze and Guattari 1987, 11)

History

The institution of academia originated in the year 1155 ACE with the publication of the *Autentica Habita* by Frederick Barbarossa, Holy Roman Emperor, according to Walter Ullman in his *Scholarship and Politics in the Middle Ages* (1975). Barbarossa had waged a number of campaigns across the Alps to subdue the city-states of the Italian peninsula and saw the Vatican as the largest impediment to the expansion of his empire. Along with military victory, Barbarossa also saw the necessity of bureaucratic unity and solicited an army of scholars to study Roman Law at the University of Bologna[1] in order to justify his empiric ambitions. These scholars, of course, needed to make the journey across the Alps and through various and not necessarily friendly regions. The *Habita* gave these scholars the same protections that traveling clergy enjoyed and thus our institution of academia was born. As Ullman points out, "Infliction of injury on a scholar was at the same time an injury inflicted on the whole public weal" (111).

Barbarossa, according to legend, fell off his horse and drowned in a shallow stream because he refused to remove his full suit of kingly armor.

Fiction

> What I warn you to remember is that I am a detective. Our relationship with truth is fundamental but cracked, refracting confusingly like fragmented glass. It is the core of our careers, the endgame of every move we make, and we pursue it with strategies painstakingly constructed of lies and concealment and every variation on deception. (French 2007, 3)

Cooking tips

About a week after the Middle East trip, I baked my first loaf of bread. It felt like a miracle, and I ate the whole loaf when it came out of the oven after midnight, some of the warm slices with peanut butter but most simply dipped in olive oil. Amidst existential terror, I was full to the brim.

Ingredients
- 3 cups all-purpose or bread flour, more for dusting
- ¼ teaspoon instant yeast
- 1¼ teaspoons salt
- Cornmeal or wheat bran as needed

Preparation
1. In a large bowl combine flour, yeast and salt. Add 1 5/8 cups water, and stir until blended; dough will be shaggy and sticky. Cover bowl with plastic wrap. Let dough rest at least 12 hours, preferably about 18, at warm room temperature, about 70 degrees.
2. Dough is ready when its surface is dotted with bubbles. Lightly flour a work surface and place dough on it; sprinkle it with a little more flour and fold it over on itself once or twice. Cover loosely with plastic wrap and let rest about 15 minutes.

3. Using just enough flour to keep dough from sticking to work surface or to your fingers, gently and quickly shape dough into a ball. Generously coat a cotton towel (not terry cloth) with flour, wheat bran or cornmeal; put dough seam side down on towel and dust with more flour, bran or cornmeal. Cover with another cotton towel and let rise for about 2 hours. When it is ready, dough will be more than double in size and will not readily spring back when poked with a finger.

4. At least a half-hour before dough is ready, heat oven to 450 degrees. Put a 6- to 8-quart heavy covered pot (cast iron, enamel, Pyrex or ceramic) in oven as it heats. When dough is ready, carefully remove pot from oven. Slide your hand under towel and turn dough over into pot, seam side up; it may look like a mess, but that is O.K. Shake pan once or twice if dough is unevenly distributed; it will straighten out as it bakes. Cover with lid and bake 30 minutes, then remove lid and bake another 15 to 30 minutes, until loaf is beautifully browned. Cool on a rack. (Bittman 2014)

Anecdotes

I wasn't going to get a job in the United States it seemed, and after a couple of weeks without word, anywhere else. I had to restrategize my job search. I figured I was most attractive as newly minted, that my value lay in bright-eyed enthusiasm if not quality or clarity of research objectives. So, I was going to delay defending my dissertation for another year, even though I had run out of funding. I could, I figured, adjunct at my university and at the community college in town, defer loan payments, and go back on the job search. These options would mean more debt and more work, and my chair had taken another job, but these details were manageable. The heartbreak, the feeling of wasted time, and the failure were less so.

I had the adjunct application in front of me when Colorado called. One of their candidates backed out and they wondered if I could interview at Cs in Las Vegas, Nevada. I could. I did. They liked how I spoke about teaching, and they poked good-natured fun at my once-again sweaty three-piece suit. Not long after, I was an instructor. I bought a Colorado t-shirt online. My family was so proud. My dissertation seemed easier. The world returned to color, and I moved to Colorado.

In my first two years as an instructor, I was lucky enough to be one of the founding members of the Conference on Community Writing.

In the lead-up to the conference, I had been soliciting potential sponsors. One of those was a local, independent talk-radio station. One of their reporters had an interest in community literacy, it turned out, and in place of a cash donation, they offered an hour of on-air interview.

I went with two of my colleagues—one tenured, the other not—first thing in the morning. I was very nervous and very early and spent nearly half an hour sitting in my car, sun rising over the prairie, sweating and writing notes. During the interview, my colleagues exhibited the poise and intellectual dexterity of academics. Their answers easily translated scholarship into arguments and language appropriate for the audience. For my part, I repeatedly screamed "um" into the mic; I continually and audibly exhaled through my nose. There I sat, unable to do the thing I had so recently felt entitled to do. All those interviewers at all those schools were right about me, it felt like, and they were right to have called someone else to the ranks of the tenure track. Everyone who heard the interview was very nice, of course, but the fantasy that I'd be called back for another or nationally recognized for my acuity or genius had fallen away. The work remained in front of me, the work of teaching and exploration and service, but that reward, that something signified by *associate professor* or authorship or even minor academic fame flickered once again into fantasy.

The conference itself was a rousing success. The energy was huge; I was proud to be a part of it. After three days of hustling, the like of which I had never before experienced, I was attending and helping facilitate the final workshop. This was a capstone for the conference, and the large convention room was full. During this meeting, I ran around manically trying to solve problems and anticipate the needs of the different workshop groups, moving writing-pad easels, negotiating working markers, holding microphones, and the like. Towards the end of the ninety minutes, after the real work of the session had quieted, one of the prominent scholars—a dedicated and wonderful scholar, a true public intellectual—pointed me out and asked the room for a round of applause for me and for the rest of conference services for the work we'd done. All the work that I'd done, the thinking, the reading, the writing—all my intellectual contributions were made invisible or already were. I wasn't a producer of knowledge. I was a mover of microphones.

My mantra, after being rejected from the tenure track, is that such labels don't matter, that even though I'll likely never be a professor, I can still contribute to the field and find an improbable but therefore sweeter recognition for my work. I am free, I tell myself, from the nonsense of the institution, and that freedom will help reveal the quality in me that has been recognized and valorized since my precocious childhood. However sidetracked, my academic identity lives within me, a private flicker of light awaiting its fulfillment. I repeat this to myself as I move desks and tables, as I grade four classes' worth of essays on bright

Sunday mornings, when I buy dry-erase markers and sit in meetings. But I also think this mantra is simply wrong, that the light within me, within anyone, craves a recognition of a different sort, a recognition that moves through me and out and back from and into the world.

Religion

> How beautiful are thy feet with shoes, O prince's daughter! the joints of thy thighs are like jewels, the work of the hands of a cunning workman. Thy navel is like a round goblet, which wanteth not liquor: thy belly is like an heap of wheat set about with lilies. Thy two breasts are like two young roes that are twins. *Thy neck is as a tower of ivory*; thine eyes like the fishpools in Heshbon, by the gate of Bathrabbim: thy nose is as the tower of Lebanon which looketh toward Damascus. Thine head upon thee is like Carmel, and the hair of thine head like purple; the king is held in the galleries. How fair and how pleasant art thou, O love, for delights! (Song of Solomon 7:1–6 [King James Version]; emphasis mine)

Wikipedia

> The term ivory tower originates in the Biblical *Song of Solomon* (7:4) and was later used as an epithet for Mary. From the 19th century, it has been used to designate an environment of intellectual pursuit disconnected from the practical concerns of everyday life. Practically speaking, it means being disconnected from the reality of the everyday life of average people because one has spent too much of their time in intellectual pursuits. A person coming from an ivory tower has difficulty judging the actions of people and life in general outside of their environment. In American English usage it is also used as shorthand for academia or the university. (Wikipedia)

Anecdotes

The woman who would become my wife always wanted a dog. She'd grown up with the creatures; I hadn't. Just before the possibility of a pet became real, I got rid of the old Corolla I had in grad school (I donated the car to National Public Radio—at auction the thing brought like four hundred bucks) and bought a new (used) car that turned out to be kind of a lemon. I was determined to be less impulsive when acquiring big stuff. "We won't take the first dog we meet," I kept saying, though I suspect Beth knew different, that her childhood had exposed her to the peculiarly intoxicating joy of dog love.

In April 2016, I had just returned from Cs, where I acted as representative of the Conference on Community Writing, meeting luminaries and talking ideas and taking congratulations and where I felt important and small and tired and energized. Beth and I took the weekend to go camping in the foothills of the Rocky Mountains in Wyoming where Beth's from, where the land rises as prairie and falls away into mountains, where the rocks have been blown into impossible balance by the ceaseless wind. Two years later we would be married just there.

While we were out under that sky, Beth's mom found a dog she wanted us to meet. It was close to the end of the semester, and we had flights to the Yucatan booked for two weeks later. And it was Sunday night, and I was on the schedule for an online writing center job I'd taken because I could only barely pay my bills. We'd meet this first dog, and we wouldn't take her home, I kept saying. We didn't have time, I said, and we were about to leave the country.

And then we met Harriet. She was wild and cute and looked into my eyes and we became/always already were rhizomatically entangled. As I type right now, my empty breakfast plate is to the left of my computer and she has a paw on my right leg, waiting patiently for the inevitable breakdown of my rules.

Backpacking

The following is transcribed directly from my journal:

> 7/21/16—campsite by pond, mile 10.9 of segment 9 of the Colorado Trail—70 degrees—cool—threatening rain.
> ... And I just don't have space for how wonderful it's been to have Harriet with me, how everything that everybody says about a dog is true. How I wanted her near me as I was praying for mercy to all gods (God) who would listen (and did listen and spared me and Harriet a lightning strike though we kind of foolishly [but kind of also smartly] camped in a notch on the ridge after Searle Pass in what was clear but soon became clearly a big thunderstorm, me clutching the creature—who only wanted regardless of weather to chase marmots & pika & dig dig dig—filthy and wet to a dog degree, taking whiskey in gulps, counting after every flash, double counting of course, given that I was given to counting fast) and feeling certain death when the count was 2 one-thousand, but relief when it was higher, shivering in every stitch I brought, my food bag a pillow. Oh and that thunder, loud and close, while I searched the stitching patterns on the inside of my tent for a sign, the no-sign peals asserted what is the only sign. Over-written. The point is I was super scared, and when the rain stopped, I went outside and the dog was happy, and I was cold and wet, and I watched a cloud come in below me over the pass and disappear.

Anecdotes
Beth and I spent our honeymoon in Fiji. The nation is comprised of two large islands and near three hundred smaller ones, about fifteen hundred miles north and east of New Zealand. On our last night, back on one of the large islands, the Fijian mainland, we took a cab to Tu's Place, a Fijian restaurant famous for its traditional fare (we had huge plates of a delicate fish in coconut and lightly fried balls of Fijian spinach). The cab driver was the talkative sort, especially, I imagine, when driving two enthusiastic, curious tourists. Not a lot of Americans travel to Fiji, and he appeared particularly proud to talk about his home island, a two-day bus and boat journey away from where he was driving us.

It turns out he was a farmer back on his island, and that his farm and his home had been decimated by Cyclone Winston in February of 2016, one of the most powerful storms to make landfall in the South Pacific in the historical record. His story focused on the darkness. The power had been blown out, and just before the full strength of the storm took his house and his farm, he and his family sought refuge in a concrete cistern his father had built. He held his year-old daughter in his arms to keep her above the chest-high water and in perfect darkness embraced her near hypothermic body while she screamed and screamed and lived.

His island suffered no casualties, he told us, unlike others. Only the buildings—but all of the buildings—were destroyed. And he told us he had come to the mainland to drive a cab until he earned enough money to rebuild his farm. He drove a taxi on the big island for six months, he said, went home, and put in the foundation. He returned and drove for another six months before earning enough to put up the walls, and our fare would contribute to his roof. He missed his family, he told us, and his island and his farm.

We thanked him for his story, paid him, and went inside for a feast while he chewed the fat and smoked cigarettes with the other drivers outside under the Southern Cross in the humidity and vegetal scent of the tropics.

Fiction
> I am alive. I am a precious jewel. I am a drop of blood. (Atkinson 1995, 333)

Philosophy
> Fire does not exhaust the reality of cotton by burning it, nor does rain use up the glass that it moistens. (Harman 2009, 143)

CONCLUSION

Writing this essay has been a valuable if a little heartbreaking exercise. For so long I had such ambition to be an Important Scholar, and in writing this essay I'm realizing that what makes me important is not the recognition of some professional body or publisher or accolades from other corners of academia. As is so often the case, the more experience I gain, the more thought and work I put into this job and my career, the more I realize that achieving my ambition is to touch those mysterious crystals of pure life, to contribute to a community, to be and to promote and celebrate being curious and kind.

At the most recent Conference on Community Writing (October 2019 in Philadelphia), Carmen Kynard gave a rousing and passionate keynote address that, among many other things, highlighted the difference between what she called the "job" and the "work." As I understand it, the job is made of the weird anxieties around committee obligations, the obsession with job titles, the endless, pointless meetings, the stultifying emotional labor of pretending to be into something we're really not into. The work, though, is why we do what we do. This is the visually obvious moment of learning in a student's eyes. The work is the luxury of the community of scholars and teachers who help us in our various inquiries, the Friday afternoons spent drinking beer and talking about critical posthumanism. The work is all those moments that don't feel like work and seamlessly and effortlessly integrate with every other moment of teaching, learning, reading, and writing.

NOTE

1. The University of Bologna, founded in the late twelfth century, has a great website (https://www.unibo.it/en); their list of notable students includes Erasmus of Rotterdam. I follow their Instagram account.

REFERENCES

Atkinson, Kate. 1995. *Behind the Scenes at the Museum.* New York: Picador.
Bittman, Mark. 2014. "No-Knead Bread." *New York Times Cooking.* https://cooking.nytimes.com/recipes/11376-no-knead-bread.
Bogost, Ian. 2015. "The Aesthetics of Philosophical Carpentry." In *The Nonhuman Turn*, edited by Richard Grusin, 81–100. Minneapolis: University of Minnesota Press.
Deleuze, Gilles and Félix Guattari. 1987. *A Thousand Plateaus: Capitalism and Schizophrenia.* Minneapolis: University of Minnesota Press.
French, Tana. 2007. *In the Woods.* New York: Viking.
Grusin, Richard, ed. 2015. *The Non-Human Turn.* Minneapolis: University of Minnesota Press.
Harman, Graham. 2009. *Prince of Networks: Bruno Latour and Metaphysics.* Melbourne: re.press.
Kynard, Carmen. 2019. "'All I Need Is One Mic:' A Black Feminist Community Meditation on the Work, the Job, and the Hustle (and Why So Many of Yall Confuse this Stuff)."

Keynote at the Conference on Community Writing, October 17–19, 2019. Philadelphia, PA.

Ullmann, Walter. 1975. *Law and Politics in the Middle Ages: An Introduction to the Sources of Medieval Political Ideas*. Ithaca, NY: Cornell University Press.

Whitman, Walt. 1855. "Preface 1855—Leaves of Grass, First Edition." In *Leaves of Grass and Other Writings*, edited by Michael Moon, 616–36. New York: W. W. Norton.

Wikipedia. s.v. "Ivory tower." October 4, 2020. https://en.wikipedia.org/wiki/Ivory_tower.

PART IV

Next Steps

13
COLLABORATION AS ANTIDOTE TO NTTF PRESSURES

Nathalie Joseph and Norah Ashe-McNalley

Though NTTF's embrace of collaboration is a widely observed fact, it is not often the focus of discussion or academic research. In this chapter, we suggest practical methods by which NTTF can start and sustain professional collaborative relationships and also present our own long-standing two-person collaboration as illustrative of some of the ways these relationships arise. In addition to collaborators having a good foundational relationship so they can build a professional partnership, positive administrative support and a department culture of partnership have a significant impact on specific collaborations.

We work at a large R1 university where the majority of the general education classes are taught by non-tenured teaching faculty, who generally teach three or four courses a semester. In other institutional contexts, both tenured and non-tenured faculty may teach similar or even higher loads. Our discussion regarding work sharing applies across a range of tenured and non-tenured contexts that emphasize teaching. Commonly, a collaborative approach characterizes much of the service and committee work teaching faculty perform within their home departments: developing coursebooks, designing new courses and curricula, developing departmental rubrics and other teaching materials, conducting teacher training, and more. In acknowledging the high workload associated with teaching-track appointments, we also want to be careful in exactly how we approach these examples of service work. Many contributions to our individual departments and fields are examples of successful and fruitful collaboration that is often highly rewarding, but much of it can also be underpaid, somewhat unstimulating, and even leave faculty feeling unappreciated.

For many non-tenured writing faculty in particular, the opportunity to work collaboratively with other compositionists has become an antidote to the high service-work component of academia. Faculty collaboration

DOI: 10.7330/9781646420759.c013

can make the work not only manageable but also intellectually and personally rewarding. Collaboration allows for a sharing of not just the academic labor of teaching and publication but also the emotional labor of time management, meeting student needs, and balancing the increasing demands of teaching-track work. While the investment required to cultivate a strong collaboration can itself be a form of emotional labor, the reciprocity it involves helps nurture not only that relationship but also the professional and personal rewards it can produce.

UNLIKELY ORIGIN FOR A SUCCESSFUL FACULTY COLLABORATION DUO

Our own collaboration began as a somewhat forced moment, though we are lucky it has developed into something far better than its strange beginnings. We are both associate professors of writing who have been working at the same institution for over fifteen years. When one of us was assigned to join an existing project on an undergraduate journal, the other had to make sure we were both up to speed on the overarching goals of the publication. The then-director of our program literally suggested the partnership in a brief hallway pause, and though we were well aware of one another's presence in our rather large rhetoric department, we certainly didn't know each other outside an occasional conversation about assignment design or class-session pacing. In taking on a collaborative approach to the undergraduate publication, we seized an opportunity to shift the progress of our university service (an explicit part of our contracts, as we explain later). We actively committed to a duo model in terms of many areas of service, as well as our academic research, and have now been successfully maintaining that partnership for nearly a decade.

At present, we collaborate on an online undergraduate journal (*Scribe*), a journal-aggregator project known as *Conduit*, conference presentations, and publications. Essentially, the bulk of our nonteaching work—the work that identifies us among colleagues in our field and builds our identities—is done as a pair. Our conference and publication work often discusses undergraduate publication, assignment design, teaching pedagogy, and the dynamics and effects of faculty collaboration. Piece by piece, we have expanded our interests as a pair, and if a topic intrigues one of us, we find a way to be open-minded about the possibility of our own commitment to that pursuit. This work of drawing individual interest into the collaboration rather than engaging in it alone (or in parallel formation) speaks to our faith in one another's abilities but also to our faith in the efficiency and productivity of this dynamic. Intriguing work is often complicated work, and faculty collaboration eases the burden and weight, making it possible to explore complex ideas with more depth and to commit to higher numbers of projects.

When our thought processes align, we are that much more motivated and forceful when creating forward momentum in our projects. When they don't, we have been able to pick up the slack for one another while also politely requesting tasks of the other when we know those tasks fall within the person's forte. In terms of work allocation, we maintain a strong sense of responsibility to one another. There is an underlying expectation of honorable behavior, pulling one's own weight, making up for the other person when she is overly taxed at any given time; the rule of thumb is to be cautious with critique and generous with praise, acknowledging that any temporary conflict is simply that—temporary. But, the challenges we encounter shift as we move through our academic careers. With one of us currently in a more administrative role, serving as writing program director, finding the time and energy to work on our joint scholarly and student-publication projects has proven to be tricky.

THE SHIFT TO PROMOTIONAL TRACKS

Our own personal shifting roles, across faculty positions and administrative ones, are an indirect result of larger institutional shifts regarding the positionality of teaching-track faculty. Over the past decade, universities and colleges have faced increasing pressure to address significant wage discrepancies for NTT and teaching-track faculty on an institutional level. Reports both inside and outside academia began to shine a light on the academy's overreliance on underpaid and unsupported adjunct faculty to provide an ever-increasing share of undergraduate instruction, particularly in general education courses like languages, mathematics, and composition (Shulman et al. 2016). The most glaring inequities were associated with adjunct faculty teaching at multiple campuses. These faculty perform their duties without sufficient compensation, office access, teaching supplies, and more. While the need for equitable pay for college faculty is often acknowledged on many fronts, the path towards implementation can pit the pragmatic concerns of NTTF about wages, benefits, and working conditions against the vaulted institutional interest of the academy. R1 universities tend to link pay and promotion to a strong research profile and demonstrable indicators of academic "excellence"—elements traditionally limited to tenure-track-professional files. As a result, successful policies for promoting better working conditions for NTTF have tended to appeal to these same sorts of institutional values—scholarly work, research, conference presentations, and publication. Tailored promotional tracks for NTTF can provide some measure of compromise between these viewpoints.

Undeniably, reducing the reliance on "freeway flyers," part-time adjunct faculty who teach the same general education courses at several campuses, is a valuable first step. But, shifting NTT faculty from part-time to full-time positions does not adequately address concerns about low wages, low morale, and lack of institutional support for research and professional development (Shulman et al. 2016). As Steven Shulman et al. (2016) write, "It is becoming clear that improved employment security alone is not an adequate substitute for tenure" (19). At R1 universities, tenure-track lines are generally privileged with higher salaries, higher raises, and more funding for research and professional development (both internal and external). As an institution, academia has a vested interest in preserving the tenure hierarchy precisely because of these benefits. This rigidity has serious implications for writing instruction, as NTTF teach most of the writing on university campuses, from 75 to as much as 95 percent (Lamos 2016, 363). While promotional lines have reduced the marginalization of teaching-track faculty, the attendant demand to cultivate a strong professional profile alongside one's teaching can often feel like tenurization without the benefits of that title. In their 2015 study of changing university guidelines around NTT, Daniel Maxey and Adrianna Kezar note that "poor working conditions and lack of support" continue to "create suboptimal conditions for teaching and learning" despite the shift towards promotional lines (568). Some teaching-track faculty complain that the more professionalized NTT model exacerbates some of the very problems it is designed to mitigate, notably the problem of unpaid and overburdening academic work.

The contracts that govern NTT appointments are centrally related to why this paradox persists. The specifics of contracts tend to differ based on the type of faculty appointment, such as teaching- versus research-track or promotional versus nonpromotional NTT. However, generally speaking, NTT teaching faculty have a contractual obligation to devote between 75 and 100 percent of their time to teaching, depending on whether or not they are on a promotional track. Contractual support for service is a good thing, but the promotional track can often require a professional and research profile that goes beyond teaching and service. In order to move up the available promotional track, faculty members must perform more work atop their existing contractual obligations to the university. Universities often expect teaching faculty to cultivate a robust research and publication profile while maintaining a heavy teaching load and to perform well in each of those roles without one giving way to the other. This is another area where collaboration can serve to ameliorate the time and stress of NTT work by providing the support and burden sharing of a productive partnership.

COLLEGIALITY AND COLLABORATION

On top of the need to develop a professional-service profile, the time burden for writing and composition faculty is particularly pronounced. Student conferencing, grading, providing commentary on drafts, and paper mark-up are all time-consuming work. Although there are tools that can be used to reduce some aspects of the workload, such as grading software, the person-to-person interaction at the heart of composition instruction takes time and energy to nurture. The benefits of a student-centered, workshop-style classroom also contribute to these noble goals but are similarly time consuming and energy draining. One means by which our own program has managed to lift some of these burdens is through a strong culture of collaboration amongst the faculty and support for that collaboration within university governance groups.

It is true that there are many aspects of teaching—chiefly, key areas like grading, office hours, and conferencing—for which the workload is not readily shareable. In our program, some relief arrives in the form of frequent discussions about assignments, materials, and best practices—elements of our work shared formally through mentoring of new faculty and coordinator positions that oversee the various composition courses. Because of the collegial nature of our department's culture, informal conversations offer further valuable opportunities for support. Interestingly, when some members of the program expressed anxiety about this culture of sharing best practices, stating concerns that others were "stealing" their work, the response was surprisingly united and supportive—ultimately arriving at a resolution that satisfied all parties. There is now a program-wide practice of acknowledgment and attribution when "borrowing" or building upon someone else's teaching materials—a fitting approach that follows the example of citation and general acknowledgement of the intellectual property of others. In our department, this informal practice of collaboration has contributed to a culture of collegiality we have come to value deeply and that has laid the groundwork for our own sustained collaborative duo over the years.

While academic collaboration in the humanities is no longer seen as uncommon, it continues to fly under the radar, unlike the life and social sciences, business, or professional schools, where it is institutionally valued. Nevertheless, there exists a large body of writing—much of it written collaboratively—on the value of academic collaboration in composition studies. Lisa Ede and Andrea Lunsford (1990, 2001) have chronicled both the rising prominence given to collaboration in the humanities and the theoretical underpinnings of such work. As collaborative work has come to take on a more central role in composition studies, it no longer can be seen, as Elizabeth Ervin and Dana Fox (1994) once suggested, as a revolutionary challenge to traditional academic institutions. Nevertheless, it remains political insofar as it proves an effective strategy for addressing institutional shortfalls. In all our research, study after study argues for the value of collaboration, both formal and informal, as integral to academic work, and for the need to promote more institutional support for collaborative research and publication in the humanities (Baldwin and Austin 1995; Ervin and Fox 1994; Lee and Bozeman 2005). Sooho Lee and Barry Bozeman's study on research collaboration touts the value of such work, particularly in terms of productivity. While they suggest the evidence may not be as clear cut as it appears, they nevertheless demonstrate that researchers who collaborate more often on their work tend to be more productive in terms of the number of publications they produce (2005, 689). This finding is particularly poignant academia; publication in particular remains an integral measure in faculty promotion. Seen in that light, academic collaboration can increase the productivity of faculty looking to develop a more robust professional profile and ultimately move up the available promotional ranks.

But, beyond the somewhat utilitarian goal of increasing productivity, academic collaboration offers meaningful occasions for the kind of intellectual engagement necessary to sustain us. Whereas the sometimes draining work of conferencing and grading can contribute to faculty burnout, the opportunity for deep and intense conversation about the work we do can renew our personal investment in the work of teaching. Moreover, faculty collaboration can expand opportunities for new and creative course design, or open up opportunities for interdisciplinary work. Collaboration can also help ameliorate the emotional labor of our work. Many aspects of our work are not formally recognized or "seen" by department chairs, deans, and upper levels of administration, nor are they easy to characterize on the documents we use to create that visibility, such as curriculum vitae and teaching and service statements.

In particular, much of the mentoring work we devote to undergraduates is explicitly omitted from our departmental dossiers: mentoring during office hours, writing recommendation letters, advising, and referring students to other faculty in order to further their academic work. As Steve Lamos notes, writing faculty put a great deal of emotional labor into cultivating a positive atmosphere in their classes around the work students must invest in their classes, "making writing processes themselves (especially processes of critically attending to issues of audience, of form and genre, and of editing) feel good and right and natural" (2016, 365). Working alongside each other, we as faculty can see and affirm for each other the work we are doing. Building a departmental habit of acknowledgement can go a long way toward making individual faculty feel as if that work is seen, appreciated, and recognized for its influential impact. Beyond that, cultivating a culture of collaboration promotes faculty supporting faculty in ways that can nurture and support student mentoring; in that sense, collaboration doesn't necessarily have to only take place in organized pairs or pods but can be actively incorporated into a department so intrinsically that it informs much of faculty interaction. We recommend our colleagues' courses to our students, or one student's work for publication to someone and another student for an internship to another.

CULTIVATING COLLABORATION

Our department is a large, independent writing program entirely made up of NTTF. The majority of our instructors are on a full-time promotional track (80/20), with some part-time faculty on yearly, renewable 100 percent teaching contracts. Anecdotally at least, the absence of tenured faculty is often cited as one of the reasons there is such a notable feeling of collegiality in the program. Faculty in our writing program have a strong sense of being in this thing together, and the distinctions between promotional ranks are not belabored. But, we must note that the lack of tenure reduces, but does not remove, the problem of intradepartmental marginalization that stems from institutional hierarchy. Part-time faculty on 100 percent teaching contracts do not have the same institutional support for teaching materials or individual professional development as do tenure-track faculty, nor are their contracts supported by multiyear appointments. As studies show (Maxey and Kezar 2015; Shulman et al. 2016), such a lack of material support has implications for morale, faculty performance, and career progress. One partial solution we have frequently observed amongst our departmental peers has been collaboration, especially between promotional-track and part-time members.

We are also fortunate that our program strives to diminish another potential source of conflict—that between the WPA and teaching faculty. In many universities, having a tenure-track faculty member overseeing a predominately NTTF and/or part-time teaching faculty is the norm. One member of our own partnership is currently serving as the first faculty director of our writing program. When our longtime director, who had been administrative staff, retired, our program opted for faculty governance and decided we wanted the WPAs to be drawn from our own faculty. In the contract for this position, the 80/20 is reversed: 80 percent administrative or service and 20 percent teaching. Notably, professional development and research are not explicitly included, although if we want to make progress towards promotion, we must continue to work on our academic profiles. That progress toward advancement means finding creative and intellectually rewarding means of uncovering the ways administrative work is also a source of meaningful research and intellectual scholarship. As for how this has affected our own partnership, while there is excitement in discovering new areas of inquiry, the shifting of our appointment contracts out of sync—one more focused on teaching, the other on administrative work—can create hurdles to working together on even the most basic level, such as balancing time commitments and finding windows of time to work and plan as a team.

MODELS OF COLLABORATION

Collaborative writing offers its own set of distinct concerns and issues. In *Collaborative Writing in Composition Studies*, Sheryl Fontaine and Susan Hunter identify the production of language and knowledge as inherently collaborative (2006, 2–7). The authors compare writing collaboratively to the act of joining existing and ongoing conversations. As writers who have coauthored work collaboratively, their discussion resonates with us. Fontaine and Hunter's point is furthered by considering the roles of author and reader. When we write alone, we must imagine our readers and make some educated guesses about their existing knowledge base and what contribution from us would be most useful or relevant for them. In collaboration, the dynamic is more fluid, with each person oscillating between the role of the author (of our designated portion of a first draft, for example) and the reader (responding to both our own production and that of our colleague).

In collaborative writing, the work is easier because the reader (literally, the collaborative partner) is more real, available for interaction and input, but the work is also more difficult because we still must approximate the gap between our collaborative partner as a reader of our work and the invisible readers beyond that person. In "Collaboration and Concepts of Authorship," Lisa Ede and Andrea Lunsford consider the ways traditional notions about "the author" must be reconsidered, acknowledging both anxiety and liberation as possible side-by-side outgrowths of that rethinking (2001, 355). Though many scholars express potential for risked agency in collaboration, a duo model ironically affords us with an increased opportunity to be individually heard. It can also be a way to add to the number of venues our individual voices reach. Nonetheless, university reward structures are stacked against the decision to collaborate, as composition scholar Joseph Harris (2001) notes. Faculty collaboration not only reduces burdens but also affords us an opportunity to perform more prolifically as individually functioning scholars. Surely, the work of doing something together necessitates a steep learning curve, but that curve pays off in the reduced stress of taking on projects and challenges together.

In addition, it is worthwhile to be mindful of the ways collaboration can be vulnerable to hierarchies that undermine or undervalue the work of some participants and to always strive to correct or counterbalance such forces. For faculty, perhaps the smoothest partnerships are self-selected, often between equally ranking members with similar levels of seniority or between members who all share a specialization of field of interest. In our case, because our rank and status is the same, the power exchange can move back and forth as we take ownership of different parts of a project that interest us as individual scholars.

The productivity of each member of a duo also carries serious stakes, as the humanities is only starting to recognize that work done collaboratively is evidence of solitary faculty production. Though collaboration does ease the process of academic production, it is important to recognize that duo-driven work supports the value and merit of individual members of a department. If one can forge a successful faculty-collaboration unit and continue to grow one's individual skills within that dynamic, the possibilities for an eased burden of one's workload and increased pathways to promotion become real motivators. Geraldine McNenny and Duane Roen (1992) lament the situational issues caused by a composition and rhetoric faculty who are outnumbered by the literary scholars in their departments. They call attention to this underrepresentation as problematic given that more rhetoricians work in collaboration than literary scholars do (295–96). This issue places an undue burden on rhetoricians and compositionists to inform their literary-scholar peers of the value of working in faculty collaboration. Though literary scholars and rhetoricians are often housed in the same department, their roles necessitate different approaches. While the literary scholar can choose to work alone, the rhetorician advances an argument with an opposition or rebuttal in mind; in that sense, for the scholar of rhetoric and composition, the author doesn't write alone but always with an avatar of their potential reader in mind. Our entire department is not only teaching-track faculty—it is entirely made up of rhetoricians. This pedagogical focus on composition informs our other professional work to such a degree that we are always working in collaboration with our potential reader, if not with an actual colleague. As such, the theoretical space occupied by rhetoric faculty lends itself very easily to faculty collaboration among those colleagues.

COLLABORATION IN SERVICE VERSUS TEAM TEACHING

Ultimately, each duo must evaluate for itself whether the output of time is worth the potential benefits of teaching together. Generally, team teaching requires a significant time allocation, as well as a strong departmental infrastructure to support it. Speaking only for ourselves, our pedagogical interests and strengths aren't as well aligned as our overall professional ones, as we generally design courses for different disciplinary cohorts. Still, we use one another as sounding boards for new assignments and overall curriculum arcs, and at times, the other's lack of knowledge can become a powerful tool in checking for clarity and understanding in our work. On the other hand, while faculty collaboration can be a powerful source of renewal, there is something to be said for the intellectual time apart. Susan Cain, author of *Quiet*, an examination of the research into introversion and society, argues that there is a time and place for collaboration with one's colleagues and that an overemphasis on collaborative work environments or group work can actually hinder certain personalities and temperaments in their attempts to be optimally productive (2012, 115–29). For us, it's not that one of our personalities benefits and the other is hindered but rather that certain portions of our work are easier to do together and others to do apart. When we do work together, we are fresh and eager and can bring new discoveries we have been exploring into the collaborative. Without time apart to pursue our own pedagogical interests, it's possible the work done together wouldn't be quite so enriching. The time apart also affords us some reflection on our collaborative workflow; we are able to return to the duo with suggestions and realizations that often enhance and increase efficiency and productivity.

Nevertheless, in many ways, the professional collaboration we do with our colleagues can inform our classroom instruction habits as well. In prioritizing a student-centered workshop-style approach to the teaching of composition and rhetoric, there are a number of avenues through which our faculty collaboration might have bearing on our students. We might consider the implications of voluntary rather than focused collaboration for our group projects. We might rethink the evaluation structure of student work and consider how that might provide hints as to how to better position faculty duos in terms of climbing promotional ranking systems.

The faculty collaboration that encompasses all the rest of our professional work does inform our individual pedagogies in substantive ways. For example, the interplay and balance between teaching content and argumentation our courses demand of us can benefit from the practice of skills obtained through faculty collaboration. Working as a duo requires learning to be comfortable with receiving constructive input from another person consistently; in the classroom, the use of a workshop-style instruction method also requires the interplay of ideas between faculty member and student, and between individual students or student groups. This sort of give-and-take doesn't detract from the authority of the faculty member in the room but enhances the strides that can be made in argumentation. With each exchange of ideas, the original argument at hand can be strengthened. Whether in the classroom or during a work session, when constructive critique is readily available, the holes or weaknesses in any prospective argument are easier to see. The interplay of collaborative thinking creates opportunities for strengthening one's original point of view. With careful handling, one's voice isn't lost in collaboration but is enhanced and accompanied by another's.

FACTORS FOR SUCCESS

Though a social or personal relationship component isn't necessary for successful faculty collaboration, it does have its benefits. In their analysis of the values that undergird successful pairings, Roger Baldwin and Anne Austin acknowledge the frequency with which their respondents cited the friendships that "blossomed" from their professional collaborations (1995, 52). The better you know one another, the rarer the disagreements or problematic assumptions that can interfere with the productivity of the professional relationship. The ease of our friendship contributes to the success of our working relationship, but friendship isn't always a clear predictor of good outcomes. Searching for more fundamental underlying factors, Shawn Bohen and James Stiles identify five elements that promote success: "clear vision, leadership, institutional commitment, financial resources, and incentives/rewards" (1998, 46). Other contributors to success include professional courtesy (including an acknowledgement of the power of doing nothing/remaining silent), strong attachment, investment, a flexible allotment of time, awareness of individual strengths, and a willingness to pick up where the other person's abilities give way. In particular, professional courtesy can take both spoken and unspoken forms. There are moments when it's appropriate to directly acknowledge the other person's ideas or contributions and there are moments when the courtesy takes the form of essentially doing nothing and allowing the other person some time to take control and pursue something a bit more single-handedly. At times, one member can make a choice or pursue a line of reasoning they feel strongly about and the other person can be willing to take that expression of strong feeling as something that should be fully explored; essentially, the other person might cede control to facilitate a process by which that idea might be fully realized. That sense of strong connection can also be used to guide decisions about who puts a particular conference presentation slide together or who writes the initial draft of an idea down on paper in preparation for a publication.

Perhaps because a sense of strong attachment or investment guides the division of our workload, we are careful to make sure revisions are a shared responsibility. In making revisions to one another's prose, we must walk a line between creating strong transitions and fitting each section into the larger project at hand and not allowing our decisive editing viewpoint to override the other's point of view. We must be mindful about not accidentally imposing our own voice over the voice of our partner. That's a much more difficult task in terms of the self-discipline required than it initially seems. Given that we have taught rhetoric for many years, it's easy for each of us to imagine ourselves as purposeful editors and legitimate guides of someone else—namely our students—as they explore argumentative prose. While that training in careful diagnostic reading is relevant to our collaborative work, we must remember not to recreate the classroom power dynamic in our working relationship with one another. We want to enhance, to help realize, to push further but never obliterate or damage or silence. It is delicate work to balance gentle critique of one another's work with the necessity of supportive feedback that both encourages and elicits engaged future contribution. Recalling Lamos (2016), this is some of the affective labor of collaboration. Part of this approach involves an awareness of one's impact on the other person's prose and voice (which is an active mindset), and part of it is also simply pulling back to not dominate the text. In many ways, it's as much about what we don't do as it is about what we do choose to do.

Logistical considerations also play a role in the success and sustainability of faculty collaboration. Establishing a productive duo takes time and patience on both sides so the relationship can progress in an organic fashion. Of course, parallel to this development is the growth of each individual member as an increasingly more knowledgeable and influential scholar in their own specialized field. As we mature as faculty in our own right, we bring stronger capabilities to the duo. The collaboration feeds our individual professional identities and vice versa. After the initial work of getting the dynamic up and running, faculty collaboration can ultimately do much to enhance and further the speed of contributions made to one's department and the field. Attention to even small tactics can aid this process. For example, working for short stretches of time that require smaller commitment in our schedules is easier, and we find we are significantly more productive if we work in a focused manner for a short period of time rather than in a multihour meeting. In addition, at the end of a working session, we often come to an agreement about the next time we'll work together. At times, this scheduling is dictated by an upcoming deadline; at others, it is simply motivated by moving various projects forward. Because time is at such a premium, scheduling consistently and well in advance ensures collaboration takes a position of priority in our working and personal lives.

As a tool, faculty collaboration is powerful and far reaching. For us as long-time members of our department, it has minimized the risk of faculty burnout and overload. It has brought a renewed interest in new challenges and made meeting those challenges less daunting. We can take on more complex and more frequent projects because we know there's a supportive colleague in place who will face those difficulties and share the workload with us. Our collaboration has become a way to make our work fresh again at a variety of intervals throughout our careers and to renew our eagerness for research and discovery. Though it is easy to become settled in one's teaching approaches and service identities, collaboration doesn't allow us to become comfortable with everything staying the same. It makes approaching research exciting precisely because it promises a fruitful partnership in uncovering the discoveries that await.

REFERENCES

Baldwin, Roger G., and Anne E Austin. 1995. "Toward Greater Understanding of Faculty Research Collaboration." *Review of Higher Education* 19 (2): 45–70.

Bohen, Shawn Jacqueline, and James Stiles. 1998. "Experimenting with Models of Faculty Collaboration: Factors That Promote Their Success." *New Directions for Institutional Research* 1998 (100): 39–55.

Cain, Susan. 2012. *Quiet: The Power of Introverts in a World That Can't Stop Talking.* New York. Broadway Books.

Ede, Lisa, and Andrea Lunsford. 1990. "Rhetoric in a New Key: Women and Collaboration." *Rhetoric Review* 8 (2): 234–41.

Ede, Lisa, and Andrea Lunsford. 2001. "Collaboration and Concepts of Authorship." *PMLA* 116 (2): 354–69.

Ervin, Elizabeth, and Dana L. Fox. 1994. "Collaboration as Political Action." *Journal of Advanced Composition* 14 (1): 53–71.

Fontaine, Sheryl L., and Susan M. Hunter. 2006. *Collaborative Writing in Composition Studies.* Boston: Thomson Wadsworth.

Harris, Joseph. 2001. "Meet the New Boss, Same as the Old Boss: Class Consciousness in Composition." *College Composition and Communication* 52 (1): 43–68.

Lamos, Steve. 2016. "Toward Job Security for Teaching-Track Composition Faculty: Recognizing and Rewarding Affective-Labor-in-Space." *College English* 78 (4): 362–86.

Lee, Sooho, and Barry Bozeman. 2005. "The Impact of Research Collaboration on Scientific Productivity." *Social Studies of Science* 35 (5): 673–702.

Maxey, Daniel, and Adrianna Kezar. 2015. "Revealing Opportunities and Obstacles for Changing Non-Tenure-Track Faculty Practices: An Examination of Stakeholders' Awareness of Institutional Contradictions." *Journal of Higher Education* 86 (4): 564–93.

McNenny, Geraldine, and Duane Roen. 1992. "The Case for Collaborative Scholarship in Rhetoric and Composition." *Rhetoric Review* 10 (2): 291–310.

Shulman, Steven, Barbara Hopkins, Robert Kelchen, Sharon Mastracci, Mehmet Yaya, John Barnshaw, and Samuel Dunietz. 2016. "Higher Education at a Crossroads: The Annual Report on the Economic Status of the Profession, 2015–16." American Association of University Professors. *Academe* (March–April 2016): 9–23.

14
COLLABORATION IS CRITICAL, BUT FURTHER CONSIDERATIONS ARE NEEDED FOR NTTF

Heather Jordan

As this collection illuminates, labor practices and expectations are changing across the academy. In this collection, Nathalie Joseph and Norah Ashe-McNalley discuss publication being the prominent marker for promotion in the academy—and what that means for NTTF specifically—and they demonstrate the importance of professional partnerships and collaboration for sharing the multifaceted labor load of NTTF in their department, which is staffed entirely with NTTF. Although their department's makeup does not entirely eliminate the institutional hierarchy, Joseph and Ashe-McNalley recognize it does help to create a culture of collaboration, which has been mutually beneficial for them.

What I hope to offer in this chapter is a furthering of that recommendation for collaboration as a way to learn and grow, and share the workload, but I also think it's important to be explicit about the power dynamics always in place in the academy. My contribution here is that of a doctorate-holding NTTF member in an English department at an R2 midwestern university with a faculty union. Our department is comprised of nearly 40 percent faculty who are tenured or on the tenure track, and the rest are contingent faculty. We certainly have faculty in our department who would agree with those in Liz Gumm's contribution in this collection who prize literature above composition and believe anything less than a tenure-track faculty line in literature would be considered Plan B, but they are certainly in the minority. In fact, our department's only remaining doctoral program is in rhetoric and writing studies, and teaching composition is definitely Plan A for those graduates, as it was for me when I was on the job market nearly a decade ago.

DOI: 10.7330/9781646420759.c014

JOB-MARKET REALITIES

We can learn a lot from just one look at the job market, as the MLA Job Information List and higheredjobs.com reveal that the limited jobs for R1 or R2 tenure-track positions with research and publication expectations often have more administrative duties and teaching requirements than those of even a decade ago. For example, back in 2010, a person on the job market for a tenure-track faculty (TTF) position could expect to be able to negotiate a 1/2 or 2/2 teaching load based on publication expectations and demands, but we are seeing more TTF jobs at institutions that require 3/3 and even 4/4 teaching loads or writing program administrator or writing center director duties on top of expectations to publish. And that is when those job openings even exist, as we know TTF lines are decreasing in favor of either full-time NTTF positions or part-time adjunct-faculty labor. The data from the American Association of University Professors reveal that "at all US institutions combined, the percentage of instructional positions that is off the tenure track amounted to 73 percent in 2016, the latest year for which data are available" (AAUP 2018). This trend is significant and does not seem to be going anywhere, so it is important for us to consider the implications if the academy hopes to sustain itself. As prominent labor scholar Seth Kahn states, "A sustainable ecology can't survive without addressing threats to its health and can sustain itself positively and healthily with care, trust, and good faith. More directly—unethical labor practices are threats. Refusing to be honest with new members of the field about the current conditions of the academy and the field is a threat" (2015, 117). My hope is that this contribution is read with care as a good-faith effort to open up dialogue about the inequity that threatens our sustainability so we might take steps toward improving the landscape rather than so many of us feeling as if we've been caught in a landslide.

Acknowledging the Hierarchy, NOT the Meritocracy

First, I clarify that as a full-time faculty member, I recognize and acknowledge I have advantages many of my adjunct-faculty colleagues do not simply because I am employed full time. I have insurance, retirement contributions from my institution, and a regular, renewable contract that provides some employment stability not only semester to semester but also year to year. And, I at least recognize these advantages puts me in a more privileged position than many highly qualified others because one area that threatens our sustainable ecology is the belief in the myth that the academy is a meritocracy. It is not.

This idea of meritocracy is certainly not the case for all tenured and tenure-track faculty. I have absolutely met countless tenured faculty who genuinely believe they are somehow more qualified or have more credentials—that they are better than I am—because they were fortunate enough to land a tenure-track position. I even have a former faculty mentor from my PhD-granting institution who, when she found out my husband and I accepted NTTF positions near family instead of doing a nationwide search and moving to where the TTF jobs were, abruptly ended our conversation at the Conference on College Composition and Communication (CCCC) and went on to talk to the recent graduates who were willing to move much farther south or west than we were, and who, as a result, landed the coveted tenure-track positions. And, to be fair, my husband and I were the first graduates from our institution who elected to limit our search for personal reasons and therefore ended up off the tenure-track line—this was back in 2010–2011, right after the market had taken a hit—but I certainly felt her dismissal. (And, that I feel such a need to include this, to somehow still offer a reason for our NTTF jobs beyond a terrible job market, is indicative that I, too, have been trained up in the narrative.)

Many tenured faculty like to give credence to this myth of meritocracy, and for good reason. They get to be the chosen ones. They can believe themselves to be "exceptional" (Kahn 2020). Though some may not consciously agree, as tenured faculty and labor activist Seth Kahn further notes, "I'm not queasy about the claim that the protections of tenure are important. . . . But when we claim them unto ourselves and don't fight for them more broadly, the practical effect is the same: we sound like we're declaring ourselves exceptional, and thus shouldn't be surprised when others think we're being self-aggrandizing and arrogant" (2020).

And, because their positions at institutions often mean training the next generation of potential tenure-line faculty, those faculty (consciously or not) tend to perpetuate the myth that if someone earns their doctorate and doesn't get a tenure-line position, they are somehow not as qualified or they are somehow less than. To address this misguided belief, I want to point to the above job-market statistics and to remind those faculty who actually believe the meritocracy myth that there are many reasons fully qualified, innovative faculty are taking non-tenure-track positions. Gumm's chapter in this collection offers further support for this real problem in the academy, and the effects are further reaching than our bank accounts, though a closer look at the monetary compensation differences is very telling.

Living with/in Tension: Demonstrating the Value of Non-Tenure-Track Work

As a non-tenure-track faculty member, I am not afforded nearly the same job security as my tenured colleagues, and I am certainly not afforded the same amount of respect across campus (the meritocracy myth is powerful), nor equal compensation for my work. Though the work I do may look a little different, the amount of labor, investment, and time demanded of me is certainly at the same level (if not higher in some cases), but the financial compensation I earn for my education and dedication to the field, and for my labor, is significantly less than most of my colleagues. And, I am not referring just to my tenure-track and tenured (TT/T) colleagues.

Recently, I happened to read John Warner's January 26, 2020, post to the Insider Higher Ed blog *Just Visiting*, "Equal Pay for Equal Work: Calculating 'Fair Pay' for Teaching—Introducing the Teaching Labor Wage Gap Calculator," in which he uses numbers from Clemson to provide a model for how institutions of higher education might provide more equitable financial compensation for their teaching faculty. The idea is to divide a tenured professor's salary by the number of courses assigned per year and then multiply that by the expected workload contribution of teaching (most tenured faculty are expected to devote 40 percent of their time to research and scholarly publication, 40 percent to their teaching, and 20 percent to service) to determine how much money they are earning per course they teach. His calculations are that a tenured faculty member gets paid $8,700 per course—$3,050 more per course than the average course wage ($5,750) would be if using his Teaching Labor Wage Gap Calculator. When one considers that the national average for adjunct writing faculty is $2,700 per course (Kahn 2017), the overage is even more appalling.

Still, I must admit that the more articles written and the more people who take up this important work, the more encouraged I become that one day the system of academia will become a more equitable landscape for all its faculty. Of course, that is, until I read the comments on the Warner post and I am reminded this is an uphill battle that will not soon be over.

As "The Shift in Promotional Tracks" section from the Joseph and Ashe-McNalley contribution in this collection points out, NTTF (what they call "teaching-track") lines often come with an 80/20 or 75/25 workload designation for which 75–80 percent of a faculty member's time is supposed to be dedicated to teaching efforts and 20–25 percent of their time is for service, and this is certainly the case for NTTF at my institution (I am on an 80/20 contract), but they acknowledge and unpack the paradox this designation creates when there are tenure-track faculty who have different workload expectations. Their chapter demonstrates what really has value in the academy, and it offers a corrective: publication for advancement on the promotional track.

But, emphasis on publication is precisely where ours is a field that muddies the waters, so to speak. Much of the research we do in our field is pedagogical research, so if we NTTF start regularly publishing on top of our more demanding teaching loads, how are we any different from our TT/TF colleagues (other than doing similar work for less pay)?

Like many of my tenured colleagues, I often set an alarm for early-morning work sessions. My work isn't always crafting a submission for publication, but it is often focused on providing substantive feedback to the multiple student projects and essays that crave encouragement and a new perspective. Or, I rise before the sun (and my own son) to rethink or rework an upcoming lesson or assignment to help further a student's understanding.

I, too, consume meal after meal in front of my laptop screen, but my meals sometimes occur with a student onlooker as I am trying to squeeze in another writing conference and the only time I could carve out happened during my body's need for nourishment.

I, too, frequently find myself in impromptu one-on-one meetings with students, but mine are often the fast-paced walk-and-talk as I'm leaving one class to scurry across campus before my next class session begins.

Once a student literally followed me into the restroom because she still had questions (and I had bodily needs), and I know I am not alone in this experience. I am quite certain this behavior (though circumvented with a simple "Please. I am going to need a moment") occurs across both tenured and non-tenure-track lines.

Recently, I ran into a fellow non-tenure-track faculty member in that same restroom. She is a newer faculty hire, someone I really would like to know better. I had done an observation of her online summer course, and whenever we meet, which always seems to be when we are taking that quick, but necessary, bathroom break, we mention the desire to grab a coffee sometime. In one exchange while washing our hands nine weeks into our fifteen-week semester, we wondered what this illusive free time is because it simply does not exist for us. And, the explanation for this reality is that I simply cannot even find time in my schedule to meet a colleague for coffee. Some of us on the non-tenured track still have aspirations of landing a tenure-track gig, or we notice inequity and want to fight for our fair share, so we're filling every free moment with our words, knowing that what really holds value in the academy is publication.

The demands on our time as university faculty are significant, and there simply are not enough hours in one day to accomplish it all. For any of us. As Jimmy Butts reminds us in his entry in *Bad Ideas about Writing* titled "The More Writing Process, the Better," "Time is our most important non-renewable resource" (2017, 109). Though Butts is reminding us here that we need to rethink our love affair with a long, drawn-out process when it comes to writing and just focus on getting the writing done, his words have resonated for me in other areas of my life. I, too, have been regularly working twelve- to fifteen-hour days, and that includes time on the weekends. Just because I don't always have published work to show for it does not mean work isn't happening. The work of teaching is different, but it is still valuable.

And, this is not to say TTF workload demands are not also increasing while institutions fail to replace and rehire TTF lines, so I do not want to misrepresent or mislead here because I know they are feeling the burden as well, sometimes even more so. To their credit, many of my TTF colleagues are stepping up where they can and are taking on overloads and doing the additional labor just now required in our department because they really don't want to exploit their less compensated colleagues.

But an associate professor friend of mine on Twitter recently remarked she wishes she had the energy of an assistant professor again, and that thread revealed what is known as "the crash of the associate professor," who, once tenure is official, often exhales for the first time in a decade. Many commented that there is nothing like job insecurity to keep one motivated. And they are absolutely right. So, I gently reminded them to advocate for their NTTF colleagues who will never have the privilege of knowing the crash of the associate. As more and more of us find ourselves on NTTF lines, fewer and fewer of us get to exhale. Or, if we do, we risk our livelihoods.

The very real lived experience of an NTTF member is that even with a faculty union, we must always be performing. NTTF are expected to do a lot more than just teach; we are expected to do so by using some of what scholar Adrianna Kezar (2012) deems to be high-impact practices (HIPs), and, although Kezar's work does shine a light on some real lived experiences of NTTF in higher education institutions (because there often is limited funding and time for professional development, and student evaluations really do contribute significantly to job security), it devalues those of us NTTF who are engaging students in HIPs by making use of our campus resources, seeking out faculty mentors, and regularly participating in professional-development opportunities, all while risking less-than-optimal student evaluations. More important, Kezar's recommendations merely serve to increase the uncompensated and often invisible workload demands of NTTF who are already overworked and significantly underpaid.

Administrative Oversight: The Trickle-Down Effect

As state and federal budgets continue to cut funding to higher education, the need to secure and justify those ever-decreasing dollars becomes increasingly more important, which often leads to some additional administrative requirements of faculty, like student-success reports or other student-monitoring programs. And, I understand the idea behind programs that serve to link current-semester faculty members with a student and their advisors because such programs would seemingly open up communication and provide a bit of a safety net of support for a student who might be struggling; however, the programs often ask a faculty member to write notes on attendance and class performance or to share any other kinds of concerns that might be of note, tasks that take up a significant amount of a faculty member's time. Also, many faculty already make the additional time to talk with students before or after class, or email them directly to open up conversations, so adding in an additional layer of administrative paperwork is repetitive, at best. Requiring a report of concerns to other campus resources, even when they are in a centralized location, becomes just one additional element in already busy days.

Last semester, for example, I issued an early alert on several students who were having some difficulties. One such student had disclosed to me that he was trying to get his accommodations transferred from high school to our university, so I clicked a radial button on a form indicating that a nonacademic concern was affecting the student and explained in a detailed note that I wanted someone from the office of accessibility services to follow up with him. It had taken a significant amount of trust for the student to disclose his learning disability to me, and my goal in issuing the alert was only to help put the support in place for him, but what happened was that an official email from my institution was emailed to him, requesting that the student email me immediately. The boilerplate language caused the student to panic, so I spent much of the day trying to reassure him he was doing fine and that I was just trying to get others to help him with his concern. I thought I was dousing a fire with water in an attempt to extinguish a flame and had unfortunately grabbed the gasoline instead.

The reality with these mandated administrative programs is that they fail to consider I am already a much better front line of engagement with the students in my courses than some boilerplate language emailed out to them. My emails are personally addressed with empathetic language and understanding.

I know more than my students' names.

I know them through their writing, which means I often know whether they are missing their beloved childhood pet, are homesick for grandma's lasagna, or are having trouble maintaining that relationship with their significant other from high school—the relationship they thought was going to last forever but isn't even going to last until Thanksgiving.

I am a safe zone for those who are learning who they will be and who they want in their future relationships.

I listen to their heartbreak, and I offer reassurance that they will be okay. Better than okay.

I email them and follow up when they miss my class because I am an actual person who cares about them as people new to our institution of higher education, and I get the opportunity to hear about the many ways they are learning about life, both in and out of the classroom.

The boilerplate directives of these administrative oversights often only serve to dismantle significant strides I have made in building trust with some of the students. If students are struggling, they need to know we care about them and their success. This knowledge will have more bearing on their decision to stay at our institution than some automated system of checks and balances ever could, especially when the automation just kicks the student back to me. If students are not reading the emails I am sending them directly, the automated emails are only going to pile up in their inbox alongside mine. This particular administrative mandate really is just additional busy work.

But this task is not where the administrative busywork ends. We enter multiple midterm grades and end-of-term assessments, and this may not seem like a lot of work initially, but the more students one is teaching and the more places there are to report information on those eighty to one hundred students, the more the work really does begin to add up. And because time is not a renewable resource, it must come from somewhere. I often get too little sleep, and by the end of the semester, my husband and I are often back to just grabbing unhealthy fast food or ordering takeout because we simply do not have the time or energy to cook a healthy meal and then also clean up the mess cooking inevitably creates. Our house is a disaster by finals week, and we then spend time on our breaks between semesters trying to put it back into some order so we can do it all again the very next semester. We are still struggling with making self-care a priority, but I am certain many educators can relate to this story.

Other Administrative Decisions: The Effects of Increasing Class Sizes

As a faculty member who was hired back in 2011, I have felt the burdens on faculty increase incrementally over these past nine years. When I started, our first-year writing courses were capped at a maximum of twenty-three students, but in the spring 2012 semester, they were actually capped at twenty students per course. CCCC has written a clear position statement that serves to highlight recommendations for maximum enrollment numbers in writing courses. It reads, "NTTF workloads should be limited to a maximum twenty students per section of first-year and/or advanced composition courses and a maximum fifteen students per section of basic (or 'remedial') writing courses. Generally, NTTF should not teach more than three sections of such courses per term" (Conference on College Composition and Communication 2016). Given these guidelines in our discipline, spring 2012 was a dream come true according to the course caps because they were held at twenty students each; however, the additional recommendation that might be easier to overlook is that these courses should be limited to three per term. And, this recommendation is significant because best practices assumes a maximum of sixty students who are doing writing-intensive work in any one semester.

Even during that dream semester of spring 2012 when the courses were capped at a reasonable twenty students per class, I taught four sections, which adds up to eighty students. And these classes required five total essays, each with the expectation of multiple drafts and revisions and cheerful encouragement from the instructor. Currently, course caps here at my institution have only increased and are already significantly higher than best practices, at twenty-five students per course. When compared with that semester in spring 2012, if I was assigned to teach the same courses again, I would essentially be teaching one more course than I did in spring 2012 because five additional students have been added to each of those four sections. And, this increase means that rather than having a maximum of sixty students taking a writing-intensive course during any semester, we full-time NTTF have one hundred students each semester who are writing multiple drafts that demand and deserve our feedback. I know this is a ubiquitous argument that is rendered meaningless to those in administration who are looking at the bottom line, but it has a significant effect on the teachers of those courses, and our lives are not meaningless.

LIVED EXPERIENCES AS AN NTTF: OUR MULTIFACETED LIVES

During any ongoing academic semester, I am busy providing feedback to students, rethinking a day's activity, contemplating a new assignment based on where I'm noticing the students are struggling, meeting with students in conferences and during office hours, and doing important committee work that is itself a significant labor demand. And, I have added this publishing goal to my agenda simply because at my core I am a writer, and when writers have something to say, we find a venue for our work.

I am a writer, but also, like fellow writing compatriot Anne Lamott, a Presbyterian, so I do take time on Sunday mornings to gather with my family at our local church. Beyond my Sunday morning ritual that represents my Christian identity, I am also a daughter to aging divorced parents, one of whom lives two and a half hours away. When my husband and I earned our PhDs back in June of 2011, we drew a circle with a six-hour drive radius from the area where we met in our master's program and only applied to those jobs. By limiting our search, we knowingly limited our career opportunities, but we wanted our son to have memories with his extended family members. Earning our PhDs in a remote location made us realize the importance of being able to drive back to our hometowns for a weekend visit. This academic year has reaffirmed for me that I did make the right choice, as my father learned in October of a cancerous tumor that decided to take up 60 percent of his bladder and that his aortic aneurysm was dangerously close to rupturing. Dad is recovering from multiple successful surgeries, and I am grateful for my laptop that travels those two and a half hours with me on weekends. Faculty have family, too.

And to think this academic year is somehow unique on the demands of our lives seems to negate and invalidate other roles I claim as part of my identity. As a mother to a young son who was being bullied by a classmate when he was only a first grader, I recognize my job does afford me some flexibility to take him to counseling appointments and the capability of advocating to get him transferred to a different elementary school within our district, but watching a once-engaged, school-loving little boy become a sullen, downtrodden six-year-old does take an emotional toll. In the years that have followed, the residue of first grade remains, so we continue our counseling and rephrase our negative self-talk, and

Mommy tries to carve out and reserve those precious after-school hours so her son knows he matters and is important and that he has value.

And yet, he still has to ask me to put down my phone when I'm trying to quickly respond to a student email or to get off my laptop and help him build a new Lego world because those work-life demands creep up and invade and take over even though we fight like hell to box them in and keep them contained.

THE CHANGING LANDSCAPE: FORGING A PATH FORWARD

This brings me to the "turn" as it were because administration is not hiring more TTF, or more full-time faculty for that matter, and we really must just get the required work done. We are being asked to remain current in a field that is continually improving and rethinking and growing and shifting, but we NTTF are given very little, if any, time to do that important reflection and engagement with the current research required of us to improve. So how do we do this important work? And, what is the effect of this shifting terrain on the future of our discipline?

Potential Reciprocal Relationships: Graduate Students and NTTF

I first learned of this collection from a (now former) graduate student in our on-campus doctoral program. Although I am not doctoral faculty, I was regularly making time to connect with these engaged scholars in an effort to build our department community, and because these students are reading the most current scholarship in our field, as an added benefit to these relationships, I was able to learn from them. I learned an immeasurable amount from my interactions, conversations, and friendships with these students. And, because I was never in a position of any authority over their degree completion, I was able to interact with these students in a different manner than my TTF colleagues can.

We built relationships and went to the movies and had writing days at Panera, and I even invited them to our family holiday party. I considered them my friends, and ultimately, by attending their grad lectures, their prospectus talks, and their dissertation defenses, I learned more about current scholarship in our field. Because I ended up counting many as friends, they sent me articles they thought would interest me based on conversations we'd had or ideas we had discussed. That was a critical step because I no longer had to sift through all the journals to learn the contemporary information on contract-based grading, for example, when I had access to graduate students who were so generous with their resources.

Our tenure-track faculty are top-notch, but they are busy rising to the new demands their own roles and positions require (and they rarely interact with NTTF since none of us are in their rhetoric and writing program), so learning from the graduate students who were enrolled in their courses became like sitting in on only the days of a graduate seminar that were most meaningful to me at a particular moment for my teaching or other responsibilities.

Believing as I do in reciprocity, and recognizing the vulnerable position I have always been told a graduate student is in because of the system that exists in academia, I absolutely looked for ways to give back. I provided feedback when requested, I collaborated on teaching materials, I wrote letters of recommendation, and I tried to help defer costs of conference travel by offering to carpool or by sharing a hotel room. And, I helped prep them for the job market by providing texts and faux interviews and advice.

Then the landslide happened.

My graduate student friends did their nationwide searches and got their tenure-track jobs, and I really and truly couldn't be happier for them. They worked hard, and they will make so many contributions to the field, and I am really proud of them.

But, then they left.

Their lives are elsewhere now, and even though they did land the tenure-track jobs, they are crafting new syllabi and learning their own new landscapes. Their teaching loads are higher than their mentors' were, and I know how exhausting that can be. I fear the landslide may be coming for them and their own students because they too will be under pressure to publish or perish while teaching ever-increasing numbers of students. I feel left behind a bit because my own sense of academic self was nurtured by the give-and-take and collaboration with graduate students and friends, and I fear that as NTTF, those chances won't come up often without building a system that rewards that kind of collaboration and sharing rather than relying on an ad hoc system of friendship. In other words, if I know it is a good thing to work with graduate students and share knowledge, why can't the system of academia more proportionally reward that? The problem is that if I want that kind of knowledge building and mentorship, I must do it myself.

The Uphill Climb

I took this job because I wanted to be close to my family. That hasn't changed, and with my dad's health, I doubt it will.

But, that doesn't mean I still don't feel the residual shame of being on the nontenure track. Being just a teacher.

Just a teacher. As if that isn't enough? What is so wrong with being an excellent teacher? Why must I consistently be devalued by my own institution and reminded I am less than because I am on the nontenure track? Why must I be reminded that my job is always at risk, that one misstep could lead to a dismissal?

As educators and scholars, we know we learn from others, whether that be by reading their published contributions in journals or collections such as this one, or through participation in portfolio-assessment groups, like the teaching circles Dauvan Mulally explores in this collection. When I first saw the call for contributions to this collection, I was excited to share my experiences working with graduate students in our PhD program because I genuinely thought it could be a potential resource for interested NTTF. Now I think it's more important than ever that we are explicit about these power dynamics and a landscape that has already changed.

Finding (and Maintaining) a Proper Support System

As NTTF, it is imperative that we each practice self-care. For example, although I often feel as if I am failing at being a parent, I am in a very privileged position to have a spouse who completely understands the demands of my job since he holds the same NTTF position at the same institution where I work, and he teaches primarily writing classes just as I do. But the workload demands can take their toll.

Because parenting is a tag-team effort, when one of us has silenced their cell and is trying to build a Lego train that stretches the length of our living room to make a little boy's dreams come true, the other one is naturally using that time to be productive and to attend to the other learners in our lives that require our time and attention, our students. It takes real effort for my husband and me to spend any kind of quality time together from August through May, but we are learning the importance of doing so. We mistakenly thought graduate school was going to be the hardest part of our academic lives. In those rare moments when our conversations move from texting each other grocery lists or food orders and we do get to actually talk with one another, we're usually so exhausted we reminisce about our graduate-school days and about how much free time we used to have. This isn't to say we weren't extremely busy and productive during our years earning our PhDs. In fact, those were some of the hardest years of our life together. It's all about perspective. It got harder in many ways.

But we still have each other.

And I recognize that for the gift I have been given.

The academic system currently in place is not sustainable. The myth of meritocracy is pervasive and corrosive, and it quickly turns a collaborative community into a competitive rivalry in which students who once supported each other become cutthroat contenders for the handful of dream jobs available every year.

And I will always be the NTTF who remains behind.

Clearly, there are many reasons NTTF take the positions they do, and gaining insight and understanding into who makes up this growing faculty cohort will hopefully get more access to representation in faculty senates and within departments and more overall equity and respect. We may not experience the crash of the associate in terms of a career trajectory, but many of my NTTF colleagues genuinely crash for at least a week or two once grades have been submitted each semester. Our bodies break down into sickness, so we swallow our ginger tea and orange juice and sleep when we can because we know the start of the next semester is just around the corner. And we often have much to do to prepare for that still.

REFERENCES

AAUP Updates. 2018. "Data Snapshot: Contingent Faculty in US Higher Ed." *AAUP*, October 11. https://www.aaup.org/news/data-snapshot-contingent-faculty-us-higher-ed#.W9Aw6flRf.

Butts, Jimmy. 2017. "The More Writing Process, the Better." In *Bad Ideas about Writing*, edited by Cheryl Ball and Drew M. Loewe, 109–14. Morgantown: West Virginia University Libraries Digital Publishing Institute.

Conference on College Composition and Communication. 2016. "CCCC Statement on Working Conditions for Non-Tenure-Track Writing Faculty." Conference on College Composition and Communication, April. http://cccc.ncte.org/cccc/resources/positions/working-conditions-ntt.

Kahn, Seth. 2015. "Towards an Ecology of Sustainable Labor in Writing Programs." *WPA: Writing Program Administration* 39 (1): 109+.

Kahn, Seth. 2017. "Redux: Contingency Is Still Worse." *Here Comes Trouble*, May 12. https://sethkahn.wordpress.com/2017/05/12/redux-contingency-is-still-worse/.

Kahn, Seth. 2020. "Tenure Isn't the Problem; Exceptionalism Is the Problem." *Here Comes Trouble*, January 25. https://sethkahn.wordpress.com/2020/01/25/tenure-isnt-the-problem-exceptionalism-is-the-problem/?fbclid=IwAR1Nvs3UGJAC86UjG4DxHl1eGSmo6DHEkPwUD8yXusTQeLci4eJaMAKGfos.

Kezar, Adrianna. 2012. "Toward High-Impact Non-Tenure-Track Faculty." *Peer Review* 14 (3): 31.

15
FACULTY COMMUNITY BUILDING
Portfolio-Assessment Groups as Teaching Circles

Dauvan Mulally

NEW-TEACHER STORY

The first time I taught composition was the fall of 2000. Fresh out of my master's program I was hired to teach first-year writing. At twenty-four, I was nervous about the challenges I would face as a new instructor. As I stared at a stack of syllabi and a list of textbooks, my eyes glazed over, and panic set in. Attempting to play it cool, I thanked the chair for his recommendations and scurried to the office I shared with five other people. I had one week to prepare a syllabus, develop assignments, and figure out how to teach writing. I tried to quell the fear by reminding myself that I possessed an English degree and had worked as a writing consultant, so I would be fine. But it turned out I was not fine.

I watched as the other faculty buzzed confidently around the department discussing their great assignments and making photocopies. I was too scared to ask for help because I did not want to be perceived as green, or worse, incompetent. On the first day, I was convinced the students could smell my fear. Twenty-eight pairs of eyes stared intently at me. The clock's slow-moving hands finally read 2:00, and it was time to start. I composed myself long enough to stammer out my name and let students know I would be their teacher. I imagined the agony of spending the semester figuring out how to teach composition. It was going to be a case of trial by fire, a solitary rite of passage I assumed most teachers faced.

Fortunately, I did not have to go it alone. After my initial terror, I discovered I would have help. My writing program required faculty to participate in weekly portfolio-assessment groups to set community standards for evaluating student writing via grade norming. Comprised of two veteran NTTF, two tenure-track professors, and me, the newbie, my group was quite diverse, from pedagogies, specialties, experience, and faculty rank to where we taught and where we attended school. These

DOI: 10.7330/9781646420759.c015

meetings were the first real interactions I had with colleagues since starting my job. I feared these meetings would expose me as a fraud because I was pretending to be something I was not—a teacher. Sensing my anxiety, they shared horror stories from their teaching days. "Don't worry," Anita advised. "You'll get the hang of it! We've all been there."

Over time these meetings became more than grade norming for me and the others. We shared tales of our lives inside the classroom, dialoguing on curriculum and trading teaching advice. My involvement in the group reassured me that my concerns were not unique and that I was not alone. We, veterans and novices, were learning to become better teachers together. The support I received from my group was invaluable during my first semester and every semester thereafter. Unfortunately, all too often the collegial scenario I experienced does not occur for many instructors teaching composition today.

STATEMENT OF THE PROBLEM

Despite calls from the Conference on College Composition and Communication (CCCC), the Modern Language Association (MLA), the National Council of Teachers of English (NCTE), and the Two-Year College English Association (TYCA) to provide NTTF with opportunities for dialogue in a professional community, the lack of communal exchange is still a problem. A consistent complaint I hear about teaching in higher education today is the lack of community. I first became aware of this issue after enrolling in a low-residency composition/rhetoric doctoral program. In speaking with numerous NTTF from my cohort, I discovered that countless writing teachers work alone without the benefit of a professional community. Yes, there are department meetings but few occasions to converse with colleagues on what is happening in our classrooms. In response to our conversations, I created an informal focus group to learn more about NTTF experiences teaching first-year composition at two-year community colleges, as well as four-year state universities and private colleges. NTTF interviewed were part-time and full-time instructors not on the tenure track. Their institutions categorized them as adjuncts, instructors, or lecturers. Several NTTF in the group reported feelings of isolation, longing for a sense of community, and receiving little support for faculty development from their colleges and departments.

Unfortunately, the amazing happenings occurring in these peers' classrooms remained there, solely witnessed by the instructor and students. Many NTTF interviewed expressed an interest in discussing teaching-related matters with colleagues. However, teachers in the focus group described how tenure systems, faculty rank, curriculum, specializations, and schedules make such interactions difficult. They admitted being starved for conversation about teaching writing. Such comments not only highlight our desire for collegial exchange but underscore how rarely professors come together locally to dialogue about our mutual interest—the teaching of college writing. Teaching should not be done in isolation; it should be a collaborative process for the good of teachers, students, and writing programs.

LACK OF COLLEGIAL EXCHANGE IN WRITING STUDIES

The literature on collegial exchange among composition teachers is a narrow thread in writing studies. A search through *College English* and *College Composition and Communication* reveals little scholarship. Bill Hendricks notes that in "mainline journals, writing about writing teachers' talk about student writing has never been a staple" (2009, 237) except for *Teaching English in the Two-Year College*'s "Instructional Notes," *College English*'s new "And Gladly Teach" feature, and the now-defunct *CCC*'s "Staffroom Interchange." Former *CCC*'s editor Deborah Holdstein further puzzles over how a field that once prized pedagogy has "less and less publication about teaching now . . . we no longer have the Staffroom Interchange section that was an assumed part of CCC, which was the opportunity to talk about 'what to do in class on Monday morning'—'Here's how I teach this; here's a new way to do that'" (2011) The profession, and its teachers, is starving for pedagogical conversation. Heather Jordan's chapter in this collection also ponders how the discipline has allowed teaching to become so devalued. Holdstein, like Jordan, feels we have lost our emphasis on pedagogy and that there are few academic spaces for teachers to share what is happening in their classrooms.

TEACHING REMAINS A SOLITARY ACT

The same silence that seems to pervade the discipline's journals has also carried over into English departments and writing programs. In "Working Alone Together," Hendricks comments on the lack of collegial exchange occurring:

> Our real work, or part of it, is teaching composition, every semester. One might expect, then, that we would have rich and ongoing discussion of what we are doing in our composition courses. That we for the most part

do not have these conversations is for me more than a trivial annoyance; the virtual silence in which we bathe ourselves feels like waste, the diminishing of our working lives. (2009, 235–36)

The virtual silence is evidence that for many NTTF, teaching remains a solitary act. This trend persists on campuses nationwide, as teaching continues to be perceived as an individualistic, self-directed, and sequestered event. Shari Stenberg and Amy Lee (2002) note that writing studies works out of what Louise Wetherbee Phelps calls an "ethic of radical individualism" that positions the composition classroom as a private place (1991, 866). Teachers may partly believe that what they do in their own classrooms is so distinctive it cannot be usefully evaluated or productively talked about with others. Another reason may be that writing teachers generally come to their careers with limited training or teaching experience besides disciplinary content and employment as a teaching assistant (Myers and Kircher 2007). According to NTTF in my focus group, this lack of instructional experience and training makes instructors wary of asking questions, seeking help from colleagues, and opening their classroom to others. As a result, NTTF may feel displaced within their departments and disconnected from tenure-track peers. Some teachers I interviewed also reported feeling invisible in their academic units and discussed how those feelings of marginalization hurt their self-esteem and drastically diminished their success as educators.

LACK OF TEACHER DEVELOPMENT

The lack of conversation across the discipline around these issues is critical to note because NTTF now comprise much of the academic labor in higher education. The American Association of University Professors (2017) reports that full-time non-tenure-track and part-time faculty make up nearly 60 percent of instructional appointments. Within the last ten years, however, scholars have amplified calls to support NTTF positions as a viable career path that no longer treats these faculty as professional underlings (Baldwin and Chronister 2001; Kezar and Sam 2010). But no matter how competent and devoted, NTTF are impacted in the performance of their duties by a lack of collegial support. Many remain isolated within the academy due to a lack of access to professional communities.

Despite their growing numbers, most NTTF are not provided with the training they need to be successful educators. Ultimately, many rely upon themselves to learn how to teach through trial and error. Capturing this frustration, a college instructor in a study on teacher development lamented, "From the day I entered this place to right now, you sort of figure out how you're gonna teach yourself" (Grubb 1999, 49). Further, few NTTF have had more than a single course in composition or writing pedagogy (Beech and Lindquist 2004; Stenberg 2005). This was essentially the case for me and NTTF peers in the focus group. Therefore, they turned to other means to learn how to teach writing.

Due to their lack of training in composition/rhetoric, many must rely upon recollections of how their favorite college instructors taught or draw on their own experiences as teaching assistants (Richardson 1997; Stenberg 2005). A few NTTF in the focus group detailed how they were handed a textbook and sent off to teach. With no training and/or mentoring, they let the textbook do the teaching. Some utilized books and professional journals to glean information, but Margaret Marshall notes NTTF have limited time for the "reading and study that would add to their knowledge base" (2008, 426). Additionally, many NTTF I interviewed admitted being unaware of journals in the field before pursuing a PhD. A small number attended conferences, departmental in-service meetings, or generic faculty-development programs offered by their institutions. Several focus-group participants reported a lack of access to professional-development initiatives at their universities because, they intuited, their departments did not seem concerned about their growth as teachers. Much has been written about the deficit in professional development available for NTTF and the importance of ongoing faculty development across ranks (Daniell et al. 2008; Schell and Lambert Stock 2001). In response to the lack of teacher-development opportunities, several NTTF from the focus group had turned to informal means.

Almost all NTTF interviewed recalled utilizing informal exchanges with others to assist with course construction, assignment development, and assessment. Hendricks's study found "teacher-to-teacher connections seem at all times in the last four decades to have flourished in a culture of informal professional exchange" (2009, 246). This contact usually transpires in hallways, at the copy machine, in the parking lot, and even in restrooms. Those I informally conversed with regarded these exchanges as valuable ways to see the classroom from other perspectives. Nearly all used these casual conversations to talk about their students, classes, and teaching approaches. Nathalie Joseph and Norah Ashe-McNalley's chapter in this collection discusses how informal collaborative practices at their institution contributes to a culture of collegiality and further highlights that teachers need time to talk with other teachers in local settings.

DISCIPLINE'S CALL FOR TEACHER COMMUNITIES

A growing body of scholarship has called for the creation of communities dedicated to examining the local contexts in which teaching occurs. Scholars report the use of a range of teacher communities (e.g., teaching circles, graduate-assistant meetings, department teaching conferences, informal mentoring, and writing groups) to promote discussion and mutual respect building within writing programs and/or departments (Davis, Provost, and Major 2009; Good and Warshauer 2008; Marshall 2008). While these communities take different forms, they remain centered on collaboration, inquiry, reflection, and community building. For instance, some programs have implemented portfolio-assessment groups (PAGs), which bring faculty together for conversations around teaching and grading. At Grand Valley State University (GVSU), my home institution, groups of four or five teachers read samples of student writing throughout the term to discuss and agree about what is an A, B, C, D, or F paper. The goal is to set fair and accurate grading standards by discussing samples from all the members' classes during the semester. This agreement between two professors on the portfolio grade constitutes the bulk of the student grade. This collaborative approach encourages the development of community standards for letter grades and allows students to self-select which papers represent the bulk of their portfolio grade. This grade-norming process continues until the end of the semester when PAGs exchange portfolios for final grading. Faculty coach students through the term as they draft and revise papers for possible inclusion in the portfolio. While often a veteran teacher or two keep the group on task, there is no recognized group leader, and all voices are expected to be treated equally. Officially, GVSU's PAGs exist to norm grading. Unofficially, they become teaching circles for instructors to reflect on their own teaching and that of their colleagues.

PORTFOLIO-ASSESSMENT GROUPS AS MODERN-DAY TEACHING CIRCLES

Although researchers (Alleman and Haviland 2017; Morrison 2008) have addressed aspects of collegiality and the isolation of NTTF, more scholarship is needed. While the informal focus group I conducted confirmed NTTF's desire for more collegial exchange in writing studies, I needed to investigate further. A limited number of studies have fully explored the communal relationships forged among teachers in PAGs (Broad 2003; Hamp-Lyons and Condon 2000). Therefore, I studied three PAGs to gather richer descriptions of teachers' experiences. Data were collected by observing weekly PAGs, conducting interviews with fourteen faculty participants, and studying program documents and teacher journals. Employing multiple methodologies (i.e., observation, journals, fieldwork, field notes, interviews, and cultural artifacts), I developed a comprehensive understanding of PAGs and their impact on teachers. During fieldwork, I took notes, audio recordings, and analyzed teaching artifacts (e.g., syllabi, journals, assignments, grading rubrics, textbooks, handouts, etc.) were analyzed.

Interviews were conducted with participants and institutional artifacts (e.g., website, mission statement, etc.) were examined over a fifteen-week semester. Teachers spent half an hour each week journaling about their PAG experience, which averaged seven hours per person. Each of the PAGs' sixty-minute, weekly meetings were electronically recorded. Ten norming sessions per group were recorded for a total of over thirty hours of audio. Transcripts from PAG meetings, journals, and participant interviews were transcribed and coded. I ultimately determined that the use of PAGs in my institution's writing program supported NTTF learning, promoted collegiality, counteracted faculty isolation, facilitated teacher development, and contributed to department community building. Furthermore, the findings reinforce the importance of NTTF dialoguing with colleagues about shared professional work.

This data-driven study based on teacher stories calls us to rise above factors that limit time and space for NTTF to get together. As reflected in this study, I, as well as my NTTF colleagues, have benefitted from PAGs. The findings address how participants (i.e., seven affiliates, four visitors, and three adjuncts) talked about their teaching within the PAGs. NTTF in GVSU's writing department include visiting, affiliate, and part-time adjunct instructors. Affiliates primarily teach in the first-year writing program on renewable three-year contracts. They teach full time on nine-month appointments and maintain twenty-four credit hours per year. Unlike part-time adjuncts, affiliates earn significantly more pay and receive health and retirement benefits.

Visitors receive three-year nonrenewable contracts and teach a full load of twenty-four credits in the composition program and the writing major/minor. They also receive salary and health benefits similar to those enjoyed by affiliates. Part-time adjuncts receive appointments to teach up to nine credits for a single academic semester for less pay and no benefits. NTTF are not eligible for nor do they accrue any credit toward academic tenure. NTTF are also not required to possess a terminal degree. Tenure-track faculty in the department teach eighteen credits per year and are focused on high-quality teaching with additional service and scholarship expectations.

MAKING TEACHING MORE PUBLIC

Participants reported using PAGs to make their teaching public and converse with colleagues about good professional practice. As some teachers in the study asserted, their lack of theoretical knowledge made it difficult at times to communicate with peers. They suggested this perceived deficiency makes some afraid to open their classrooms to observations for fear they will be negatively judged. Other NTTF described how they preferred to be in control of their courses and keep their teaching private. Veteran affiliate Clare suggested, "If someone sees teaching as private, individualistic, and isolated, then he or she probably also sees it as authoritative. Indeed, the whole classroom experience may promote a sense of hegemony since most instructors by necessity become little dictators when it comes to choosing what's read, when it's read, and how long the paper will be in response to what's read." Fortunately, by making the drafting and grading process more public, PAGs appear to help teachers relinquish their pedagogical privacy.

New visitor Sierra understands why this sharing of pedagogy can make some teachers uneasy but claims PAGs break down the privacy associated with teaching. Instructors often commented how PAGs made teaching public property rather than a private, isolated activity. Most participants claimed PAGs allow them to collaborate but still feel they are masters of their classrooms. Affiliate and former teaching assistant Michelle noted that "portfolio grading opens up the classroom to one's peers. It is part of the portfolio-grading process to become aware of what is taking place in the classroom of the group members." PAGs appear to challenge the notion of teaching as a solitary activity because of their collaborative nature. NTTF in the study appreciated hearing about what was happening in other instructors' classes and how transparent members were in sharing their teaching practices and concerns with peers.

The study findings highlight how the cooperative dynamic of PAGs seems to make teaching more reflective. Pat Hutchings (1996) maintains that teaching needs collegial exchange and publicness. Therefore, because their teaching was more public, study participants appeared to become reflective by examining their own practices through the lens of other teachers. Seasoned affiliate Bethany affirmed how "constructive [it is] to hear what assignments have succeeded and which ones were more to perform. Many reported how easy it is to fall into a teaching routine and permanently remain there. Affiliate Michelle stated, "With this grading system, I find myself forced to keep up with the current trends and constantly change my assignments and experiment with how I teach to become more effective." PAGs appear to encourage instructors to keep up with current trends in the field. Adjunct Mike emphasized that he relied on PAG members for updates on the latest developments in composition and recommendations on reading materials. Others, like veteran affiliate Felicity, indicated how PAGs led them to change assignments and experiment with how they teach.

Besides preventing stagnation and staying current, PAGs also appeared to keep instructors excited about teaching writing. Participants reported that teaching the same course every semester can be tedious. Visitor Sierra divulged that participating in PAGs "prevents burnout among seasoned professors and helps to regulate and educate professors who are new to the . . . process." Further, NTTF conveyed that PAGs were the primary way they stayed motivated to teach first-year writing. Seasoned affiliate Cynthia stated, "I usually feel encouraged and energized by my interactions with my group and motivated to put positive effort into my teaching." Teachers in the study indicated they felt participating in PAGs was a growth-enhancing experience. While their motivations differed, participants' overall goals seemed to be the same—they desired a professional space where they could learn from other educators and gain support.

Participants also described seeking out other teachers for advice on how to handle classroom issues. Long-time affiliate Clare suggested she found reassurance that "other members of the [portfolio] group face the same sort of classroom and work-related issues [she does]." NTTF described their biggest teaching challenge is often addressing a problem happening in their writing classrooms. In all three PAGs studied, I observed teachers discussing their struggles with various issues (e.g., student engagement, attendance, classroom management, etc.). They appeared to want counsel from colleagues on how to effectively deal with these situations. By commiserating with others, NTTF seemed to communally solve the issues they faced. The findings highlight how engaging in collegial problem solving serves as a valuable instructional practice.

IMPACT BEYOND PEDAGOGY

The results also reveal how participating in PAGs seems to provide teachers with a supportive community that offers more than pedagogical benefits. The collegial conversations in GVSU's PAGs appear to serve as an antidote to teacher isolation, promote collegiality, and motivate department community building. Much of the literature on developing strong teachers in higher education stresses faculty isolation as a major problem (Alber 2012; Hendricks 2009; Kezar 2005). In these scholars' studies, instructors reported feeling isolated from peers and receiving little or no professional support from colleagues. One of the current study participants helped crystallize this problem. Karen, a new visitor, commented, "Being a teacher can mean some very isolated days, even though they may be filled with classes; although you talk constantly to students, it's not quite the same interaction . . . the autonomy associated with this profession is one of its biggest challenges." Several NTTF shared prior experiences outside of GVSU in which they did not see colleagues for weeks, rarely met with others to discuss teaching outside faculty meetings, and in some cases were completely ignored by other professors. Many lamented that limited contact with other teachers made them feel marginalized. According to adjunct Phillip, "Teaching composition can be a slightly isolating experience; you only catch rare glimpses of what other instructors are doing, assigning, etc., in a few meetings a week or by snooping around the copy machine." NTTF participants noted they did not feel as though they were part of a community before participating in GVSU's PAGs and thus felt alone in their profession.

Seasoned affiliate Scott experienced this lack of connection with coworkers firsthand while teaching at another college: "I would go to colleagues' offices to ask questions and was repeatedly told they did not have time to speak with me. They were 'too busy' to give me five minutes of their time. Their responses made me feel like I was alone in the department." For study participants, this treatment often led to lower job satisfaction and poor morale. Rebecca Alber (2012) found seclusion from colleagues caused teachers to feel worthless, alone, or even unhappy. Instructors in Alber's study were often cut off from a valuable learning resource in their other workplaces: other teachers. As affiliate Felicity posited, "Colleague relationships have a great impact on my teaching," and collegial conversations do influence her decisions in the classroom. Numerous NTTF expressed similar observations during my study, noting that connection with peers was extremely vital in their teaching careers.

IMPLICATIONS

Today as I see new teachers arrive in GVSU's Department of Writing, I feel they are in good hands. I know they will be supported, mentored, and taught by the same colleagues that nurtured me and continue to nurture

When NTTF do not have time to talk to other instructors, they seem to miss out on developing better ways to teach.

IMPACT ON TEACHERS AND THEIR PEDAGOGY

The study findings also demonstrate how the group talk that takes place in GVSU's PAGs appears to impact teachers and their pedagogical approaches in first-year writing. Instructors seemed to use PAGs to develop as teachers, gauge their effectiveness as educators, and try new pedagogical approaches. Newer participants shared that it was sometimes difficult to identify where, when, how, and why things went awry in their courses. NTTF recalled feeling both anxious and excited to share what they were doing in their classrooms with others. New visitor Adam appreciated the teaching-oriented conversations he had. He stressed, "[It's beneficial] learning how other teachers teach lessons or what essays they assign. This is helpful because it allows me to get new ideas. Often, in this line of work we work alone. So, it's hard to figure out what new ideas to try." Adam and others commented that they found PAG discussions often led them to think more deeply about their assignments and course design.

PAGs also seemed to aid in the development of veteran instructors. Seasoned NTTF in the study suggested that dramatic changes in the student population, technology, and pedagogy make it difficult to keep up with trends and reinforced the need for development opportunities and support from colleagues. Mike, a long-term adjunct agreed, claiming, "Personally, it's always a benefit for teachers of different academic backgrounds and levels of experience to get together to discuss student writing. Through the years, I have learned so much from the diverse views of many different people." The more experienced teachers disclosed how even new instructors taught them something. For instance, I observed third-year visitor Susan ask first-year visitor Karen about her conflict-based narrative assignment. She was impressed with how Karen's narratives showed struggle compared to her own narrative assignment. Susan suggested, "Hearing what people actually do in their classes—both the major assignments and the smaller in-class assignments—is useful. It's helpful to hear what works and what doesn't." Because Karen shared her assignment, Susan was able to decide whether there was a more effective option for her students. Belonging to PAGs seems to help NTTF gain the collegial support they need to try new strategies and take risks in their teaching.

Teacher participants described numerous advantages of opening up one's classroom. Some discussed how PAG membership pushed them challenging from my peers. I think only positive results can be obtained from making teaching more public." Sharing teaching practices with others allows NTTF to take personal ownership of their teaching. As the research results seem to indicate, PAGs can potentially allow teachers to learn from their own teaching practices in multiple ways.

DIALOGUE ABOUT PROFESSIONAL PRACTICE

In addition to calling for teaching to be more public, organizations such as CCCC, MLA, NTCE, and TYCA continue to advocate for opportunities for reflective dialogue in a professional community. As this study documents, NTTF are eager for genuine, meaningful conversation with colleagues. Yet many continue to lack formal or informal means for this type of collegial exchange. The limited resources these teachers face make fulfilment of this desire challenging. According to Landthem Camblin and Josephy Steger (2000), there is an expectation that teachers stay current in the field and develop new skills on their own. NTTF in my study complained about experiencing stagnation and a lack of motivation at their former teaching posts, largely because they received little to no professional-development support from their departments or colleges. Therefore, they were left responsible for their own development as educators. Further, research confirms that to improve teaching, professors need more opportunities to investigate and query their own and others' practices, philosophies, and knowledge (Cochran-Smith and Lytle 1992; Hollingsworth and Sockett 1994). Numerous PAG participants revealed they had no opportunity at other workplaces to observe their peers' teaching.

Examining the contexts of their experiences as composition teachers seemed to enable NTTF participants to collaborate in a critical dialogue about their teaching. Faculty communities, like GVSU's PAGs, have the potential to nurture norms of collaboration and exchange that increase instructors' opportunities to improve classroom practice (Little 1999; Louis and Marks 1998). Third-year visitor Susan stressed that the collegial discussion that occurs in PAGs is extremely useful: "Talking is really useful to get a sense of what others' expectations and ideas are. I appreciate hearing these things from others because I always get a better sense of what my own expectations are, and I can pass this all on to my students." Many in the study appeared to use PAGs to reflect on their teaching methods by vocalizing with others what they do in the classroom. By doing so, they seemed to discover new ways to improve their practices by viewing themselves through the eyes of other teachers.

me on my teaching journey. However, I wish others could experience the power a collaborative teacher community has to connect, challenge, awaken, and inspire teachers. Countless writing instructors, especially NTTF, continue to work alone without the benefit of a supportive professional community. I join others in our field (Elbow and Belanoff 1986; Marshall 2008; Richlin and Cox 2004; Wetherbee Phelps 1991) calling for the formation of teacher communities for writing faculty.

As this study documents, PAGs hold great potential to serve as modern-day teaching circles where teachers feel less alone in their careers. The data confirm that PAGs can be an effective form of faculty development because novice and veteran instructors alike gain much-needed support from colleagues, share teaching stories, reflect on their own teaching, and find motivation and inspiration to change their practices. The results demonstrate the tremendous impact PAGs have on the teaching of first-year composition and the development of writing teachers at GVSU. NTTF in this study had a palpable desire for collegial exchange, which I believe was effectively met by their membership in PAGs. We must find more ways to meet teachers' needs for collegiality and membership in local communities. These professional exchanges need not take the shape of PAGs, but the study's implications are that teachers need local spaces within their departments where they can dialogue with colleagues about their mutual interest—the teaching of college writing. Creating teacher communities is one way to fill this void for NTTF in writing studies. I would not be the writing teacher I am today without my teaching circle—GVSU's portfolio-assessment groups.

REFERENCES

Alber, Rebecca. 2012. "Six Ways to Avoid Feeling Isolated in the Classroom." *Edutopia*, January 9. http://www.edutopia.org/blog/avoid-teacher-isolation-stay-connected-rebecca-alber.

Alleman, Nathan F., and Don Haviland. 2017. "'I Expect to Be Engaged as an Equal:' Collegiality Expectations of Full-time, Non-Tenure-Track Faculty Members." *Higher Education* 74 (3): 527–42.

American Association of University Professors. 2017. "Trends in the Academic Labor Force, 1975–2015." American Association of University Professors. March 2017. https://www.aaup.org/sites/default/files/Academic_Labor_Force_Trends_1975-2015.pdf.

Baldwin, Roger G., and Jay L. Chronister. 2001. *Teaching without Tenure: Policies and Practices for a New Era*. Baltimore: Johns Hopkins University Press.

Beech, Jennifer, and Julie Lindquist. 2004. "The Work before Us: Attending to English Departments' Poor Relations." *Pedagogy* 4 (2): 171–89.

Broad, Bob. 2003. "What We Really Value: Beyond Rubrics in Teaching and Assessing Writing." *All USU Press Publications* 140. https://digitalcommons.usu.edu/usupress_pubs/140.

Camblin, Landtham D., and Josephy Steger. 2000. "Rethinking Faculty Development." *Higher Education* 39 (1): 1–18.

Cochran-Smith, Marilyn, and Susan L. Lytle. 1992. *Inside/Outside: Teacher Research and Knowledge*. New York: Teachers College Press.

Daniell, Beth, Laura Davis, Linda Stewart, and Ellen Taber. 2008. "The In-House Conference: A Strategy for Disrupting Order and Shifting Identities." *Pedagogy* 8 (3): 447–65.

Davis, Danielle Joy, Kira Provost, and Amanda E. Major. 2009. "Writing Groups for Worklife Balance: Faculty Writing Group Leaders Share Their Stories." In *To Improve the Academy: Resources for Faculty, Instructional, and Organizational Development*, edited by Judith E. Miller and James E. Groccia, 31–42. San Francisco: Jossey-Bass.

Elbow, Peter, and Pat Belanoff. 1986. "Portfolios as a Substitute for Proficiency Examinations." *College Composition and Communication* 37 (3): 336–39.

Good, Tina Lavonne, and Leanne B. Warshauer, eds. 2008. *In Our Voice: Graduate Students Teach Writing*. New York: Pearson Longman.

Grubb, W. Norton. 1999. *Honored but Invisible: An inside Look at Teaching in Community Colleges*. New York: Routledge.

Hamp-Lyons, Liz, and William Condon. 2000. *Assessing the Portfolio*. Cresskill, NJ: Hampton.

Hendricks, Bill. 2009. "Working Alone Together: Labor Agency and Professional Exchange in the Teaching of Composition." *Pedagogy* 9 (2): 235–60.

Holdstein, Deborah. 2011. "Interdisciplinarity after Three Decades: A Conversation." *Writing Instructor*. December 1, 2011. https://eric.ed.gov/?q=The+writing+instructor&id=EJ959706.

Hollingsworth, Sandra, and Hugh Sockett, ed. 1994. *Teacher Research and Educational Reform*. Chicago: University of Chicago Press.

Hutchings, Pat. 1996. *Making Teaching Community Property: A Menu for Peer Collaboration and Peer Review*. Washington, DC: American Association for Higher Education.

Kezar, Adrienne. 2005. "Moving from I to We." *Change* 37 (6): 50–57.

Kezar, Adrienne, and Cecille Sam. 2010. "Non-Tenure-Track Faculty in Higher Education." Special issue, ASHE Higher Education Report 36 (5): 1–91.

Little, Judith Warren. 1999. "Organizing Schools for Teacher Learning." In *Teaching as the Learning Profession: Handbook of Teaching and Policy*, edited by Linda Darling-Hammond and Gary Sykes, 233–62. San Francisco: Jossey-Bass.

Louis, Karen, and Helen Marks. 1998. "Does Professional Learning Community Affect the Classroom Teachers' Work and Student Experience in Restructured Schools?" *American Journal of Education* 106 (4): 532–75.

Marshall, Margaret J. 2008. "Teaching Circles Supporting Shared Work and Professional Development." *Pedagogy* 8 (3): 413–31.

Morrison, Joshua D. 2008. "Faculty Governance and Non-Tenure Track Appointments." *New Directions for Higher Education* 143: 21–27.

Myers, Janet C., and Cassandra Kircher. 2007. "Teaching without License: Outsider Perspectives on First-year Writing." *Teaching English in the Two-Year College* 34 (4): 396–404.

Richardson, Virginia, ed. 1997. *Constructivist Teacher Education: Building New Understandings*. Washington, DC: Falmer.

Richlin, Laurie, and Milton Cox. 2004. "Developing Scholarly Teaching and the Scholarship of Teaching and Learning through Faculty Learning Communities." *New Directions for Teaching and Learning* 97 (March): 127–34.

Schell, Eileen E., and Patricia Lambert Stock, eds. 2001. *Moving a Mountain: Transforming the Role of Contingent Faculty in Composition Studies and Higher Education*. Urbana, IL: NCTE.

Stenberg, Shari, and Amy Lee. 2002. "Developing Pegagogies: Learning the Teaching of English." *College English* 64 (3): 326–47.

Wetherbee Phelps, Louise. 1991. "Practical Wisdom and the Geography of Knowledge in Composition." *College English* 53 (8): 863–85.

ABOUT THE AUTHORS

Brendan Hawkins is a PhD candidate at Florida State University, where he teaches first-year composition and histories of rhetorical theory. Occasionally, he babysits two quirky golden retrievers, Mardi and Janeway.

Heather Jordan earned her PhD in June 2011, just two weeks after her husband earned his and almost two years after their son was born. Since then, both Drs. Jordan have been non-tenure-track faculty with a short commute to family.

Nathalie Joseph is an associate professor of writing at the University of Southern California. She has worked collaboratively with Norah Ashe-McNalley for many years on various projects, including student-run publications, research, and conference papers.

Julie Karaus is the assistant director of the University Writing Center and a WAC consultant at Appalachian State University. She is happiest when hiking in the woods with her dog.

Christopher Lee is a tenure-track instructor at Snow College. He holds a graduate degree in American studies and taught composition at Utah Valley University as a lecturer for eight years.

John McHone is currently an adjunct instructor in the English Department at Western Carolina University, though he has taught at numerous four-year institutions and community colleges throughout North Carolina since graduating with his MA in English in 2011.

Dauvan Mulally is a senior affiliate professor in the Department of Writing at Grand Valley State University, where she teaches first-year composition and directs the department's internship program.

Seth Myers, PhD, is a senior instructor at the University of Colorado at Boulder. An award-winning teacher, his work focuses on critical, inclusive, reflective pedagogy and multimodal rhetorics.

Liliana M. Naydan, associate professor of English at Penn State Abington, is author of *Rhetorics of Religion in American Fiction* (Bucknell UP 2016) and coeditor of *Out in the Center* (Utah State UP 2018) and *Terror in Global Narrative* (Palgrave Macmillan 2016).

Linda Shelton has been a senior lecturer in the English and Literature Department at Utah Valley University since 2000, teaching lower- and upper-division courses. She received her undergraduate and graduate degrees from Brigham Young University.

Erica Stone is an assistant professor of English and the associate director of General Education English at Middle Tennessee State University. Her most recent scholarship has been published by *WAC Clearninghouse*, 4C4E's *Spark*, and *Community Literacy Journal*.

Elizabeth J. Vincelette, PhD, is a senior lecturer in the English department at Old Dominion University. Her past experience as a writing center director informs her classroom, as well as her work instructing colleagues in professional-development workshops.

Lacey Wootton is a Hurst Senior Professorial Lecturer, director of the writing studies program at American University, and a PhD student in writing and rhetoric at George Mason University.

ABOUT THE AUTHORS

EDITORS

Jessica Edwards teaches critical race studies, composition studies, and technical and professional writing at the University of Delaware.

Meg McGuire teaches digital writing and technical and professional writing at the University of Delaware.

Rachel Sanchez teaches composition and technical writing at Washington State University.

AUTHORS

Norah Ashe-McNalley is the current director of the USC Writing Program and a longtime associate teaching professor at the University of Southern California.

Sarah E. Austin is the director of student affairs and registrar at the US Air Force Academy and Preparatory School and a PhD candidate at Texas Tech University. She has published in *Feminist Teacher, Present Tense, BWe*, and *Forum: Issues about Part-Time and Contingent Faculty*.

Rachel Azima is writing center director and assistant professor of practice in English at the University of Nebraska–Lincoln. Her work has appeared in *ESQ and* the *Journal of Commonwealth and Postcolonial Studies* and is forthcoming in *The Writing Center Journal*.

Megan Boeshart Burelle is the Old Dominion University writing center director and a composition lecturer. She is a PhD student at Old Dominion and is working on an online-tutoring dissertation.

Peter Brooks, University of Washington Bothell FYC lecturer, received an MEd from Arizona State University, and worked in Student Affairs before returning to academia for an MFA (NMSU) and PhD (UWM).

Dr. Angie McKinnon Carter, a senior lecturer at Utah Valley University, analyzes writing-conference discourse and teaches first-year composition. She enjoys illustrating the writing process, especially revision, using Marvel-derived metaphors.

Denise Comer is a professor of the practice of writing studies and director of first-year writing at Duke University.

Jessica Cory, a newly termed English instructor (step up from lecturer) in the English Department at Western Carolina University, is also a PhD student in English at the University of North Carolina Greensboro.

Liz Gumm is associate director of writing for UC San Diego's Sixth College. She teaches first-year composition, literature, and mindful rhetoric in the Culture, Art, and Technology writing program.

INDEX

A

AAUP, 22–23, 24, 56, 134, 208
academia, 15, 20, 60, 63, 76, 77, 119, 122, 123, 124, 146, 151, 165, 181, 182, 188, 193, 195, 196, 198, 210, 218; outside, 15
academic writing, 148, 156, 162
activism, 43, 56, 57, 66, 68, 73; social activism, 99
activity theory, 33
adjuncts, 8, 25, 26, 29, 42, 46, 47, 48, 49, 53, 54, 55, 56, 64, 66, 73, 74, 81, 87, 90, 91, 92, 93, 94, 95, 96, 97, 98, 100, 110, 119, 120, 122, 123, 124, 125, 127, 129, 132, 133, 134, 143, 145, 146, 158, 159, 162, 163, 164, 167, 168, 169, 171, 172, 173, 179, 183, 195, 196, 207, 208, 210, 222, 227, 230, 231, 232
administration, 3, 5, 8, 16, 20, 32, 33, 38, 47, 48, 59–63, 67, 68, 74, 75, 83, 84, 85, 87, 88, 98, 109, 112, 113, 114, 116, 118–121, 124, 126, 129, 132, 134, 136, 137, 138, 140, 141, 142, 151, 155, 156, 159, 164, 169, 171, 198, 215, 217
administrative oversight, 214
administrative requirements, 213
advisor, 95, 150, 213
allies, 60, 66, 67; administrative, 99–100; student, 143; tenure, 81, 99, 100, 101
ambition, 82, 182, 188
American University, 73–74
annual review, 9
anxiety, 31, 34, 36, 38, 129, 138, 140, 141, 152, 180, 197, 201, 222
assistant professor of practice, 15, 17, 18, 22
assistant professor, 4, 15–17, 18, 21, 24, 47, 54, 165, 168

B

Baldwin, Roger, and Anne Austin, 203
Barnard's Contingent Faculty Union-UAW Local 2110, 56
Bartholomae, David, 34
benefits, 9, 10, 26, 31, 43, 44, 45, 47, 48, 49, 51, 68, 75, 84, 88, 98, 119, 123, 126, 128, 129, 132, 134, 139, 141, 143, 163, 164, 165, 166, 167, 168, 171, 195, 196, 197, 202, 203, 227, 231; health, 227; retirement, 227
Berubé, Michael, and Jennifer Ruth, 23
biracial identity, 20
Bizzell, Patricia, 36
Bogost, Ian, 178
Bousquet, Marc, 59, 61, 66
Bowen Report, 148
Brady, Laura, and Nathalie Singh-Corcoran, 25
Brooklyn College CUNY, 56
Butts, Jimmy, 212
bylaws, 18, 19

C

Camblin, Landthem, and Joseph Steger, 229
Carter, Christopher, 63, 65
Carter, Genesea, 54
Cassuoto, Leonard, 23
Caswell, Nicole, Jackie Grutsch McKinney, and Rebecca Jackson, 32
chair, 16, 17, 19, 75, 81, 82, 110, 111, 115, 132, 135, 138, 141, 169, 183, 198, 221
Chickering, Arthur, 26
child care, 80, 84
Christian identity, 216
Chronicle of Higher Education, 23, 73, 87, 126, 148, 168
cisgender, 28, 54, 127, 178
Coalition on the Academic Workforce, 47
coffee shop, 63, 66, 151, 177, 202
Coley, Jonathan S., 67
collaboration, 6, 18, 32, 101, 143, 193, 194, 195, 197, 198, 199; academic, 201; culture of, 229; faculty, 200–203; impact on labor, 205; norms of, 218; vulnerable, 207; with graduate students, 205; 207; within NTTF, 226
colleagues, 3, 6, 8, 17, 18, 19, 20, 23, 24, 26, 30, 31, 33, 35, 59, 60, 73, 74, 76, 84, 87, 88, 90, 96, 97, 98, 99, 101, 112, 115, 117, 121, 122, 125, 131, 132, 136, 137, 139, 142, 149, 152–155, 158, 184, 194, 199, 202, 203, 208, 210, 211, 212, 217, 220, 222, 223, 224, 226, 227–233;

238   INDEX

tenured, 19, 23, 24, 26, 30, 74, 99, 131, 132, 139, 184, 210, 211, 212, 217
collective bargaining, 24, 54, 56, 158, 161, 170
collegiality, 139, 180, 197, 199, 225, 226–227, 232, 233
Collins, Gail, 79, 85, 86
Colorado, 181, 183
committee chair, 16, 17, 19, 75, 81, 82, 110, 111, 115, 132, 135, 138, 141, 169, 183, 198, 221
community college, 16, 46, 90, 95, 96, 97, 119, 123–125, 133, 134, 145, 149, 179, 183, 222
community, 3, 7; academic, 232; campus, 155, 156, 157, 163; collaborative, 43, 51, 63, 99, 101, 139, 145, 146, 151, 152, 153; contingent/NTTF, 221, 222; department, 183; intuitional, 233; lack of, 10, 18, 19, 28, 33, 37; literacy, 226, 227, 229, 231, 232; professional, 188, 217, 220; teaching, 233; writing program, 153
composition, 19, 30, 33, 34, 43, 45, 49, 57, 61, 63, 76, 77, 78, 90, 92, 93, 94, 99, 108, 116, 119, 120, 121, 132, 133, 139, 145, 146, 147, 148, 149, 150, 151, 154, 163, 177; classroom, 195, 197, 198, 201; courses, 225; field, 224; FYC, 227; program/department, 202, 203, 207, 215, 221, 222, 223; teaching, 229, 231, 232, 233
Conference on College Composition and Communication (CCCC), 42, 50, 68, 159, 209, 215, 222, 229
Conference on Community Writing, 183, 185, 188
connections, 3; between institutional spaces, 90, 92; to others professionally, 151, 225
contingent faculty, 3, 4, 5, 8, 10, 21, 23, 24, 29, 30, 31, 34, 38, 42, 43, 48, 49, 50, 51, 53, 54, 55, 56, 57, 59, 60, 61, 62, 63, 64, 66, 67, 77, 90, 92, 93, 94, 95, 98, 99, 100, 101, 131, 132, 135, 138, 139, 146, 155, 157, 158, 159, 207
contingent spaces: for communication, 4, 6; community, 8, 9, 37, 39, 54, 56, 90, 91, 92; institutional, 136, 150, 152, 154, 163, 166; liminal, 101; need for, 93, 96, 97, 98, 99, 100; office, 231; voices, 233; work, 202
contracts, 3, 4, 9, 10, 15, 22, 23, 44, 45, 48, 51, 52, 53, 54, 55, 60, 73, 75, 83, 87, 96, 108, 109, 110, 115, 121, 124, 126, 129, 133, 134, 139, 148, 160, 161, 162, 163, 164, 166, 167, 168, 170, 171, 177, 194, 196, 197, 199, 200, 208, 210, 217, 227; nonrenewable, renewal/renewable, 44, 48, 53, 55, 133, 166, 168, 170, 177, 208
Crenshaw, Kimberlé, 5
critical thinking, 46, 98

D

Denny, Harry, 64
department chair, 9, 15, 18, 47, 83, 112, 125, 132, 134, 140, 141, 198. *See also* chair
Dickens, Charles, 97
dissertation, 116, 138, 183, 217
domestic, domesticity, 77, 78, 79, 80, 81, 127
Duke University Thompson Writing Program, 158, 161, 162, 166, 168, 169, 170; unionize, 168, 169
Duke University, 159, 160, 161, 161; NTTF, 169; faculty union, 171
Duqesne University, 64

E

Edwards, Kristen, and Kim Tolley, 167
Elbow, Peter, 36
emotional health, 146
emotional labor, 29, 30, 31, 32, 33, 35, 36, 38, 39, 40, 48, 49, 61, 83, 85, 188, 194, 198, 199
empathy, 32, 36, 38, 39, 74, 158, 170, 214
employment-at-will, 98, 100
English: developmental, 46; field, 119, 120, 121, 122, 136, 139; jobs, 47; language 185; literature, 141, 145, 147, 148; major, 17, 108, 110, 111, 112, 116; professional identity, 149; teaching, 52, 54, 61, 77, 94. *See also* English department
English department, 8, 17, 18, 26, 77, 108, 112, 121, 122, 136, 148, 207, 223
Eodice, Michele, Anne Ellen Geller, and Neal Lerner, 61
ethical, 38, 97, 109; standards for NTTF, 114; working conditions, 116
evaluation, 21, 29, 74, 84, 85, 98, 108, 109, 113, 114, 115, 116, 117, 135, 142, 203, 212, 213; student, 74, 84, 98, 113, 117, 135
Evans, Nancy, 35
Everingham, Christine, Deborah Stevenson, and Penny Warner-Smith, 86
existential, 182
expertise, 50, 54; disciplinary, 21; disrespect of NTTF, 153, 154; professional, 54, 143; writing, 167
extended family, 216

F

faculty senate, 32, 73, 75, 76, 82, 121, 132, 220
family, 5, 6, 9, 25, 37, 45, 51, 77, 80, 81, 120, 122, 126, 127, 128, 148, 149, 163, 168, 177, 183, 197, 209, 216, 217, 218
Federici, Silvia, and Arlen Austin, 65
feedback, 37, 49, 154, 155, 163, 205; providing student, 211, 215, 216, 218
Fels, Dawn, 21, 26, 59
female, 65, 66, 73, 76, 77, 81, 152
feminine, 76, 77, 86
feminism, 65, 79, 85. *See also* second wave feminism; third wave feminism
4/4 teaching load, 15, 109
freeway flyers, 163, 196
Freudian, 77–78

G

game studies, 38
Gehrke, Sean J., and Adrianna Kezar, 136, 138, 139, 141, 142, 196, 199
Geleuze, Gilles, and Felix Guattari, 178
Geller, Anne Ellen, and Harry Denny, 61, 67
generational divide, 147
Gilliam, Alice, 29, 32
Gladstein, Jill, 109; and Brandon Fralix, 21
graduate students, 9, 20, 77, 113, 116, 116; collaboration with, 173, 217, 218, 219; as instructors, 147–155, 159, 162
Gramsci, Antonio, 4
Grand Valley State University, 226, 230
Grusin, Richard, 177, 178
Guerra, Juan, 155

H

Harvey, Jerry, 34
Hendricks, Bill, 223, 225, 232
hierarchy: academic, 221; faculty, 223; institutional, 199, 207; tenure, 196
higher education, 5, 23, 25, 38, 43, 47, 48, 50, 54, 55, 57, 62, 64, 65, 74, 85, 91, 92, 95, 99, 101, 119, 132, 136, 143, 159, 160, 166, 167, 210, 212, 213, 214, 222, 224, 232
Hochschild, Arlie, 28, 30, 31, 32
Holbrook, Sue Ellen, 76, 78
Holdstein, Deborah, 223
Hollingsworth, Sandra, and Hugh Sockett, 229
hope, 4, 31, 38, 53, 57, 91, 96, 125, 129, 148, 180
hopelessness, 129, 145
Hughes, Bradley, 16; with Paula Gillespie

and Harvey Kail, 61
husband, 18, 38, 209, 214, 216, 219
Hutchings, Pat, 228

I

Inland Empire University, 145
instructors, 3, 8, 9, 26, 30, 31, 32, 34, 35, 36, 37, 38, 39, 40, 45, 46, 49, 53, 55, 64, 74, 91, 93, 95, 97, 114, 122, 129, 131, 133, 134, 140, 145, 147, 148, 150, 152, 153, 154, 155, 156, 157, 162, 177, 179, 181, 183, 199, 215, 221, 222, 224, 225, 226, 227, 228, 229, 230, 231, 232, 233
International Writing Center Association, 68
interview, 19, 31, 32, 43, 47, 48, 53, 79, 90, 92–98, 120, 135, 147, 180, 183, 184, 218, 224–22
invisible, 6, 28, 29, 33, 35, 40, 43, 49, 59, 60–61, 65, 99, 115, 118, 131, 133, 138, 143, 178, 184, 201, 213, 224, 234
Isaacs, Emily, and Melinda Knight, 59
isolation, 8, 139, 156, 157, 222, 223, 226, 227, 232
ivory tower, 180, 185

J

job description, 23, 45, 53, 107, 108, 109, 110, 111, 113, 114, 116, 134
job insecurity, 163, 212

K

Kahn, Seth, 66, 90, 91, 92, 100, 129, 208
Kelsky, Karen, 149
Kezar, Adrianna, 131, 132, 134, 138, 139, 143, 212, 213, 232; and Cecile Sam, 131, 132, 135, 143; and Tom DePaola, 56
Kirsch, Gesa, 49
Kolb, David A, 36
Kynard, Carmen, 188

L

labor movement activists, 66
LaFrance, Michelle, and Anicca Cox, 92
Lake, Danielle, and Joel Wendland, 99
Lakoff, George, and Mark George, 4
language, 3, 4, 5, 8, 18, 31, 34, 35, 36, 38, 78, 93, 99, 133, 154, 171, 184, 195, 200, 213–214
lecturers, 3, 18, 29, 30, 31, 60, 62, 108, 110, 112, 113, 114, 115, 119, 120, 121, 122, 127, 131, 132, 133, 134, 135, 136, 137, 138, 139, 140, 141, 142, 145, 146, 147, 148, 149, 150, 151, 152, 153, 154,

155, 157, 164, 168, 179, 222
Legleitner, Rickie-Ann, 54
Lerner, Neal, 64
LGBTQ, 64
Listserv: department, 149; IWCA, 111; WPA, 8
literacy, 38; emotional literacy, 60–62, 64, 132, 178, 181, 183
literary studies, 19
literaure, 9, 74, 75, 82, 84, 93, 119, 149, 150, 151, 152, 154, 177, 207
lived experiences, 49, 50, 159, 160, 170, 172, 212
loan payments, 183
Lorde, Audre, 5
Lunsford, Andrea, 36

M

MacKenzie, Gordon, 33
Maisto, Maria, Joseph McCartin, and Jacob Swenson, 43
Marshall, Margaret, 109, 225, 233
Marxist/Marxism, 60, 62, 64–66, 65
masculine, 77, 78, 128
master frame, 63, 65
Master's Degree: MA, 25, 44, 120, 125, 145, 150, 162, 167; MEd, 216, 221; MFA, 167
Maxey, Daniel, and Adrianna Kezar, 196
McCarver, Virginia, 85, 86
McIntosh, Peggy, 101
McKinney, Jackie Grutsch, 21, 32, 65
McTaggart, Robin, 94
mentor, 6, 9, 16, 20, 21, 39, 59, 61, 66, 67, 81, 91, 110, 117, 138, 141, 146, 147, 150, 151, 156–157, 209, 212, 218, 232; formalized/informal, 226; lack of, 218; policies, 199; of students, 150, 197, 199
meritocracy, 208, 209, 210, 220
metaphor, 4, 73, 74, 76–79; of having it all, 76; of school marm, 79, 80, 81, 82, 85, 86, 87, 88, 91; of sad women, 76
military, 44–46, 53, 54, 182
Miller, Susan, 76, 77, 78
MLA Committee on Contingent Labor, 101
MLA, 8, 54, 90, 91, 101, 162, 208, 222, 229
motherhood, 76, 77
Muller, Eric, 156

N

narratives; NTTF, 32, 90, 91, 142, 143, 230; personal, 67; student, 36
National Labor Relations Board, 56
National Science Foundation, 54
National Survey of Student Engagement, 30
neoliberal, 42, 56, 74, 86–87, 132
non-tenure-track faculty (NTTF), 3–8, 10, 20, 21, 25, 29, 30–33, 35, 37, 39, 42, 44, 45, 47, 49, 55, 56, 71, 73, 74, 79, 85–88, 90–95, 97–101, 107, 109, 110, 112, 113, 114, 116, 117, 119, 120, 121, 126, 127, 129, 132, 133, 134, 135, 136, 138, 139, 140, 141, 142, 143, 146, 158, 162, 164, 172, 193, 195, 196, 199, 200, 207, 208, 209, 210, 211, 212, 213, 215–222, 224–233; professional development, 91, 101; university system, 93, 94, 95. *See also* contingent faculty
nonevents, 37
North Carolina, 120, 123, 125, 126; adjunct labor, 92, 94; at-will state, 98, 100

O

O'Grady, Helen, 91, 92
office hours, 134, 197, 199, 216
Olson, Gary A., and Evelyn Ashton-Jones, 107
Omi, Michael, 4
opposition, 63, 66, 151, 177, 202
organize, 56, 60, 63, 66, 84, 111, 151, 155, 161
otherness, 20

P

Padavic, Irene, and Barbara Reskin, 59, 65
parent, 29, 38, 51, 57, 85, 120, 127, 145, 166, 181, 216, 219
part-time faculty, 3, 16, 59, 73, 74, 95, 99, 110, 199, 224
participatory action group (PAR), 90, 94, 99
pay equity, 24, 26
pedagogical approaches, 230
pedagogy, 62, 92, 112, 122, 132, 133, 223, 228, 230; teaching, 194; writing, 36, 154, 161, 165, 167, 171, 225
people of color/faculty of color, 4, 54, 64
performance evaluation, 108, 109
performing, 32, 84, 107, 127, 167, 212
Perry, William, 36
PhD, 9, 19; committees, 20, 45, 46, 54, 55, 76, 111, 116, 119, 122, 145, 146, 147, 148, 149, 150, 161, 163, 167, 179, 181, 209, 216, 219, 225; doctoral program, 20, 207, 217, 222
Phelps, Louise Wetherbee, 224
portfolio assessment, 219, 221, 226, 233
portfolio assessment groups (PGA), 219, 221, 226, 227, 228, 229, 230, 231, 232,

233
postdoctoral as NTTF, 45, 158, 161, 162, 163, 164, 165, 166, 167, 168
privilege: class, 168, 169, 170; institutional, 23, 42, 64, 101, 110, 164, 171, 196, 212; of literature, 153; personal, 24, 42, 43, 44, 47, 54, 100, 178, 208, 219; power, 172; race, 101; voting, 135, 169
professional development, 47, 48, 51, 136, 141, 142, 145, 163, 166, 196, 199, 200, 207, 212, 225, 229
professional identity, 3, 5, 6, 61, 67, 84, 146, 147, 152, 168, 205
professional space, 92, 96, 97, 231
professional, 4, 6, 8, 9, 17, 20, 21, 26, 29, 30, 32, 34, 35, 39, 42, 49, 54, 61, 68, 80, 84, 85, 86, 88, 91, 92, 96, 97, 100, 107, 108, 109, 111, 116, 117, 119, 120, 131, 132, 133, 134, 135, 138, 141, 143, 146, 147, 148, 149, 150, 151, 152, 153, 154, 155, 156, 163, 166, 168, 178, 188 193, 194, 196, 197, 198, 202, 203, 204, 222, 224, 225, 227, 228, 229, 231, 232
promotion, 3, 7, 8, 29, 38, 39, 74, 75, 109, 114, 116, 121, 135, 136, 137, 138, 139, 140, 141, 142, 143, 195, 196, 198, 199, 200, 201, 203, 207, 210, 211
public-service professionals, 32
publish, 7, 20, 23, 30, 42, 49, 54, 57, 63, 64, 98, 100, 109, 120, 122, 129, 135, 138, 143, 145, 148–149, 150, 155, 178, 188, 194, 195, 196, 197, 198, 199, 204, 207, 208, 211, 212, 216, 218, 219, 223

Q

qualitative data, 90, 94
quality-enhancement plan, 107

R

R1, 15, 20, 22, 25, 179, 193, 195, 196, 208
R2, 207, 208
race: intersection of, 4, 5, 36, 178; identity, 154
racial identity, 20, 46
racism, 5, 153
Ratcliffe, Krista, 39
relationship: adversarial, 170; collaborative, 193; composition to literature, 78; to contingent positions, 10, 29; end of, 180; between faculty, 74–75, 115, 164, 226, 232; maintaining, 45, 214; personal, 77, 203; professional, 39, 66, 100, 204, 205; reciprocal, 217; to space, 29; strained, 137; with students, 36, 37, 47, 152

reappointment, 34, 38, 39, 84, 85, 114
reciprocity, 194, 218
relational, 83, 86
research, 6, 7, 17, 19, 22, 23, 26; research-active, 90, 91, 92, 93, 94, 96, 98, 99, 100, 109, 111, 112, 113, 116, 120, 122, 125, 133, 134, 136, 148, 150, 161, 162, 163, 165, 166, 178, 183, 193, 195–198, 200, 202, 205, 208, 210, 211, 217, 229; research-based, 46, 49, 53, 54, 57, 62, 64, 82, 85; research center, 32, 36, 44; research-centered, 31
responsibilities, 80; administrative, 151, 164; family, 9; NTTF, 8, 109; service, 10, 66, 76, 117; teaching, 21, 218
Reynolds, Nedra, 91, 92, 99
rhetoric, 4, 5, 36, 62, 204; alternative careers, 170; of choice, 85; collective bargaining, 19, 177, 202, 203, 222, 225; composition and, 179; department, 201, 202; framing, 63; listening, 60; power, 39, 66, 67, 68; professor of, 194; rhetoricians, 207, 218; situation, 133, 138, 142, 149; and writing studies, 3
Rhodes, Georgia, Kim Gunter, and Elizabeth Carroll, 99
Robinson, E. Ian, 62
Rocky Mountains, 179, 186
Royster, Jacqueline Jones, 49

S

Salem, Lori, 32
Schell, Eileen, 78, 92, 98, 132, 138
scholarship, 3, 5–8, 15, 22, 25, 29, 31, 33, 35, 37, 38, 45, 49, 51, 56, 57, 85, 94, 109, 113, 120, 122, 131, 132, 137–140, 142, 150, 166, 179, 181, 184, 200, 217, 223, 226, 228
scientific-management theories, 77
second wave feminism, 81
self-care, 156, 215, 219
service, 4, 6, 7, 19, 21, 22, 30, 32, 51, 66, 73, 74, 75, 81, 82, 84, 85, 86, 87, 107, 109, 110, 113, 115, 118, 120, 131, 135, 137, 138, 139, 140, 142, 159, 166, 184, 193, 194, 196, 197, 198, 200, 202, 205, 210, 213, 225, 228
sexism, 5, 60
Seymour, Daniel, 35
shared governance, 23, 132, 136
silence, 7, 29, 133, 138, 143, 170, 204, 219, 223, 224
Simpson, Jeanne H., 68, 109, 110
Slaugher, Anne-Marie, 80, 86
Snow, David A., and Robert D. Benford, 60, 62, 64

Southern California, 145, 181
spouse, 18, 47, 119, 219. *See also* husband; wife
Stenberg, Shari, 225; and Amy Lee, 224
Strickland, Donna, 63, 77
student affairs, 17, 29, 30, 49
student development, 35
student evaluations, 74, 84, 98, 117, 135, 212, 213
sustainability, 24, 208; lived reality, 57
Swathmore's National Census of Writing Data, 109
syllabus/syllabi, 98, 218, 221, 227
system, 3–6, 8–10, 23–25, 30–35, 39, 43, 45, 48, 55, 56, 62, 78–81, 84–88, 90–93, 96, 98, 115, 117, 122–125, 127, 135, 136, 149, 151, 153, 159, 163–165, 168, 171, 172, 177, 203, 214, 218, 220, 223, 231

T
teacher scholar activism, 56
teacher training, 146, 151, 193
teaching at multiple institutions, 46. *See also* freeway flyers
teaching intensive, 23
teaching, 4, 5, 6, 7, 8, 9, 16, 17, 18, 19, 22, 23, 25, 26, 29, 30, 46, 47, 48, 50, 51, 53, 55, 61, 62, 73, 74, 78, 81, 82, 85, 86, 94, 96, 97, 98, 99, 113, 115, 120, 122, 123, 124, 125, 126, 134, 135, 136, 137, 139, 142, 143, 145, 147, 149, 150, 151, 152, 153, 154, 155, 156, 157, 162, 177, 178, 180, 181, 183, 184, 188, 193, 194, 195, 196, 197, 198, 200, 202, 205, 210, 214, 215, 218, 223, 224, 227, 228, 229, 230, 233; assistants, 149, classroom, 66, 81, 132; circles, 219, 226, 232, 233; composition, 77, 116, 120, 148, 203, 207, 222; contracts, 121, 199; evaluation, 114, 117; feminine work, 77; first-year writing, 84; graduate, 147, 225; load, 15, 24, 44, 45, 75, 78, 108, 109, 111, 123, 166, 179, 208, 211; multiple positions, 46, 47, 128; portfolios, 114, 140, 115, 162; of writing, 32, 60, 65, 74, 161, 163, 165, 167, 231
technology, 96, 230
tenure, 4, 5, 7, 8, 9, 17, 19, 22, 23, 25, 26, 32, 54, 55, 60, 61, 62, 63, 64, 66, 67, 73, 74, 75, 76, 80, 82, 83, 84, 85, 87, 88, 91, 98, 99, 100, 110, 111, 112, 113, 119, 120, 131, 132, 134, 135, 136, 138, 139, 140, 141, 148, 149, 150, 153, 154, 156, 159, 162, 164, 165, 167, 168, 169, 180, 184, 193, 196, 199, 207, 209, 210, 211, 212, 223, 227. *See also* Tenure Track

Tenure Track (TT), 3, 5–10, 15, 17, 19–26, 30, 31, 42, 44, 46, 47, 49, 53, 54, 55, 59, 62, 66, 91, 99, 100, 109, 110, 112, 119, 122, 129, 132, 133, 134, 135, 136, 137, 138, 139, 140, 143, 149, 153, 168, 177, 179, 180, 181, 184, 191, 196, 199, 200, 207, 208, 209, 210, 211, 212, 217, 218, 221, 222, 224, 227. *See also* tenure
term faculty, 3, 73, 74, 75, 76, 81, 83, 84, 85, 88
terminal degree, 23, 63, 119, 120, 227
The Nonhuman Turn, 177
third wave feminism, 86
time, 3; full-time, 55–57, 59–61, 63, 66, 73, 74, 76, 80, 82, 84, 86–88, 90, 91, 93, 95–97, 99–100, 107–115, 119–128, 131–143, 145–156, 160–163, 166, 169, 170, 177, 179–183, 185, 186, 194–197, 199, 200, 202, 204, 205, 208–213, 216–217, 221, 222, 225, 227, 230–232; half-time, 16–21, 28–35, 37, 39, 43–44, 46–47, 48–52, 54; part-time, 3 4, 6, 8, 9
trauma, 31, 35, 36, 40
Two-Year College English Association (TYCA), 222, 229

U
Umbach, Paul, and Matthew Wawrzynski, 91
unethical, 50; labor practices, 208
union, 57, 60, 63, 87, 135, 158, 159, 160, 161, 165, 166, 167, 207, 212. *See also* unionize
unionize, 24, 56, 57, 158, 159, 160, 161, 164, 165, 167, 168, 169, 170, 171, 172. *See also* union
University of Delaware, 24
University of Denver, 53
University of Mississippi, 73
University of Washington, 53
unsustainable: academic system, 55, 220; dependence on adjunct, 91, 97; labor conditions, 171
US Bureau of Labor Statistics, 93
Utah Valley University, 132, 134, 135, 137
UW-Madison Writing Center, 16

V
Vojtko, Margaret Mary, 64, 123
voting, 23, 131, 135, 169
voting rights, 3, 6, 101, 135, 164, 172. *See also* voting
vulnerable, 28, 34, 43, 49, 85, 99, 110, 113, 201, 218

W

Wardle, Elizabeth, and Doug Downs, 33
Warner, John, 43, 210
Weisser, Christian, 57
Westin, Charles, 147
white, 4, 20, 28, 42, 54, 101, 146, 165, 178
Whitman, Walt, 178
wife, 125, 185
Wilson, Julia, 80, 83
Winant, Howard, 4
Wootton, Lacey, and Glenn Moomau, 101
women, 40, 42, 60, 61, 64, 67, 75, 76, 78, 79, 85, 88; disparities between men and women, 33, 54, 80, 81, 84, 127; emotional labor of, 33; women's work, 59, 60, 66, 77, 78, 83; women and gendered spaces, 65, 76, 86. *See also* feminism
workload, 7, 19, 21, 39, 43, 48, 49, 50, 52, 53, 54, 85, 93, 112, 115, 132, 133, 146, 150, 152, 178, 193, 197, 201, 204, 205, 207, 210, 211, 212, 213, 215, 219
writing center director, 16, 17, 18, 19, 20, 21, 22, 64, 107, 108, 113, 116, 208
writing center, 16, 17, 18, 20, 21, 22, 25, 26, 32, 48, 59, 60, 64, 65, 66, 67, 68, 94, 95, 107, 108, 109, 110–115, 116, 117, 118, 124, 186; work/workers, 59, 60, 61, 64, 65, 66, 67, 114, 116
writing faculty, 32, 68, 73, 74, 75, 76, 77, 78, 79, 81, 82, 94, 158, 159, 160, 162, 163, 164, 165, 170, 193, 199, 210, 233
Writing Program Administrator (WPA), 76, 108, 158, 208
writing studies, 4, 26, 42, 50, 147, 153, 167, 207, 223, 224, 226, 233
writing center administration, 16, 32, 59, 119

Y

Yoshino, Kenji, 64
Youn, Ted I. K., 146, 148

www.ingramcontent.com/pod-product-compliance
Lightning Source LLC
Chambersburg PA
CBHW031104080526
44587CB00011B/813